1/4

KOSHER
EMOTIONS

KOSHER EMOTIONS

A GUIDED TOUR OF THE HEART

SHMULEY BOTEACH

Hodder & Stoughton

LONDON SYDNEY AUCKLAND

First published in Great Britain in 2000

10 9 8 7 6 5 4 3 2 1

British Library Cataloguing in Publication Data
A record for this book is available from the British Library

ISBN 0 340 73567 8

Typeset by Avon Dataset Ltd, Bidford-on-Avon, Warks

Printed and bound in Great Britain by
The Guernsey Press Co. Ltd, Channel Isles

Hodder & Stoughton
A Division of Hodder Headline Limited
338 Euston Road
London NW1 3BH

**To my children
Mushki, Chana, Shterni, Mendy, Shaina, and
Rachel Leah**

*Ancient Jewish mystics said that the intellect is
the parents and the emotions are the children.
Just as parents give birth to children, the
intellect gives rise to the emotions. And
as children bring joy to parents, so do the
emotions enliven the intellect.*

Contents

Acknowledgements

I want to thank my friends at Hodder, specifically Charles Nettleton, and my commissioning editor, Judith Longman. This book is the product of their encouragement and endurance, however much they deny it. Every creative act is a challenge, especially writing a book, and rarely does an author have a team of people who so believe in him and his message like I have in Charles and Judith. They steadfastly pursued me to publish with Hodder and have stood by me every step along the way, even when my last book was given by the Labour Party as a gift to all those who voted for the Conservative Party. Before I joined Hodder, Charles was the all-powerful head of religious books. But after he backed my last book, he now has a far more important assignment, wandering the halls of Hodder with a little tray uttering his mantra, 'Would you like milk and sugar with that?'

I also wish to thank Holly Pinchevsky-Cin who helped order, edit, shape and somehow smooth my material for the final manuscript and offered a great many invaluable suggestions. Her hard work on the final text allowed me to devote my time to the far more important task of working on my tan, which has now reached an advanced state of perfection that even George Hamilton would envy.

I also wish to thank my wife Debbie for all her support and encouragement without which I could never have completed this project. You may not know this, but writing is hard work, and halfway through this book I was on the verge of quitting and going back to my day job of working as a male model. It was only when Debbie walked into my study one night at midnight and saw me hard at work on the keyboard and said to me, ever so lovingly, 'Don't tell me that you're still working on that same drivel?' that I somehow mustered the inspiration to complete the book.

Finally, I pay homage to the Master of the Universe, God Almighty, for the infinite blessings that He has always showered upon me. Although after the publication of *Kosher Sex* all my friends abandoned me, my congregation deserted me, my wife denied knowing me, and my children burned me in effigy, nevertheless my laptop still works and I feel like the luckiest man in the world.

In a serious moment, God *has* showered infinite blessing upon me and I hope that I am always found worthy by utilizing those blessings for the furtherance of Godliness and goodness.

Rabbi Shmuley Boteach
April 2000
New York City

PART ONE

Why This Book and
What Are the Emotions?

Introduction

I grew up as an emotional kid in an emotional family, watching how emotions paradoxically created both love and heartbreak, bonding and separation. I understood from an early age that the inability to be in command of our negative emotions made us like a car careering out of control. Everyone in my family suffered permanent injury from our frequent emotional collisions. My father unwittingly alienated the wife who loved him because he could not always control his frustration. My mother gradually became more withdrawn because she could not always contain her hurt. And, sadly, my siblings and I spent too much of our childhood occupied with meaningless distractions because we could not always hold back our tears.

Controlling our negative emotions is certainly an important factor in achieving and maintaining emotional health, but this is only one side of the equation. In order to reach our full potential, we must understand the whole palette of emotions that comprise the human personality. Moreover, we must develop and refine those emotions that lead us to love and joy, goodness and happiness, inspiration and exaltation.

This is not as easy as it may seem. Most of us talk nonstop about how we feel but are unable to penetrate the core of our emotional selves. One reason is that there is much confusion surrounding what emotion is. I think, indeed, that there is a profound misunderstanding of emotions and how they fit into our lives. Ask ten people to define love and you probably will receive ten different answers, ranging from comradeship, to lust. Similarly, many pop psychologists will tell you that getting anger off your chest is the key to equilibrium, others that stifling anger until it subsides is the key to preserving relationships.

Another issue that has been grossly misrepresented is depression, perhaps the most talked-about modern emotion. Although the drugs used to treat depression are commonly known, do we really know what depression is? In his otherwise excellent book *The Road Less Traveled*, M. Scott Peck tells us that depression is a necessary emotion, that it is an essential part of development and growth. But this is a superficial understanding of depression. In truth, nobody can *feel* depressed because depression is the absence of feeling, a numbness to all sensation. True emotions pull us outside ourselves and attach us to the external world, allowing us to create relationships. But emotional highs are similar to thought, pulling us inside ourselves. That is what makes them false emotions.

The secret to success

There are many secrets to succeeding in life – the attainment of knowledge, discipline and hard work, making friends, creating strong and stable relationships. None of these goals is achievable, however, without understanding and harnessing the power that our emotions can generate. For example, if you possess no *love* of learning, you will hardly acquire much knowledge. If you cannot control your *anger* and do not show *compassion* for others, you will scarcely be able to develop friendships. And if you cannot rein in your *lust* for strangers, you will be unable to sustain a loving and meaningful relationship.

Those who have the tools to develop and employ the appropriate emotions have the ability to live a life rich in the three aspirations that form the very stuff of our humanity: meaning, happiness and goodness. On the other hand, those who allow their emotions to run the show squander this potential. Although they may be gifted in other important areas, if they have runaway emotions their locomotive will not only miss the station but entirely derail.

The current pre-eminent example of such emotional derailment is President Clinton. A man of phenomenal talent and energy, his record shows that he is one of the most successful American presidents of the twentieth century. He has balanced the budget, overseen a period of great prosperity, brought peace to many troubled regions, and imparted inspiration to millions of Americans through his expert oratory and human empathy. Yet he may be most remembered by history for his scandalous relations with his intern Monica Lewinsky.

Did he know that his affair with Monica was wrong? Of course he did. As a man of high intellect who regularly attends church, he was certainly aware of the seventh commandment. Did he know that he might get caught? Of course. As a career politician, he had watched others destroy their promising careers with illicit affairs. So why did he do it? Some of his defenders say he suffered from an addiction to sex, others that he had a poor self-image. Even Hillary forwarded a rationale for her husband's infidelity: that because he had been abused in his childhood, because his mother and grandmother had fought over him, his life became a constant battle to please all women (but like many other husbands he did not necessarily make his wife part of that equation).

I must, however, beg to differ with all these explanations that render the president a victim to circumstances. I contend that the primary reason President Clinton fell from glory and allowed himself to be dragged in the mud of the media was because he had no grasp of the power of his emotions. A man of great passions, he kindled a fire that burned out of control and ended up consuming his presidential dignity. Had he understood the difference between love and lust, between long-term commitment and short-term pleasure, he would have reserved himself a coveted position in world history, thereby preventing untold damage and misery to his family, his nation and himself.

When the emotions paralyse the intellect

If the failure to control the emotions happens to world leaders, it certainly happens to laymen too. Dominic was a businessman who owned a small women's designer label, a man content with the living his two London stores provided for him and his family. A wealthy American tycoon whose wife fell in love with Dominic's clothes offered to invest eight million dollars into the company to vastly expand the business. Whereas most people would have signed up immediately, Dominic went home to consider the offer.

Dominic became engulfed in worry: the business at the time was a sure thing, so why tamper with it? He worried the whole night about the possibility of a huge failure following his small success. He worried all the next day too. That night, he declined the American investor's offer. The investor was in shock. After all, Dominic need not put a dime down and his whole business was worth only a million dollars. This man was going to give him a seventy per cent equity stake amidst his investment of eight times the value of the company. But Dominic lost the opportunity of a lifetime because his anxiety and fear got the better of him.

Frances was a pretty woman who married Marty out of pure and unadulterated love. He was an accountant at a small firm, and she was very happy with his simple lifestyle. Many years later, Marty's elderly father had a stroke and fell into a desperate financial crisis. Marty decided to leave his profession and go into business in the hopes of making enough money to support his parents as well as his wife and kids. He opened a liquor store that quickly mushroomed into twenty branches, making him highly successful.

Frances, however, could not handle his success and became exceedingly jealous of any woman who spoke to Marty. Her jealousy eventually became so strong that she forbade Marty to employ any woman under the age of forty at the head office with him. In response, Marty started to spend more and more time away from home. The end result, unfortunately, was a divorce after eighteen years of marriage and four children. Had Frances brought some reason to bear on her fits of jealousy, she would have stayed happily married, but the happy life she once knew was torn to pieces.

These examples describe people whose lives were destroyed because they allowed their emotions to overtake their reason. At the other end of the spectrum are those people who are unable to show any emotion at all. Mr Schwartz was a Holocaust survivor who lived down the road from me in Miami, a man who became like an uncle to me after my parents divorced. He grew up in Hungary with five brothers and two sisters, all except one sister being annihilated at Auschwitz. After emigrating to the USA, he married and had two children, both near my age. Strangely, he seemed much closer to me than to either of his sons, which made them resentful. When he walked to synagogue he would pass by my home and offer to walk with me, even though he often left his own sons at home to come on their own.

It was not until many years later that I understood the paradox of this man. He could not let himself love his sons for fear of losing them too. He could only love strangers, whose loss he could tolerate. Understandable as that might be, however, he still has a very poor relationship with his own children because of his inability to show emotion. Mr Schwartz has the greatest excuse in the world for lacking emotion, but no excuse will replace the relationship with his children. What he does not realize is that every act of love involves taking a risk: when we love – whoever we are – we make ourselves vulnerable; we expose our soft underbelly and allow for the possibility of real pain and hurt. The fear of loss or rejection makes it impossible to love. Love and fear are antithetical emotions.

Identifying our inner will

How many opportunities have we surrendered because we could not control our emotional response? How many beautiful moments have we squandered because we could not generate an emotional connection? Having passionate emotions is like being strapped to a rocket. It is truly fantastic. It can catapult you to the mountain top. But what happens when we have no guidance system, when our emotions are out of control? We end up in destinations that we never planned, in strange and unpleasant environments.

As a Rabbi who counsels people on many areas of life, I have noticed something about people as they age – that nearly all have woken up in that unplanned and unfamiliar destination. Their emotions have led them into uncharted territory where they are often miserable and alone. Because of this, nearly all have lived their lives with feelings of regret.

There are two ingredients to happiness. The first is the total integration of self, our internal will and external situation being in harmony with one another. For example, if my inner will is to be a good and decent person, I will not find myself sitting among people who are slandering others.

The second key to happiness lies in our being the complete architects of our own destiny rather than letting fate map our course. It is impossible to be happy when we feel inhibited and guarded. Indeed, when our inner potential is not made manifest, we feel imprisoned. One of the greatest sources of human frustration and misery is the feeling that we could *be* so much more, that we could *do* so much more with our lives. But our emotions sometimes prevent our promise from seeing the light of day.

What mainly prompted me to write this book is the glaring discrepancy between what we want to be and what we eventually become. All the great truths of the world are out there, and most people are quite able to distinguish the good from the bad. We possess an innate sense of right and wrong. When we make mistakes, it is most often due not to a lack of knowing which way to go but to an inability to steer our life in the correct direction. For example, it is fair to assume that a hundred per cent of those who marry do so with the intention of remaining married for the rest of their lives – so why do only half of them make it to the finishing line, even fewer with a smile on their faces? Why can we not follow things through? Why can we not fully integrate our heads with our hearts?

To ensure that we end up exactly where we wanted to be all along, it becomes vital to identify our internal will as early as possible. In each of us there are two levels of desire. First there is what we want, and second, in the words of the Spice Girls, what we *really, really* want. Our emotions often operate on the first level, what I call our external will. I believe that it was President Clinton's external will, his desire for a quick, cheap thrill, that motivated his affair with Monica Lewinsky.

The deeper level of desire, our internal will, is not what we desire at the moment but the ultimate goodness we seek for ourselves in the long term. I suspect that President Clinton's internal will actually desired him to be a great and respected president as well as a loyal husband and father. Unfortunately, however, the internal will often becomes obscured by the more ephemeral, external will. The soft, silent voice of our inner desires is often smothered by the din of our sensate lusts.

The triangle of life: map, captain and ship

In order to identify and penetrate our deep, internal will, we must first gain a more thorough understanding of our emotions. To do this, we must first examine the three essential tools upon which all success is predicated, which share a triangular relationship.

1. A spiritual road map, composed of goals and values, as well as a destination to reach (values)
2. A vehicle to take you to your destination (emotion)
3. A guidance system to steer you there (intellect).

Let us consider the first leg of the triangle. The values imparted to us by our parents, coupled with those goals which we ourselves determine to be valuable and our religious faith, all represent important fixed markers on this map. These should be denoted with large stars. They determine what we want to be in fifty years' time.

The second leg of the triangle is the intellect, the critical guidance system that helps steer us along life's trajectory. Intellect is about examining the possibilities and choices that are open to the individual. It tells us what can be done and what cannot be done, when to go forward and when to retreat. In other words, it sets limits upon us, and paves the path upon which we travel.

The final leg of the triangle comprises our emotions, the very motor of life. Without this we would be like a burnt-out jalopy strewn on the side of the road. We may be in possession of the map, indeed several maps, but they are useless if our engine stalls. Unlike our values and our intellect, which keep us steady, our emotions have the power to release us and set us free to live our dreams.

Goals and dreams,
determined by *values*

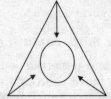

Engine to push us forward   Guidance system to reach
– *emotions*   goals – *intellect*

When these three legs are fully integrated and work in harmony, the result is a rich and successful life, not only in terms of commercial prosperity but, more importantly, in terms of internal prosperity. Our lives have the potential to be deeply rewarding, knowing that we have achieved our dreams and lived according to our principles; in other words, our inner will has been satisfied. But when any of these three elements is missing or out of sync, our life is marred by confusion and we usually end up either stalled or lost.

Consider a second analogy to illustrate this idea: Emotion unguided by intellect is like a ship without a captain. We end up either shipwrecked against the rocks or in a destination that is completely off course. For instance, our heart wanted to be in Egypt but the heart had absolutely no idea how to get there so we ended up in Timbuktu.

Likewise, intellect unaffected by emotion is like a ship without an engine. We know exactly where we want to be, what we want to do. We even know exactly how to get there. But we're out of gas so we haven't the means to reach our destination. This is why so many cerebral people who lack passion never end up fulfilling their dreams. They lack the motivation. They end up at a standstill, paralyzed by inertia.

Finally, if we have a great mind and a strong heart but no values, ideals, or religion, then we have no stars by which to set the trajectory of our ship. We can have a great captain and all the horsepower in the world but where will we go without directions? How will the captain set his course? How will we navigate in a world without beacons? The sea is large and unfriendly to those who do not know its ways. Smooth sailing is not easily achieved.

Passionate against passion

For eleven years at Oxford I watched brilliant people analyse the actions of others, treating the emotions as nothing more than an impediment to be overcome, an obstacle to intellectual development and pure, detached reason. Indeed, passion was approached with a distrust bordering on contempt.

I once attended a lecture by a distinguished visiting American professor. He spoke with great passion on the need to recreate a global volunteer organization for peace, a sort of United Nations of the people. He fortified his arguments with vast erudition and a deep understanding of twentieth-century history. When he had finished, some of the audience stood up to applaud – but only his fellow Americans. After the lecture, I asked a British friend of mine whether he had enjoyed the lecture. 'Not a bit,' he told me. 'Did you see how excited he was about his topic? How can you expect him to remain objective when he is that involved?'

My friend believed that 'getting emotional' meant, by definition, clouding one's judgement and guaranteeing intellectual error. He believed that objectivity should be preserved at all costs. To me, the reverse is true: when we divorce emotion from intellect, we guarantee *emotional* error. Truth must not only be apprehended, but also experienced. When we remove our subjectivity, we become, in the words of Simon and Garfunkel, a rock that feels no pain, an island that never cries.

Sadly, this is what I witness so often at many intellectual bastions like Oxford. I see brilliant people who, instead of going out and committing their lives to important causes, cloister themselves in their ivory tower, devoting themselves to academic and theoretical minutiae. They are brilliant captains in breathtaking ships, but sadly marooned somewhere on a sandbar with no engine to pull them off. The phenomenal contribution they might otherwise have made to the world remains unrealised.

Values without value

Peter had the terrific attributes of a great mind and a warm heart but lacked values. Consequently, anything he did wrong he could instantly rationalize and justify. When he cheated on his girlfriend, far from feeling remorseful, he construed his bad behaviour as something good. He reasoned that infidelity can make partners in an intimate relationship appreciate each other more. 'Absence makes the heart grow fonder, Shmuley,' he said.

When I left him in the USA, he was an Orthodox Jew deeply devoted to Jewish observance. By the time he visited me a year later in Oxford, he had dismissed his Judaism to become a Machiavellian. The year after that he had returned to Judaism, but this time as a Jew for Jesus, preaching a strange mixture of Jewish Christianity.

Throughout all of this, Peter made no apologies for his constant fluctuation, instead accusing me of stagnation: 'We all have to grow, Shmuley. As I experience new things in life, I see higher truths and respond accordingly.'

Unfortunately, while Peter was both intellectual and emotional, his boat had no beacon to direct him to any tangible goals. He still continues to waste his life floating from one philosophy to the next, the various religions and ideologies to which he exposes himself seeming only to confuse him further.

So, your life is like a ship surrounded by stormy waters. The captain of the ship is your intellect. The wind in your sails is your emotions, pushing the ship to its destination, and the fixed stars above are your values and faith, which allow you to navigate the stormy seas. Critics will challenge that this metaphor is too simplistic for something as complicated as a human life, and to this I plead guilty, but I believe that the essentials of life are a lot simpler than we make out. It only gets confusing once we lose our way.

For example, the emotions should never serve as a guiding beacon. Contrary to Freud's theory, which posits the pleasure principle as the prime mover of human behaviour, we are not meant to do what we feel all the time. To use Freudian terminology, the id is not supposed to dominate the ego. Instead, we are meant to feel *what we know we should do*. We are meant to be passionate about the path that our intellect, based on our value systems, dictates us to follow. Our minds must determine what is good and what is evil, but our emotions must cause us to gravitate towards good and to reject evil. If this critical order is lost, we end up with a life turned upside down. Suddenly 'right' and 'wrong' become meaningless euphemisms for 'like' and 'dislike', and morality is turned on its head.

Unfortunately, for many of us, precisely the opposite occurs: *we do only that which we feel*. We undertake only those things which are pleasurable and satiate the immediate needs of the senses.

The path to joy and love

As I see it, ours is a generation that does not aspire to true emotional joy. Modern men and women lack the capacity to feel intensely and do not live passionately, which means being dedicated to and consumed by a cause. Indeed, when we find something so special that we are prepared to dedicate our lives to it, we feel joyous because we have found meaning for our existence.

Placing ourselves at the centre of our own existence is a recipe for unhappiness and dissatisfaction. No human being, even the most oversized ego, truly takes themselves so seriously that they can be passionate about dedicating their every waking moment to their own agenda. The natural human tendency is to aspire to those things which are larger than life and greater than our selves. Then, the many bumps and hurdles we will experience along the way all become worthwhile.

The opposite of joy is self-absorption, when the walls of the psyche begin to cave in under the weight of our own perceived importance. Ours is the generation of selfishness and independence. We are afraid of falling in love too much, afraid that we will lose our selves before we have found them. We are afraid of committing too early lest we miss out on other opportunities that would benefit us more.

In a radio debate, a famous female columnist once excoriated me for glorifying the virtues of parenthood and marriage. 'The Rabbi should be rightly condemned for trying to impose his morality on the whole world,' she thundered. 'What's right for one person is not right for another. I personally have never had any maternal instinct swell up inside me, and I am quite proud of that. I don't like and don't want children, and if I had them I could never pursue the things that are really important to me, like writing and the arts.'

Confused that she would *brag* about having no maternal

14

instinct, I countered, 'I am a man, yet even *I* have a maternal instinct. It's the part of me that can at times shove aside my own egocentricity and derive greater pleasure from giving than from taking, from nurturing rather than manipulating.' Her response was to walk out of the studio abruptly, but not without one parting shot. 'What the Rabbi is really saying is that he is a weak individual who needs others to support him so that he can stand up straight. He is a coward who is afraid to live alone.'

That's what love has come to in the modern era. Instead of its being like the wings of a dove, allowing us to soar, it is considered an illness that makes us feeble. Loneliness and vulnerability, once acknowledged as humanising emotions, are today dismissed as unimpressive weakness. Once upon a time, human beings were not afraid to show their soft spots to their human brothers and sisters. Today they mask their dependency on others under thick layers of defence mechanisms, thereby allowing their ego to roam unchecked.

Such selfishness precludes the possibility of joy and love, the two highest emotions. We have to feel free and alive in order to experience joy, and the same is true of love. When all the love we have to share is incarcerated deep within our being, constraints of the ego are sure to limit our experience of joy. Even though we feel as if we are about to burst, we still do not let ourselves go for fear of growing too dependent on another.

Joy is predicated on freedom and comes about when we are liberated from the imprisoning walls of the ego, yet there are those who prefer the protective walls of a self-enclosed fortress to the open air of a loving relationship. We therefore need to re-educate ourselves to understand our true emotional needs if we are to be freed from the shackles of the self.

Peering beneath the hood

It seems ironic that we spend so much time and energy trying to master our actions but almost no time trying to cultivate the engine behind them. The book you are reading is dedicated entirely to the motor of human advance. I want this book to help us find penetrating insights into our most important organ, our heart, and our most important system, our emotions, so that we can remain fully in control of our ship. The captain and the stars have received more than their fair share of attention throughout history. There are tens of thousands of studies on the intellect and millions of books about religion and other value systems, but very little attention has been paid to our emotions.

My aim in this book is twofold. First, I wish to demonstrate the supremacy of the emotions over the intellect by showing how the sublimity of humankind is celebrated through the heart rather than the mind. Human beings are referred to as *Homo sapiens*, a kind of thinking ape. From a Jewish perspective, however, it would be far more accurate to refer to humanity as *feeling* beings. It is not our introspective cognition that most distinguishes us from the apes but our extrovert ability to forge emotional connections with our fellow beings. It is man's ability to impact upon the people around him that represents his crowning glory. By leaving a permanent imprint on his environment, man achieves immortality.

Judaism has long held that man's greatness lies not in his ability to think but in his ability to act. The mind is valuable as the guidance system directing the emotions. Thus, the emotions do not facilitate the needs of the intellect, but the intellect is the vehicle for the emotions. In other words, our minds are the means to an end rather than the end itself.

The pursuit of knowledge and understanding is certainly valuable. However, if it does not lead to acts of goodness, which, according to Judaism, is one of the three pillars upon which the world stands, intellectual attainment is meaningless. The ancient Rabbis of the Talmud said, 'Great is the knowledge that leads to action' and 'He whose deeds exceed his wisdom, his wisdom shall endure, but he whose wisdom exceeds his deeds, his wisdom will not endure.'

My purpose is better to equip the reader to understand and thereby refine his emotions by explaining the mind–heart interplay. First, we must show the vital connection between the mind and the emotions and how they can never be understood as contradictory, but rather are complementary.

Happiness cannot be achieved without a full integration of the emotions and the intellect. The source of all human unhappiness is internal conflict and tension, our outer actions not according with our inner convictions. It is when what our mind knows to be right contradicts what our emotions feel to be pleasurable.

As humans we often see ourselves as hybrid beings, buying into the false dualistic notions that were first taught by the ancient Persian philosopher Zoroaster.

Other religious thinkers have taught the same idea. The medieval Christian scholar Nicholas of Cusa called it *coincidentia oppositorum* ('union of opposites'). Since the opposites coincide without ceasing to be themselves, this also becomes an acceptable definition of God. The Hindu *jivanmukta*, the liberated individual, is he who is liberated from duality. The Tantras refer to the union of Siva (a Hindu god) and Shakti (Siva's consort) in one's own body and consciousness, and provide appropriate practices to this end.

Judaism rejects the Zoroastrian belief in dualism: Judaism is a monist tradition that asserts the underlying unity in all of creation. Living a life predicated on a false mind–heart dualism virtually guarantees inner dissent and unhappiness. How can we feel whole when we are fundamentally divided? In order to achieve nirvana, we must gain an understanding of our heart that will lead us to govern our emotions.

Second, we must show how the mind and the emotions must be integrated in order to allow us to live the lives we choose. Thus, we must define what an emotion is, explain what distinguishes it from intellect and show how the two are meant to operate in tandem. The secret to success is to be *who* we want *when* we want. To do this, we must acquire the ability to control and summon at will the proper emotion for the proper occasion.

To some, this goal will seem highly elusive and unrealistic. Others will question whether it is a recipe for self-mechanization and cliché, or even impossible to achieve. After all, isn't it the very nature of the emotions that they come naturally and spontaneously? My answer to all of the above is an emphatic no. The emotions are, contrary to popular belief, not beyond the realm of our control. The Kabbalah says that the mind is like a gardener who plants seeds in the heart; from there grow the emotions. In other words, we reap what we sow.

My great hope is that this book will serve as a map to chart the deepest desires of our heart, because while the heart has the awesome potential to breed wonderful attachments, it also has, by its subjective nature, the potential to create confusion. On our journey, we will examine the mosaic of appropriate and inappropriate emotion so that the positive ones can be emphasized and the negative ones purged, or at least managed. We will also examine how to maintain a healthy emotional balance.

We will begin the tour on one side of the spectrum with depression, which does not really belong on the map at all. It is the absence of emotion. It draws us inwards and condemns us to a life of solitary confinement. We will culminate the journey with joy and love, the holiest, most exhilarating and transcendent of the emotions. Whereas depression is the most dehumanizing of emotions because it deadens our spirit, joy and love are the most humanizing because they unburden us from the weight of selfishness and link us to our fellow human beings.

2

The pride of the intellect

One definition of man is 'an intelligence served by organs.

Ralph Waldo Emerson

Man is an intelligence, not served by, but in servitude to his organs.

Aldous Huxley

In my second year as Rabbi at Oxford, Thomas walked into my office. Although he was technically not Jewish, since his mother was not Jewish, he still had a great love for the Jewish community and wanted to help me build up the L'Chaim Society. I told him that he could help with the tedious work of sending out the weekly mailing every Sunday afternoon. In the days before megacopy machines, this was a wretched job that involved photocopying three thousand sheets of paper, folding and stapling them, and finally sticking an address label on each. Yet Thomas came religiously every Sunday and helped me like a real trooper.

After a few weeks, I discovered that Thomas was a Rhodes Scholar from Tennessee who had been a child prodigy. He had completed high school at twelve, finished university at seventeen, and completed his PhD in astrophysics at twenty-two. 'With a mind like yours,' I asked him, 'why would you waste five hours every Sunday volunteering to do such menial work as sticking papers together?' 'It's simple,' he answered. 'My father is a great professor and has won prestigious international awards for his work. Everyone loves him, that is, everyone but me. He has a great

19

mind, but an underdeveloped heart. He never gave me time or attention. So I have decided to develop my heart more than my mind. I want to care for people so that I don't end up lonely like my father.'

When we consider what distinguishes humanity from the animal kingdom, we usually think first of the human mind. We pride ourselves on our intellect, even referring to ourselves as *Homo sapiens*, thinking man, because we believe that what most distinguishes us from the beasts of the field is our ability to think rationally.

But this emphasis totally ignores the emotional component of the human personality, the emotions being from this point of view the antithesis of the intellect. Whereas the mind is cold, objective and detached, the heart is subjective and involved. And whereas the mind is logical and just, the heart is passionate, instinctive and obsessive.

But are we distinguished from hedgehogs because we can invent calculus, or do we invent calculus in order to create water purification plants and save lives? Is the truly special human organ our head or our heart?

The mind according to Moses Maimonides

According to the man considered by most to be the greatest Jewish thinker of all time, the vote would clearly be for the head. Born in 1135 in Cordoba, Moses Maimonides was the supreme theologian of medieval Jewry at the end of the historical period known as the Golden Age of Spain, two hundred years before the expulsion and subsequent dispersion of the Jews from the Iberian Peninsula. A Renaissance man in his day, he excelled in disciplines from philosophy to medicine and Jewish law, writing extensively on each subject. It was his ambition to make knowledge understood and loved by all the Jews, not just the select few scholars who guarded the entry to its gates. He is considered only second in greatness to his biblical namesake.

According to Maimonides, the meaning behind the enigmatic biblical passage that affirms man as having been created 'in God's image' is that man, like God and unlike the animals, is a creature capable of higher thought and deduction. While Maimonides regarded God as the Supreme Intellect, he held that man resembled God in this capacity, albeit at a far inferior level. Indeed, in *The Guide to the Perplexed*, he specified the intellect as man's defining characteristic: 'The true perfection of man [is] the possession of the highest intellectual faculties . . . it gives him immortality, *and on its account he is called man*' (my italics). To Maimonides, the purpose of human life was the objective pursuit of knowledge and the disinterested worship of God; we were meant to devote our lives to intellectually apprehending the deity.

Furthermore, Maimonides explained that the great material abundance promised in the messianic era was designed for no other purpose than to liberate man from his earthly pursuits and thereby grant him the time to fathom his Creator. In the messianic era, God would remove all the needling problems that today prevent us studying. There would be no ageing limbs, no spoiled crops, no clothes to be washed. Thus, we could get on with the really important work of raising our minds to ever higher levels of understanding.

Most of us today would tend to agree with this. Read any self-help book and you will see endless arguments on the need to attain higher consciousness. Millions of people meditate daily, retreating into their own private world of reflection. Woody Allen once said that he considered his brain to be his second-favourite organ. (By the first favourite, of course, he did not refer to his heart.) We tend to reserve our real respect for our minds, which may be why Albert Einstein and Sigmund Freud were two of the most respected and influential men of the twentieth century.

Intellectual versus emotional relationships

To understand the distinction between heart and mind, imagine a romantic relationship. There are two reasons why a man and a woman can get together in this way. The first involves the mind. Why do they love each other? Because they *understand* each other. They share common interests and try to fathom each other's depths. Although this is of itself not a bad thing, it is incomplete. No man or woman would ever be happy in a relationship of the mind because there are always aspects of the other's personality that are beyond rational understanding. Moreover, our capacity to understand is limited. We barely know ourselves, much less a stranger who invades our lives. The problem is further compounded by the vast gulf that separates men and women, who are different to their very core. The mind, in its profoundly inward orientation, cannot extend itself sufficiently to reach into someone else's gut. Couples who have intellectual relationships will always be missing the joy of experiential love. What a hug or a kiss conveys can never be matched by words.

The second kind of romantic relationship is where the love is based on the spiritual and mysterious human force we call attraction. This love is expressed in the couple's mutual desire to identify and accommodate each other's will. They feel each other. There is a mutual exchange of energy.

But there is a further point about relationships. When love is only intellectual, it remains objective; but is it good to be objective about your spouse? There is a point in marriage when objective evaluation must give way to subjective attachment. The very definition of love is to be subjective. You must learn to be content within your relationship and stop comparing your spouse to strangers.

Jack and Hillary had been married for four years. Although they were not very compatible in terms of interests, they were deeply in love. Their mutual attraction was so powerful that it overcame all their differences. As the years passed, however, this attraction began to wane, and Jack seemed distracted when other women were around.

As they drifted further apart, Hillary, who was an exercise

nut, told Jack that she wanted to buy a trampoline. He protested that he had not married a jumping jelly bean and dismissed her idea as absurd. Buried beneath his banal protests was a real fear that his wife's newfound craze would change her for ever. Maybe she wanted someone younger and more alive than him. Hillary, in return, could not believe that her husband was so obstinate about an item that was not even expensive.

Unable to resolve their dispute, they came to me for mediation. 'I could do this,' Jack said. 'I'd buy it for her in a minute if I could just understand it, but it's just so ridiculous.' Hillary's response to her husband was, 'You used to love me Jack. Now, you're trying to understand me.'

Hillary was right on the mark with her assessment. Whereas Jack once felt a deep emotional bond with his wife, it was now slowly becoming an intellectual bond. As neither had made a sufficient ongoing effort to sustain their deep attraction for each other, they started grasping at straws. They commuted their love from the experiential to the intellectual in a desperate effort to stay married.

In which bond do you think the couple was closer? Of course, we all want both types of bonding in our relationships. We want to be both lovers and best friends, to be both physically desired and profoundly understood. But do we want to achieve unity of the mind or of the soul?

Intellectual matchmaking

Studies show that the majority of people choose their spouse based on compatibility, thus electing for the 'intelligent model' of coupling. It seems that people fear that, once they run out of conversation, they will grow bored of each other and their love will wane. Because we have so little control over our emotional lives, we have come to believe that a relationship must be built on intellectual rather than emotional foundations.

Shere Hite became one of the world's most famous sex researchers when she made the discovery that more than eighty per cent of men date women to whom they are strongly attracted but will not marry them. Instead, they marry women with whom they share much in common. They marry the mind rather than the total personality. I contend that this is one of the main reasons why the divorce rate today is so high. Intellectual bonds can never be as strong as emotional bonds.

When I wrote *The Jewish Guide to Adultery*, a how-to book about restoring passion to a dormant marriage, my next-door neighbour was a features writer for *Vogue* and I asked her to write an article on the book. 'I like you, Shmuley, but I wouldn't write anything about your book,' she said. 'I violently disagree with your point about passion being the critical point in a marriage.' 'What then is the most important thing?' I asked her. 'Good communication,' she said. 'But how does that differ from normal friendship?' I asked. 'It doesn't. Your spouse is meant to be your best friend, closer to you than anybody else. But at its core, it's still friendship.'

This is precisely how Maimonides believed man's relationship with God should be. Far from feeling some mystical, rapturous force in which the soul is inexplicably drawn to the Creator, Maimonides wanted us all to be theologians. Since man's greatness lies in the fact that he possesses cognition, he could reach an intense love of God only through the purity of thought attained by the perfection of ideas. Any tampering of the mind's pure temple with emotion would lead only to contamination.

From this point of view, the emotions have no place in religion or life because they distort our rational observations. It comes as no surprise, therefore, that Maimonides viewed the emotions, especially libidinous ones, with the gravest suspicion. In *The Guide to the Perplexed*, he wrote:

> *Intelligent persons must, as much as possible, reduce these [physical] wants, guard against them, feel grieved when satisfying them, abstain from speaking of them, discussing them, and*

*attending to them in company with others. Men
must have control over all these desires, reduce
them as much as possible, and only retain of
them as much as is indispensable.*

The history of emotional degradation

This tradition of promoting the mind and denigrating the
emotions has had a long history in Western civilization.
Since ancient Greece, scholars have been respected more
than activists.

Religion especially has seemed to have some severe hang-
ups with the emotions. Monastic religion would entirely
purge us of our emotions in the name of ascetic piety. For
two thousand years, in the spirit of Thomas Aquinas,
Catholicism's greatest thinker, Christianity has trumpeted
theology. Like Maimonides, Aquinas tried to reconcile
revelation with reason, writing the five proofs of God's
existence, the first of which was based on Aristotle's *Meta-
physics*. And like Maimonides before him, Aquinas also held
that the emotions were not to be trusted because they pulled
us in directions that were often sinful. In *Summa Theo-
logica*, he outlined *concupiscentia* – lust, in today's lingo –
as the material principle of original sin. In sum, emotional
engagement was always problematic because it could lead
to illicit desire. Better to snuff out that fire than risk its
burning out of control.

This view also accounts for the bum rap that sex has
traditionally received from virtually every religion, with the
exception of Judaism. This is especially true of Christianity,
St Paul summing it up in his famous pronouncement: 'To
the unmarried and the widows I say that it is well for them
to remain unmarried as I am. But if they are not practising
self-control, they should marry. For it is better to marry than
to be aflame with passion' (1 Corinthians 7:8–9). Marriage
and sex are treated at best as a device with which to rid
ourselves of passion rather than be aflame with it.

Finally, this tradition of denigrating the emotions still

continues in academic circles, especially in Britain. When I served as Rabbi in Oxford, I organized every year a debate between science and religion that would usually draw upwards of one thousand students. On most occasions, the science side was represented by the eminent Professors Peter Atkins, author of the strong critique of religion *The Creation*, and Richard Dawkins, regarded by most as the world's most celebrated atheist, and leading evolutionist. Atkins and Dawkins – who, although adversaries, I came to admire and respect – objected to the study of not only religion, which they dismissed as myth, but also poetry as a serious pursuit, comparable to science. In their view, all emotional investment pulled man away from the hard truths of scientific fact. Needless to say, robbing life of the colour and vibrancy of more emotional pursuits leaves a heartless corpse.

3

The holiness of the emotions: a second view of man

Some men see things as they are and ask why. Others dream things that never were and ask why not.

George Bernard Shaw

Man is to be found in reason, God in the passions.
G. C. Lichtenberg

Because of the seemingly eternal, almost normative, religious disdain for the emotions, it seems proper to enquire whether or not it is acceptable for homo spiritus – religious man – to be passionate. Do emotions have any real place in religion? Does sexual passion figure among the aspirations of those who wish to lead a spiritual life? In short, are our emotions something to be proud of or are they the beast in man?

Contrary to the rationalist school of thought, there is an alternative view of man that privileges the subjective over the objective self. From this point of view, the intellect is actually the most confining piece of equipment we possess. In the essay 'Self Reliance', Ralph Waldo Emerson wrote that 'man is ... clapped into jail by his consciousness. As soon as he has once acted or spoken with éclat, he is a committed person, watched by the sympathy or the hatred of hundreds, whose affections must now enter into his account.' In other words, once we commit ourselves to a thought, we become prisoners to that thought, the mind focusing only on the art of the possible.

Few of you will remember the NeXT computer, developed

by Steve Jobs after he departed from Apple. I was one of the few people who used it. It was the greatest computing innovation of the late eighties and early nineties, but it did not catch on. When one of NeXT's engineers was quizzed on how Jobs continually brought great innovation to computing, he responded, 'Steve has no real training in computer engineering. He's an autodidact. As such, he doesn't know what can't be done.' But as much as intellect and knowledge opens worlds, it also closes them off.

However, when our passions are in gear, fuelled by our emotions, we are driven to conquer the impossible. It is inspiration rather than intellect that causes us to overcome obstacles. It was the messianic dream of redemption that inspired the Jews to return to their homeland after two thousand years of wandering and exile. It was emotion, not intellect, that caused man to envision landing on the moon. Like so many other human achievements, it was a *dream*, one at the time divorced from reality. Our emotions, however, ignore 'reality' and make us latch on to irrational hopes that lift us far beyond our wildest imagination.

Whereas our intellect firmly grounds us on the earth, our passions allow us to touch the stars. As Robert Browning so beautifully put it, 'A man's reach should exceed his grasp or what's a heaven for?' Our capacity for thought is limited, but our capacity for love is boundless. All those who achieved greatness throughout history may have had great minds, but they had even greater hearts, throwing caution to the wind and overcoming hurdles that others said were unassailable. Thus, while the mind can get you to think, only the heart can persuade you to march.

Therefore, despite Maimonides' unquestionable authority, and despite the fact that he is my favourite Jewish thinker, I must beg to challenge his opinion here, as others have before me. The greatness of being human lies not in our ability to think but in our ability to feel. What makes us human is our capacity to form relationships through emotional bonding. *This is unique to the human condition.* Animals do not get together to love but rather to survive.

In other words, our ability to love one another is our crowning achievement, something that cannot be replicated by any other organism on this earth. When two animals copulate they produce offspring, but when men and women perform the same activity, they make love, becoming one flesh in the process. It is no accident that humans are the only species (with the notable exception of the Bonobo monkeys) that procreate face to face.

The intellect isolates; the emotions connect

We have so far established that the emotions are superior to the intellect because they lead to action. Even more importantly, the emotions are superior because whereas the intellect isolates us from the world, emotions connect us to it. When we need to think about something, we journey on our own. We do not include others in the solitary process of contemplation.

As a young man studying to be a Rabbi, I was taught that man's greatness lay in his ability not to withdraw into a solitary, independent world of thought but to be drawn outside the realm of his own experience. Only the emotions, therefore, can lead to an enlargement of the self. As such, the ancient rabbis declared that while study and knowledge are important, they are significant only in so far as they inspire man to act justly. Indeed, the greatest Jewish heresy is to live purely for oneself; as the great Talmudic sage Hillel said, 'If I am only for myself, than what am I?' The mind might understand another's pain, but the emotions allow us to *feel* another's pain. This is why the emotions are sublime.

We never equate a lack of intelligence with a lack of humanity, but we do speak this way about people who have lost their ability to feel. If a man dressed in a designer suit passes a woman on the street with a starving baby and refuses to hand her some money for food, we consider him monstrous, lacking even basic humanity.

But the same would not be true if he could not understand Einstein's theory of relativity. It is our emotions, therefore, that make us fully human.

Similarly, male–female relationships are predicated not on our intellectual ability to understand each other but on our emotional capacity to connect: without compassion, we could never sympathize; without empathy, we could never forgive; without love, we could never become one with the other.

From this point of view, the way to understand the critical biblical pronouncement that man is created in the image of God is that it is precisely our ability to feel and love that makes us like God. God is not the great Thinker, He is the great Life-Giver. The Bible does not describe God as the cold and indifferent Being in the sky who watches as humans suffer through life's torments, but as a Being profoundly affected by human misfortune and pain.

When the Jews suffered during the destruction of the Temple in Jerusalem the Midrash teaches that God suffered and was exiled with them. There is a story about Rabbi Josse who went into a destroyed building in Jerusalem and met Elijah the Prophet. Elijah asked Josse, 'Did you hear anything in the building?' Josse responded, 'Yes, I heard a wailing voice saying "woe is it to the sons that because of their sins I destroyed my house and burned my place and exiled them among the nations." ' Elijah then rejoined, 'By your life, it is not only at this instant that this voice says this, rather every day, three times a day, at the times that the Jewish people enter the synagogue and answer Amen, God bends his head and says "Lucky is the king that they praise him so in his house and woe is to the father who has exiled his son. Woe to the son who has been exiled from his father's table." ' God is profoundly affected by human suffering.

Thus, we must finally reject the Cartesian model of 'I think, therefore I am', and replace it with 'I love, therefore I am; I feel, therefore I am'; because those who cannot feel have ceased to live.

The heart transforms us

Another way to understand the verse 'Man is created in the image of God' is to say that man has no fixed nature. Just as

God is infinite, so can man be. We are all empowered with freedom of choice. There is no predestination. Instead, we all have the potential to rise above our innate dispositions and be anything we desire.

Our genetic programming – our survival instinct – leads us to be selfish. A leopard cannot help but devour a zebra. Give him all the training in the world. Sit him in an ethics class. Show him pictures of the zebra's kids and tell him how they'll be orphaned. It's all a waste of time. A leopard cannot change its spots. But humans can choose to rise above their programming and not take advantage of weaker elements. Suddenly, hurting others is the equivalent of hurting ourselves. And this is really the bottom line: we are likened to God in our ability to love and feel for one another.

It comes as no surprise, therefore, that the love of one's fellow man plays so vital a role in ethics and religion. In Judaism, the commandment of Leviticus enjoining us to 'Love your neighbour as yourself' is the greatest of all the commandments, the second greatest being 'Love the Lord your God'. If one cannot transcend his limitations to feel for another earthly being, certainly he is unable to touch a celestial one, the love of the former serving as the first step towards embracing the latter.

This leads us to a powerful rule for success: *the heart is stronger than the mind because only the heart can change us as a person*. In nearly every case, those who showed early promise but never succeeded in developing their fullest potential failed to do so not entirely because they did not think right but because they lacked the motivation and the inspiration. They could not fire up their emotions, the essential engine of human advance. Or, alternatively, they could not rein in their emotions so their engine overloaded.

In sum, while there are those who believe that human greatness lies in our ability to build castles of the mind, others believe that our greatness lies in our ability to build bridges of the heart and soul connecting us to the creatures and the Creator. This is clearly my world view. The term *Homo sapiens* captures our ability to think, that of 'homo spiritus' encom-

31

passes our ability to transcend the self, extending horizontally by connecting with our human brothers and sisters, and vertically by connecting with the Creator of all life.

Real living is an attempt by man to be larger than himself, greater than merely a conglomeration of cells and tissues. In this grand mission, there can be no greater weapon in man's armoury than his emotions, which empower him with the hunger as well as the capacity to leap to the highest heights. What makes us uniquely human is not our ability to create ideas but our ability to create relationships – to love, to commit, to react to the world outside and shape our destinies based on our unique and subjective involvement.

Thoughts retreat, emotions entreat

The primary difference between the mind and the emotions is that the former pulls us into ourselves while the latter draws us outwards. Thought is, by definition, a solitary activity, noise and the presence of others actually impeding our ability to think clearly. That is why libraries are so quiet. By the same token, meditation is never a collective activity.

Those who privilege the mind over the heart do not realize that they are simultaneously endorsing a view of life in which the world does not matter. What really matters to them is the inner world of man. Mental constructs end up outweighing hard reality.

The heart is exactly the opposite. Feelings are like silk threads attaching us to things outside ourselves. The heart has become the ultimate symbol for the emotions because the heart is not an independent entity. It is a pump that exists only for the other organs of the body, driving blood and guaranteeing the body's survival. The same is true of human beings: our greatness lies in our ability to pump up and impact on our environment.

Human beings possess the unique spiritual capacity to extend themselves beyond the boundaries of their own concerns and actually relate to another. Think about your parents for a moment. Which would you prefer, a father who is far more concerned about his own mental development, or a father who sacrifices himself and invests his time in you? Who is the true hero?

In *Why I am Not a Christian*, Bertrand Russell wrote that the Christian faith is guilty of promoting personal salvation at the expense of world redemption. He makes the point that none of the Christian saints were canonized for works of public utility; instead they are remembered for their martyrdom or their saintly lives of prayer. While I believe that Russell's argument goes too far, it is ironic that Christianity, which promotes the idea of love above all else, should embrace a view of life that seems sharply at odds with the emotional ideal. While good works, connecting to the world outside, are important in Christianity, they are never as important as faith, which is a matter of the intellect.

Christianity is based on the idea that the head is higher than the heart, so many people cherish heaven above the earth. They want to lead saintly lives on earth merely to achieve a place in heaven. Heaven is the domain of the head. Thus, part of the ongoing degradation of our emotions is a simultaneous degradation of life here on earth.

There is an ancient rabbinic legend about how Moses argued with the angels over bringing the Torah down to earth as they wanted to keep it up in heaven for themselves. Moses argued, 'What do you need the Torah for? You're perfect. You cannot fulfil these commandments. You can't honour your parents, you don't have parents to honour. You can't keep the dietary laws of *kashruth*, you don't eat. And you don't need to be admonished not to sin because you have no propensity to sin.'

For those who believe in the emotions, earth is the place to be. In heaven, we cannot build relationships, make love or create families; we cannot feed the hungry nor comfort the bereaved. In heaven, we cannot improve our lives: we can only contemplate the glory of God. While the intellect pulls us towards heaven and away from earth, the emotions enjoin us to create heaven on earth.

4

How the emotions transform the self

One of the most critical features of emotion is that it has the power completely to transform our personality.

Samantha grew up in fear of her father because of his violent temper. When he blew up, he would throw things and yell until the rafters shook. By the time she became a student at Oxford, her parents had divorced and she was deeply estranged from her father. In an effort to re-establish his relationship with Samantha, her father started to come up from London nearly every weekend. At first, Samantha treated him politely and tried to make time for him in the hope that once he got his fill he would eventually stop visiting. When he persisted, however, she told him that she had no desire to be close and asked him not to come any more. 'I have lived without you since I was a little girl, and I find it difficult now to learn to live with you,' she said.

Her father called and asked me to intervene on his behalf. I urged Samantha to forgive her father and acknowledge the effort he was making to change. 'That's just it,' she told me, 'I do recognize how nicely he's behaving. In fact, he's nicer now than he ever was before. But you should see him when he loses his temper. He is a completely different man. When he does that, I don't know who he is and he frightens me. I don't want to be around when that side of him comes out again.'

Similarly, when a man loves a woman, his emotions adorn and embellish her. No matter what her age, she appears in his eyes to be in the full bloom of her youth. The moment he loses interest in her, however, he suddenly notices every imperfection. When love fades, she goes from being light as a feather to being an unbearable burden that he must carry all the time. Joy, or its absence, can make us respond to the same person or situation in entirely different ways.

I have many times become agitated over something petty. While I am in the throes of exasperation, the issue involved seems all important. When someone tells me to calm down, I just become more irritated. My wife will say, 'Why are you getting upset about this? It's not such a big deal,' and I think to myself, 'But this is the most important thing in the whole world!' After the wave of anxiety has passed, however, I wonder what all the fuss was about. How can this be? What changed? Did the subject at hand instantly undergo some type of metamorphosis? The answer is, of course, that it was not the issue that changed, but me.

The Talmud succinctly states that when a man dances at his son's wedding, he happily dances with even his worst enemy, so great is the transformation in him as the warmth of love in his heart melts the hatred away. This emotional 'melting' occurs because the joy produces such a strong sense of unity with all around us that there is no place for the alienation that hatred engenders. This is why we love receiving good news – it lifts us out of our drudgery. On the other hand, bad news pulls us down, and everything that then happens is tainted.

A recent study proved what every young twenty-something male knows by experience. If you take your date to a really scary movie, she is far more likely to agree to go to bed with you. Yes, this is a contemptible form of manipulation. But it works because, after being given a great fright, our natural defences fall as we seek to be embraced by a warm and protective human being.

The seasons of the soul

The physical world changes so vastly in the seasons of the sun that it becomes almost unrecognizable from one to the next. Look at a forest during winter: the ground is frozen and white, the trees barren, the wildlife hidden in underground dens. Come back a few months later, however, and the scene has changed remarkably. The sun is shining and the earth is bright. The trees are covered with leaves, and you can hear the sound of squirrels and deer as they frolic in their natural habitat.

In the same way that there are seasons of the sun, there are seasons of the soul. When we experience, like Richard III, the 'winter of our discontent', we are almost unrecognizable to the self we experience in summer. When our hearts are cold, when our souls are grey with despair, we are like a barren wilderness. Conversely, when our compassion nurtures the seeds of human friendship, we are like an orchard on a warm summer day.

We know that living in a climate with seasonal changes has its ups and downs, but as Oscar Wilde said, 'variety is the spice of life.' Just ask anyone who lives in Seattle how they feel about living in a place where it rains three hundred days a year. Despite the amazing beauty of Mount Rainier, a backdrop to the south side of the city, it becomes entirely obstructed from view when the sky is full of clouds. Indeed, it is no coincidence that despite Seattle's recent popularity as an up-and-coming place to live (it has thrice been voted America's most livable city), it still has the highest suicide rate per capita in the USA. The grey winter can seem endless, making it ripe territory for depression.

Similarly, ask anyone from Texas how they feel about living in a place that suffers intense heat and blinding sun for a good part of the year and they will tell you about their imminent plans to escape to Colorado. But anyone who lives in a region where there are four distinct seasons will tell you how much they enjoy the freshness of spring-time, the warmth of the summer sun, the brilliance of the leaves in autumn, and the briskness of the winter snow.

Just as the earth must eternally burst forth with new life, so too must the human personality for ever reinvent itself. Personalities that do not dance stagnate and become rigid like a rod. From this point of view, flux is good as it means that we have a variety of tools to respond to life. Certainly, a wife wants her husband's moods to change. She does not always want him to be lustful and passionate; just as often she needs a companion with whom she can talk.

The downside of emotional fluctuation, however, is that it makes us unpredictable. The same wife who appreciates her husband's emotional flexibility does not want his mood swings to cause her uncertainty over where she stands with him. Being married to a very moody spouse is everyone's worst nightmare and, from my counselling experience, the cause of much marital discord.

Consider the climate shift in a place like Australia, where the weather can diverge radically from the seasonal norm. In the middle of a summer heat wave, the temperature can drop to freezing, and in the middle of the winter, you can have a day of intense heat. In psychological terms, we would label this kind of weather manic. Unfortunately, although science has achieved great things, we still cannot control the weather; but we do have some say when it comes to our emotional make-up. In the words of Bishop Fulton J. Sheen, 'Each of us makes his own weather, determines the color of the skies in the emotional universe which he inhabits.' The very key to success – one of life's greatest and most critical challenges – is to find the golden balance between spontaneity and predictability.

The challenge of living in the physical world: finding balance

As a young rabbinical student, I remember reading stories about medieval monasteries. While the monks were, of course, Catholic, I remember feeling a begrudging sense of respect, even envy, for their level of commitment. Here

I was studying to be a Rabbi, yet I lived with all the pleasures of the modern world. Instead of donning uncomfortable hair shirts, I wore decent cotton shirts that were regularly laundered. Instead of undertaking a vow against laughter or silence, I occasionally watched a video and had a good time with my friends. Moreover, while we could not have sexual relations because we abstained before marriage, we always hoped that we would, God willing, marry one day and have a warm female presence in our lives. We were not sworn to celibacy for life, like monks. It was hard to imagine how there were men of God who actually renounced all material pleasures – including sex – in His name.

It was only when I grew older and more mature that I understood the truth. The ascetics had actually taken the easy way out while I had chosen the more difficult path. Extremism is comparatively simple to adopt, but moderation takes great discipline and willpower to achieve. Cloistered in a monastery, the monk's faith is not challenged by that from which he has retreated. He is never confronted with people who have radically different views from his own and is thus never pressed to change or compromise. The rest of us, on the other hand, must struggle daily to uphold our principles and maintain our morality. Thus, while renouncing the earth in favour of the heavens does involve substantial material hardship, it does not involve the hardest of all workouts – bringing equilibrium to our contradictory and conflicting impulses.

Consider too the pacifist. It is difficult to be a pacifist because, when someone hits you, you must refrain from retaliating. You may even get killed to uphold your principles. However, the position is easy to maintain because there are no pangs of conscience involved. You are never torn between two equally good arguments. You do not have to look in the mirror and wonder whether you have become a monster after what seems to be a necessary retaliation.

In his chilling book, *Dawn*, Elie Wiesel depicts a

Holocaust survivor who has joined the pre-Israel Haganah defence movement. The new combatant has captured a British soldier whom he must kill as soon as the sun rises in retaliation for the British execution of Jewish prisoners. Wiesel hauntingly describes how all the ghosts of the Jewish soldier's murdered relatives taunt him how he himself has become a murderer. Such is the ferocious agony of having to reconcile opposites.

The extremist will never know the gratification of synthesis, the drawing out of the best of both worlds. Because their perspective is so narrow and limited, extremists – like workaholics – are immensely boring people.

The wisest of all men, King Solomon, recognized the great difficulty involved in achieving the critical balance. In the book of Ecclesiastes, he suggested that the key to succeeding in life was to know that there was a proper time for everything:

> *For everything there is a season, and a time for every matter under heaven: a time to be born, and a time to die; a time to plant, and a time to pluck up what is planted; a time to kill, and a time to heal; a time to break down, and a time to build up; a time to weep, and a time to laugh; a time to mourn, and a time to dance; a time to throw away stones, and a time to gather stones together; a time to embrace, and a time to refrain from embracing . . . a time to love, and a time to hate; a time for war, and a time for peace.*

In sum, the secret to living a successful life – one that is happy, healthy, productive, engaging and stimulating – is to find the proper balance between heaven and earth, ego and selflessness, joy and seriousness, indulgence and sacrifice. And within that great challenge there is nothing so difficult or so important as harmonizing the intellect with the emotions.

Synthesizing the emotions and the intellect

Embedded within each person are opposing forces that constantly up-end one another. The intellect is cold and objective. It examines and evaluates but rarely commits. The emotions, on the other hand, are heated and subjective, committing even before any examination or evaluation. While the emotions can be beautiful, they can if unguided also be deadly. It is the role of the intellect to guide the emotions from where they should be repulsed to where they should be attracted.

A metaphor in the Kabbalah is that the three faculties of intellect – wisdom, understanding, and knowledge – are the parents who give birth to the emotions. The intellect is designed to bring rational and principled thought to bear on human situations. Depending on its conclusions, it is then meant to send a signal to the heart to give birth to the proper emotions. Like parents who must guide their children to life-affirming goals, the intellect must develop the proper passions and steer the individual to healthy aspirations. The mind must lend instruction on that which is beneficial and holy, and that which is immoral and destructive.

In other words, our minds must determine what is good and what is evil, but our emotions must cause us to gravitate towards the good and reject the evil. The mind can guide but only the heart can compel us to act. Without intellect, the emotions are like a bunch of spoiled brats; they have all the energy and limitless curiosity that we so adore in children, but they end up making a total mess.

Whereas in other philosophical systems the emotions are perceived as facilitating the ends of the intellect, the very opposite is true in Judaism. The intellect is designed as a means by which to guide and give rise to positive emotion, which, in turn, compels the individual to act in accordance with Divine will. As a Rabbi whose object it is to help young people to become more involved with their religious traditions, I have discovered that there are three possible ways – three 'c's' – to interest people in religion: coercion, convenience and conviction. You can force people to be religious, and many traditions have burned people at the stake or beheaded them for transgressing religious truths. Alternatively, you can embrace religion out of a sense of convenience (which is how most religious people were raised). Or, you can embrace a religious life-style out of a deep-seated sense of conviction and belief.

Of the three possibilities, only the last provides sufficient stimulus to harmonize the inner soul of man and the outer world upon which he seeks to leave an impression. If man acts without inner conviction, although he may undertake a virtuous action, he will not have changed inwardly in the slightest and the religious exercises will all be for nought. But conviction means that we do the right things for the right reasons. And for this, a passion for goodness is essential.

Samantha, whom I quoted at the beginning of this chapter, was right. Our emotions are the most crucial part of our lives because they directly determine the kind of people we will be. If you have a bad temper that regularly erupts, you are an angry person. If you act kindly with a soft heart, you are a compassionate person. Whichever emotion you most often exhibit will become the defining characteristic of your being. Thus understanding and controlling our emotions is key to becoming the people we want to be.

5

Expressing emotion

My great religion is a belief in the blood, the flesh,
as being wiser than the intellect. We can go wrong
in our minds. But what our blood feels and
believes and says, is always true. The intellect is
only a bit and a bridle.

D. H. Lawrence

My definition of emotion is any inner movement – an internal disposition – which requires external release. Our thoughts pull us deeper into ourselves while our emotions pull us outside ourselves. And yet some people have real trouble expressing their emotions. To understand our emotions better, let's look at the quintessential paragon of logic, *Star Trek*'s Mr Spock. I had the pleasure of hosting Leonard Nimoy – the actor who created and played Mr Spock for twenty years – at our L'Chaim Society where he gave a lecture to a capacity audience. In 'real life', Leonard Nimoy is anything but the emotionless Spock, but the unique character he portrayed still fascinates fans. What is it about Spock that so intrigues us, and why has the Vulcan who appears so dispassionate become such a cherished cultural icon?

While Spock supposedly had no emotions, he always demonstrated a great level of decency. Without so much as a smile, we knew how warm his friendship with Kirk was. We even knew that there was some sort of affection for Dr McCoy despite their constant bickering. Perhaps Spock's most endearing quality, however, was the repeated sacrifice he displayed for his fellow crew members on the Starship Enterprise, the most notable being in the famous ending to the film *Star Trek II*: in an effort to save the ship from destruction, Spock sacrificed himself and died from radiation poisoning.

Thus, contrary to popular belief, Spock *did* have emotions; they just were not overtly pronounced. By the same token, just because a person does not smile, this does not mean they are emotionless. It only means that they have great difficulty expressing their emotions. Or may be they have been so hurt in life that they do not trust anyone enough to show them. Conversely, someone who smiles all the time may do so insincerely. But the very existence of a friendship is always proof of a deep emotional bond, no matter how Spock-like two friends may appear when speaking with one another. As we said in Chapter 3, the very essence of the emotions is shown in the human ability to connect with something outside itself.

But Spock wasn't married

Even though Spock had a deep friendship with Kirk, it would be very difficult to imagine him as a husband or a father. His children would want to play, and he would respond, 'But that's not logical!'

A middle-aged couple once came to me for counselling. The wife began the conversation, 'My husband never tells me that he loves me!' The husband responded, 'I told her I loved her on our wedding day twenty years ago. If anything changes, I'll let her know!' That is an intellectual expression of love which, while apparently satisfactory for one partner, leaves much to be desired for the other. Such a statement, unfortunately all too common, is based on an erroneous understanding of emotion.

In terms of expressing feelings, there are two principal ways in which our hearts differ from our minds. The first is the need for expression itself. Thoughts are by definition internal. While you can of course *choose* to reveal your thoughts, there is no intrinsic need for this and it is, in fact, unnatural to do so. The second is that intellectual truths are constant. Two plus two equals four is a universal truth that, when unexpressed, is no less potent.

But the same is not true of the emotions. First, emotions need to be released; without expression they are nothing. Every emotion first involves an internal movement, an inner disposition, which naturally fights to flow out. In the same way that it is not natural for thought to be revealed, it is unnatural for emotions to be stifled. If someone tells you, 'I'm quietly emotional, I don't express my feelings', you would say, 'No you're not, you're just acting English!' Emotions are not meant to be kept to oneself. If someone tells you they are happy for you but does not show it, you really have to question whether they mean it. Maybe what they are saying is, 'I'd really like to be happy for you but I'm envious.' No matter what the truth is, if they do not show it, it certainly will not last.

Second, emotions are not eternal in the way that intellectual truths are. Without care and nurture, like flowers in a garden, emotions rapidly evaporate. If you do not work on expressing and sustaining love, you will lose it. Fortunately, this can also be of benefit: if you choose to do nothing about your anger and just let it subside, it will pass without causing great harm.

With the exception of anger, however, the emotions may as well not exist if they do not cause us to act. Too many parents nowadays tell their children that they love them, yet rarely show it. We all know the great adage 'Actions speak louder than words'. By continuing to place their careers, their lives, their needs before those of their children, these parents are really saying that they love themselves more. In such circumstances, the emotions are basically indistinguishable from thoughts; they remain internal, affecting the individual but never his surroundings.

Emotional stoppages

James's mother died when he was seven. His father married a widow with three children, a tough woman who favoured her own children over James. Because James grew up feeling unloved, he learned to fend for himself. Grief-stricken with loneliness, he fell in love with Joy and married in his early twenties. His marriage quickly began to unravel because, although he loved his wife, he was an emotional cripple who was unable to show that love. Consequently, Joy felt neglected and hurt.

James protested that he loved her with all his heart but had difficulty showing it. When he asked me for advice, I told him that we are not meant to know how to show love, it is just meant to happen. What he had done was to create an artificial blockage because he had learned how to shield himself in protective armour. Because he had never learned how to take the armour off, it became like a second skin. 'Take away the armour,' I told him, 'and you'll see how your love will pour out. Learn how to be vulnerable and don't be afraid of being rejected.'

King Solomon said, 'Wisdom makes one's face shine, and the hardness of one's countenance is changed' (Ecclesiastes 8:1). When we are healthy, what we feel on the inside automatically finds expression on the outside. Wisdom makes our faces glow; joy makes our countenances shine. Psychologist Mihaly Czikszenmihalyi from the University of Chicago describes this as 'the state of flow', a state in which the individual can experience a rare sense of heightened consciousness and a desirable air of self-fulfilment.

When unhealthy, on the other hand, we experience an emotional roadblock. Our emotions come up against a great internal dam that prevents them flowing naturally. Removing this barrier is essential to achieving wholeness. The ancient Rabbis said, 'If you have to, go out and buy a friend.' The underlying message here is that no matter what, we all need someone with whom we can express our emotions, a recipient who allows us to express the full gamut of our inner world.

How the emotions work

In the same way that ligaments connect muscle and bones, emotions serve as the link connecting thought and action. An emotion causes an internal commotion. Something occurs to us on the inside that must find expression on the outside. When someone is truly happy, they cannot help but act upon it. Indeed, the goal of the emotions is to inspire us to find that outlet in action.

I have a relative who won several million dollars in the Florida State Lottery. (He has, incidentally, since become my favourite relative.) I asked him what he did when he heard the news. 'I sort of just sprang to my feet. It happened by itself. I wasn't in control.' Similarly, when someone falls in love, they rush to tell their friends. This is because falling in love is not a cerebral act; it is purely emotional.

The same is true of pain. When we hurt ourselves, we automatically cry. The tears just arrive on their own. A woman in labour automatically screams because the pain of the contractions is so hard to bear. Her mind simply cannot override the command of nature.

The Bible contains numerous examples of people who acted upon their emotions. Bilaam's hatred of the children of Israel was so great, for example, that he saddled his donkey and ran out to curse the Jews. Similarly, Pharaoh's hatred for the Jews was so intense that he ran to chase them into the Red Sea. This was not typical protocol for the ruler of Egypt who had an army and servants to do his bidding, but his emotion was so strong that he could not help but act upon it. Responding to positive emotion, we find that Abraham's love for God was so great that he ran to perform the sacrifice of his son Isaac, however questionable the command might have been. In a similar vein, Joseph's love for his father Jacob was so great that he dashed out to greet him even though he was the viceroy of Egypt and should not have rushed out to greet a subject.

We can almost always tell what a person is feeling by their facial expression. If they are angry, they look angry and steam seems to come out of their ears. Unless we are Spock, we usually cannot help but show what we feel. But look at someone's face and the chance is that you will have absolutely no idea what they are thinking: our thoughts are buried under layers of clothing, but we wear our emotions openly on our sleeves.

To be sure, I am not saying here that we have to express every emotion. Later I will discuss whether it is better to release all emotions – including the negative ones – or to bottle them up and hold them inside. But even if we choose to bottle up our emotions rather than have them explode like a tidal wave, we are still *choosing* to do so. The unhealthy state I describe in the next chapter relates to people who cannot express their emotions *even if they choose to* because they have an internal emotional blockage.

6

The difference between true and false emotions

True emotions, as we have stated, must be released. False emotions are, in contrast, imitations that share some characteristics of the genuine article but nevertheless differ radically. Pity is an example of a false emotion. When we feel pity for someone we feel sorry for them but we do not have any real desire to help them. Pity allows us to distance ourselves from a person's misfortune. It lets us off the hook by telling us, 'There, there. Isn't it terrible to see that person hungry? And it's so good that you feel bad about it.' Like thought, pity draws us inwards: we cordon off a part of our heart in order to experience the pain but we do not let it spread beyond that. Indeed, we are almost happy that it happened to them and not to us.

Compassion is the antithesis of pity. Compassion is a true emotion because it leads to real acts of benevolence to alleviate another's plight. We pull out our wallets almost intuitively because we cannot bear to witness the suffering of our human brother or sister.

Consider also the difference between true joy and an emotional high. Both promote an internal feeling of warmth and pleasure, but instead of demanding external release, an emotional high causes us to withdraw into a blissful state of numbness, what we call being mellow. So many young people today take drugs because they want to be high. They don't want to feel. What they really want is to numb the pain. Little do they realize they are really achieving a low.

When I went to visit Matt in his dorm at Oxford, I noticed

the door was open. I knocked a few times, and when it seemed that he still did not notice me, I entered. The room was filled with the pungent scent of marijuana. And there was my friend lying on his bed, smoking one of the biggest joints I had ever seen. When he saw me, Matt just said, 'Wow, man. You want some?'

Slowly, it dawned on him who was staring at him. 'Oh my God, it's my Rabbi.' 'What are you smoking?', I asked him. It was too late to deny it. 'Weed, man. The Lord giveth. The law taketh away.' Then, in a moment of panic, he said, 'Hey, Shmuley, you're not gonna let my folks know about this, are you?' I had him cornered. 'Not if you come to study Torah with me for an hour each day for the next four years.' A fate worse than death as far as he was concerned, but certainly not worse than his parents' wrath. 'It's a deal brother,' he said, as he safely stored away the holy herb.

At one of our classes, Matt asked me what was really wrong with smoking pot. 'It makes me high, man. It feels good and releases stress. And it's green and natural too.' I begged to differ: 'When you smoke marijuana, you feel nothing. That's why you like it. It makes you *stop* feeling. Whatever pain you were in, you stop feeling it. But feeling is something that pulls you out of yourself. When you smoke, it's like curling up into a little ball, all soft and snuggly in a womb of your own. And it's wrong because it makes you exchange a real high – the kind that comes from the joy of giving – for a false high, the kind that comes when you tell everybody to go to hell.'

Where I live in the New York area, there is an epidemic of eligible bachelors who will only date models. A girl with a kind heart and a strong mind counts for nothing with them unless it is all wrapped up in a 36DD chest. I call these men drug addicts because they are addicted to the instant, visual high that comes from seeing an object of beauty. They exchange the experience of a true emotional high – the product of being in love with a woman of merit – for the false high of arousal by a long pair of legs. (A temporary arousal that lasts just about as long as it takes for an even longer pair of legs to walk by.)

False emotions deaden the soul

These false highs are not just about the body being purged of emotion but about the body being purged almost of life itself. Sure, it sometimes feels good to stop living because life can be stressful and agonizing. But never confuse an emotional high with true emotion. The essence of emotion is that it overtakes us and leads us to positive action. If feeling does not connect us with something outside us, it ain't real. How many men who date for the thrill of having a beauty object on their arm ever really connect with them? And isn't it a shame that so many women continue to provide this aesthetic drug by becoming ever slimmer and wearing more make-up, instead of providing the real medicine of feminine comfort and warmth?

Cynthia disagreed with me. 'You're wrong about your definition of emotions, Shmuley. Let's say you've gone through a painful relationship. You take some time to recover, but you're still all battered inside. Then you meet a guy and he wants to love you. But you won't let him because of all the pain. So here a real emotion, pain, *prevents* you connecting with someone outside yourself. And you're saying that real emotions connect you with someone else.'

'What you're saying, Cynthia, confirms my point. A guy shows you love,' and it didn't take a genius to know she was talking about herself, 'and the *natural* reaction is to reciprocate. The appropriate response to being shown love is to respond with love. But here you consciously suppress what you want to show. You are acting in reverse. You are connecting, but you are inverting the connection in order to minimize the risk of further pain.'

When we refrain from showing emotion

Make no mistake about it, consciously suppressing emotion that should be displayed will undermine all your efforts at a successful and fulfilling life, whatever the excuse. Alan owned a glasses business with about thirty employees. After years of expansion, he hit upon hard times and had to lay off half his staff. But a group of ten employees who had been with him from the beginning, and who really cared about him, told him that they would take an amazing fifty per cent reduction in their wages until he got back on his feet. Alan, who was looking at another appalling balance sheet at the time, raised his eyes, thanked them quietly and went back to his reading.

His employees were deeply hurt. Here they were showing a dramatic sacrifice for him, and he couldn't even get up to thank them. Alan later apologized to them, saying that he was so miserable that he could not show any appreciation to anyone. But it was too late. Four of the employees had already submitted their CVs to other employers.

There is no quicker road to the unravelling of our relationships than refraining from expressing necessary emotion. In fact, refraining from showing love is even worse than showing hatred. I use the word 'refraining' because it shows that emotion is natural and instinctive. In the Book of Proverbs, King Solomon says that the heart is like looking into a mirror: what you show it, it shows you. When you show someone love, there is usually an automatic and reciprocal emotion of love. Refraining from it is a conscious choice, and that choice to hold back is far more damaging than even actively doing something to harm your relationship. The foundation of every relationship is the regular exchange of affection.

Emily had been married to Jonathan for ten years. One night she came home to find him in their matrimonial bed with a prostitute. She gathered her belongings, took their young baby and went to stay with her mother. Jonathan tried to get her back. First, he unconvincingly attempted to tell

Emily that it was not his fault. He argued that the woman rang the doorbell and forced him to have sex with her. He was raped against his will. For some inexplicable reason, Emily did not believe him. Then Jonathan begged her to come back. He confessed that what he had done was unforgivable but still implored her forgiveness. Emily wouldn't budge.

I went over to see her and joined in beseeching her forgiveness for her husband: 'Even if he is a jerk, he is still *your* jerk. He is your husband and you love him. Why don't you take him back?' 'That's just it,' she told me. 'If I loved him, I would take him back. But I don't love him. He is a cold man, never showing me any appreciation. The telephone and television receive all his time and attention. This marriage is empty. I can't forgive a man for whom I feel so little.'

Jonathan had lost his wife not for the bad he had done, but for the good he had not done. He had destroyed his marriage not because of his illicit passion but because of the total lack of passion he had shown to the right woman. When there are strong bonds of affection created through years of showing emotion, you can usually get through the difficult moments of a relationship, but when these do not exist, any rupture is bound to separate you.

No more cavemen

I loved John Gray's *Men Are from Mars, Women Are from Venus*, even though so much of the book was pilfered from my own writings on relationships (mercifully, I decided not to sue). However, the point he makes about men going into their caves and not wanting to discuss problems is, while true, just not acceptable. A significant number of the couples I have watched divorce involved husbands who simply could not talk about their problems. Their wives, rather than understanding them being closed off, wondered about their own role in the marriage. 'Am I just a cook and a maid?' Shelly asked me. 'He doesn't share things with me and he won't let me comfort him.' Husbands who do not express their feelings to their wives deprive not only themselves of much-needed comfort, but also their wives of allowing them to share their nurturing instincts.

My father was always a loving man, but he could never show much emotion. He had a very painful childhood in Iran, living in abject poverty with twelve siblings, and everything he attained in life came by the sweat of his brow. He is a good man who not only struggled to support himself and his family, but also supported those of his siblings who could not earn a living. It took me many years to understand the buried pain that made him so unemotional on the outside. As I grew older, we vastly strengthened our relationship, but so much precious time had been lost.

Sure, I am partly to blame because I was judgemental of him. After all, I was a spoilt kid raised with everything I needed in America. I was not grateful of how hard he worked to pay for my schooling and my upbringing because to me it was all expected. But that did not alter the simple fact that his five children all needed his love. And when kids do not receive the love they need, they learn to become introverted themselves. There comes a time in the life of a family when we must end the generational cycle of pain.

Every action demands an appropriate response. If you live with a loving spouse who is kind enough to build a home for you and give you children, yet you show no emotional response, you have not created a relationship. The emotions are like strings. Every emotion ties you to something outside yourself, either positively or negatively. But if you have built no bonds, it becomes very easy to drift apart.

To succeed in the field of human relationships, you must always respond with the appropriate emotion. If someone shows you kindness, you must first *feel* and then *show* them appreciation. If they show you contempt, you have the right to show them disdain, although it is far wiser to choose to rise above it and show them compassion.

Advice for emotional cripples

For those who have either been hurt by life or born with a very shy and retiring nature, there is hope. First, if you are a man, a woman often loves this type because it makes her feel necessary. She feels that you need her in order to learn how to express your emotions. In this way she is your personal redeemer, your own private messiah.

Second, here is some simple yet profound advice on how to release your emotions: when you do not feel comfortable expressing some emotion that is building up inside yet you know it is appropriate, do it anyway. Force yourself the first few times, and little by little you will gnaw away at the emotional barrier until it has gone.

Both Aristotle and Maimonides explain that there are two kinds of human nature. The first encompasses our natural inborn character traits. Modern scientists would call this our genetic make-up. Some people are born passive, with a kindly disposition, others aggressive with a strong competitive streak.

But there is another kind of human nature, an *acquired* one, by which we have the potential genuinely to change ourselves. Indeed, it is one of Judaism's strongest beliefs that repetitive habit ultimately becomes second nature. By practising the same action over and over again, the deed becomes ingrained into our programming to the point where its performance becomes automatic and instinctual. So what begins as something we *do* ends up as something we *are*.

How nurture changes nature

Take someone who is born with a self-centred streak. When she passes a beggar on the street, her natural reaction is to walk straight by and curse 'the freeloader' under her breath. But one day, motivated by a sense of guilt or shame in the face of other onlookers, she gives the beggar a few coins. The next day she does it again, and the next day. Soon it becomes automatic. Then, she ends up as a compassionate person who *cannot help* but contribute some coins whenever she walks by someone in need. She then becomes transformed from someone who *gives* charity to someone who *is* charitable. This new inner compassionate feeling will then need continually to be released.

Just as brushing our teeth should not be done only when we feel particularly hygienic, we cannot practise kindness only when we feel compassionate. By the same token, a husband and wife who only show each other affection when they *feel* romantic will quickly drift apart.

For better or for worse

A couple married for sixteen years who had recently been experiencing severe problems in their marriage came to see me. The wife complained of a cold and inattentive husband who could not shut off his business worries once he came home. The husband responded by describing his wife as insensitive and ungrateful. 'I admit that I'm cold to her lately,' he said, 'because my business is in dire financial trouble. How can she expect me to be in a loving mood when everything I built is teetering on the brink of collapse? Haven't I always provided for her? I can't talk to her about it because she would never understand.'

I told him that affection between husband and wife cannot be reserved for moments of financial prosperity. Life is filled with ups and downs, and any man who sinks into a world of his own while walking through the valleys will not have a wife left with whom to share the precious joy at the peaks. 'Take your wife into your confidence, lean on her and tell her of your woes. Married life must be shared throughout all moments.'

This is the same advice I gave to Harold, who had divorced his wife when his young son was only four years old. Consequently, he was not around much as the boy grew older. After his son's eighteenth birthday, Harold told me that he wanted to start being a father. 'I want to change. I want to show love to my son. But for the life of me, Shmuley,

I honestly don't feel it. I know he's my boy and all, but I just don't feel close to him.'

'Never mind what you feel right now,' I told Harold. 'Just go and do the right thing. Spend time with your son. Go to ball games together. Believe me, after a while you'll see that all the love in your heart will swell up and you'll start feeling close to him again.'

There are times in our lives when our heart needs some jump leads, a little electrical spark to get the old engine running again. That spark is the spark of a good deed, which switches our heart back to the 'on' position.

PART TWO

Emotional Fundamentals

Innocence

THE FOUNDATION OF ALL EMOTION

*The lover of nature is he whose inward and
outward senses are still truly adjusted to each
other; who has retained the spirit of infancy even
into the era of manhood.*

Ralph Waldo Emerson

There is no aphrodisiac like innocence.

Jean Baudrillard

Why am I writing a chapter on innocence when, according
to the criteria I established earlier, innocence is clearly
not an emotion? We said that an emotion is an inner disposition that requires external release, something on the
inside that has to flow to the outside. Innocence, on the
other hand, is a state of being, a character trait.

I include this discussion because innocence serves as the
support system underlying all the emotions. Indeed, it is the
pillar upon which all true emotions rest because it empowers us to authenticate what we feel. Simply stated,
emotion presupposes our ability to be touched, our capacity
to be moved. This in turn means that at all times we must be
like a blank piece of paper that has never been written on
before. Let me explain. The premise of this book is that
what makes us truly human is not our ability to think but
our capacity to feel. If we cannot feel truly and deeply, we
are nothing more than glorified apes. And if we lack innocence, we cannot feel truly and deeply, because innocence
allows us to respond to our feelings naturally, while the lack

of innocence makes us respond to our feelings in contrived and artificial ways.

Nancy, an attractive woman in her middle twenties, asked me if I could introduce her to a nice Jewish man. I invited her to our home for a Sabbath meal, and she ended up meeting a pretty decent guy. He took her out once but would not do so again. I introduced her to another man, and he also took her out once but not a second time. Then the same thing happened with a third man. I couldn't understand why. On the surface she seemed like a really good catch: physically attractive, highly intelligent and educated, and from a good family. So what was the problem?

I called her to see how she was doing. 'Why do you ask,' she said, which struck me as odd. Why was she being so defensive? 'Well,' I said carefully, 'we're friends and it's polite for friends to enquire as to their mutual well-being.' I then asked her how things were going at work. 'They're fine. Why would you think there are any problems?'

So that's the reason men aren't interested in her, I thought to myself. She is entirely on the defensive; heck, I couldn't even ask a simple question without feeling attacked for doing so. Later, however, I realized that I was wrong. Men quickly lost interest in her not because of her defensiveness or paranoia, but because they saw that she had lost her innocence. None of her responses came from the heart; they were all guarded and contrived. As such she was less real, less human and therefore less attractive.

I asked her why she had such a problem with trust. 'Well,' she said, 'all men have an agenda. They're interested in only one thing. They don't want to get to know you, they just want to use you.' It was almost as if she had made it her business to outsmart men, to show that she could be just as manipulative as she felt they were. Something had obviously happened that had robbed her of her innocence.

Defining innocence

There is nothing so beautiful in life, nor so attractive, as innocence. You can go to Disney World and be awed by the incredible Magic Kingdom that cost billions of dollars. You can go to New York City and be amazed by the skyline of buildings that scrape the heavens. Yet you will never consider these places as beautiful as a colourful canyon at sunrise or a snow-capped mountain at sunset. There is a purity to nature that can never be attained by human ingenuity or artificial manipulation. Similarly, a woman today can change every part of her face and body with plastic surgery, but the moment a man discovers her breasts are made of silicon, he will usually not find her as attractive.

Let us define innocence by first considering its opposite. Guilt is the opposite of innocence only in the legal sense of culpability; innocence as a character trait has nothing to do with blamelessness. The opposite of innocence is artifice, when we bury our innermost selves under layers of pretence.

In contrast, what makes the innocent person so deeply attractive is the openness of their heart. Because their soul is translucent, you can see right through to their core. And innocent people disarm us. Because they are so natural, they invite us to behave naturally around them, allowing our deepest selves to be manifest. They possess the unique gift of making us not take ourselves too seriously as they never invite competition. Similarly babies, the most innocent creatures of all, bring out the best in even the toughest people because they force us to be genuine. With adults, we mask our truest selves because we seek approval and fear humiliation.

Unskilled in the art of manipulation, the innocent person accepts the humanity and infinite worth of every individual. With no agenda other than sharing and openness, the innocent person allows us to lessen our guard too. The manipulative person, on the contrary, sees others as the means by which to achieve his own selfish ends. He therefore causes the person he is interacting with to raise their defences and be on the alert.

Innocence is about living honestly, not pretending to be something we are not. It is to be transparent in every situation and act honestly and genuinely. Indeed, this is perhaps the greatest problem that couples today suffer from – because they are not honest with themselves, they find it hard to be honest with others. When we live in a world of such masquerade, it becomes hard to trust, and the cycle perpetuates itself. After a while we all begin to forget who we are and our relationships dissolve.

Nakedness and childhood: living honestly

Innocence is usually associated with nakedness and childhood, but what do these latter two states have in common? The essence of nakedness is the absence of external embellishment in terms of clothing; that of childhood is the absence of external embellishment in terms of intellect. Both nakedness and childhood represent our most natural selves before we get covered up in artifice. Naturally trusting and optimistic, children do not perceive the ugliness in the world even when it surrounds them. Consequently, they do not exercise the tools of the more mature cynic: sarcasm and doubt.

Tell a child that the moon is made of green cheese and he will believe you. It is only after he reads in a book how this is not so that he will become corrupted. Because he now knows that people have the capacity to lie, he will not trust what you tell him next. Consequently, it will be necessary for you to prove yourself to him. You will have to bring outside support – facts, studies, statistics (all tools of the intellect) – in order to prove that what you say is true. In other words, intellect will be required to compensate for loss of innocence.

Put another way, the more we lose our innocence, the less emotional we are and the more intellectual we become. Take a man and a woman who start dating. She lets her emotions go and allows herself to fall in love with him. They go to bed, and she never hears from him again. The next time she dates a guy, she will be on her guard. Because she will not naturally trust him, he will have to prove his love.

When we lose our innocence, our emotions always suffer the most. Emotions are meant to be automatic and intuitive, never contrived. They are all about letting go and allowing ourselves to feel. So, whenever we are immersed in an environment where there is no trust, we train ourselves not to feel.

Consider the Garden of Eden narrative as a metaphor for the compensation of innocence with intellect. Before Adam and Eve ate from the Tree of Knowledge, they were in their most natural state. They were naked physically, but also naked in another way: like innocent children, they had nothing to hide. Emotionally honest with themselves and with each other, it was truly Paradise. It was only after eating from the tree that they attained the self-consciousness and intellect that taught them how *not* to be natural. Whereas before we could say that they were ignorant but blissful, after consuming the fruit they learned how to lie. So when God came to Adam and asked him if he ate from the tree, he responded by placing the blame on Eve. He lied. He became manipulative. He tried to hold someone else accountable for his own shortcomings. Eve, in turn, blamed the snake. She lied. Their great sin was that they manipulated the truth with the intellectual power of reason, and in so doing, they lost the ability to be natural and honest with God, with one another and with themselves. And we have lived with that sin of artifice ever since.

When they later shrouded themselves with fig leaves, they covered not just their physical nakedness; this Victorian interpretation is entirely superficial. The deeper meaning is that, in covering themselves, the first man and woman of the world concealed their beautiful souls. That part of them which was most natural, most open, now became cloaked under layers of self consciousness and pretence. They shut off the child within. They became adults. It is traditionally understood that the punishment for Adam' and Eve's sin was that man would have to labour to earn a living and that woman would have to labour to bear children. However, the truly greater punishment that remains with us to this day is that both man and woman have actively to labour in order to regain the paradise of emotional honesty and trust that they formerly knew.

This state of paradise that Adam and Eve experienced has its equivalent in human development: we call it infancy. Like the Garden, in that all of our needs are tended to without having to ask, infancy is the state of existence before language and culture show us how to act. It is man in his most natural state, a state of harmony between our inner and outer selves. We say what we mean, and we mean what we say. When a baby is happy, he laughs; when he hurts, he cries. There is no filter of culture or civilization, no pretence, only absolute honesty. It is not until a baby grows older and studies the responses of his loved ones that he begins to learn how not to conceal his emotions in order to gain approval.

As an aside, I find it extremely problematic how most parents knowingly or unknowingly encourage their children to lose touch with their emotions. What is the typical parent's first reply when their child cries from hurt? 'Oh, you're okay, it's not that bad.' Why not let the child try to explain how he feels? What if it *is* bad? When the child says, 'I'm hurt, Mummy,' a better response is to affirm his feelings with, 'Yes, I understand that you are hurt, Joey, and I'm here to comfort you.' Better for the child to learn emotional honesty than how to please others at the expense of his humanity. Later, when he is more mature, he can learn how to summon the correct emotion on command, rather than conceal the wrong emotion due to social censure.

Innocence versus experience

To be naïve means to be unspoiled by the world, to approach life with eyes that are eternally new. Why do we love to awaken on a winter morning and look out to a garden covered with fresh snow? Because we see a pure world that allows *us* the opportunity to leave *our* tracks. George Eliot said, 'The happiest women, like the happiest nations, have no history.' Because you have no past, there is nothing to jade your senses. The opposite of innocence, then, is not just experience, as William Blake would have it, but bad experience, experience that robs us of wonder and trust.

Mr Williams was one of my favourite teachers in high school. Although all the students in my class hated him, I thought he was like a rough diamond. I loved history, and Mr Williams made it come to life. He spoke of the kings and queens of England as if he had known them personally. When he taught us about the heroic death of Nelson at Trafalgar, he did so with tears in his eyes.

There was a curious discrepancy, however, between his manner during and after class. Although alive to the nuances of history in the classroom, after class his heart turned to ice. If he were unfeeling all the time, the students would simply have dismissed him, but because he was unpredictable – warm in class but indifferent if you were hit by a bus on the street – they felt he was disingenuous. I, too, couldn't figure him out.

One day I glimpsed a picture of him in army uniform in his briefcase so I asked him if he had ever been a soldier. 'I don't want to talk about it,' he frigidly responded. I wouldn't let go, however. 'When were you a soldier? Can't you tell me?' Finally, after much cajoling, he told me that he had served two tours of duty in Vietnam. 'I watched a lot of my buddies die. I saw them ground up like hamburger meat. And if you'll excuse me, I don't like talking about it.'

It was then that I understood what I felt to be true all along. The real Mr Williams was the emotional guy in the classroom who really did care about his students. However, because of the pain of witnessing the deaths of his fellow soldiers, he created an impenetrable barrier between himself and the world, one that made it difficult to love. Through no fault of his own, Mr Williams had lost his innocence and thus became incapable of feeling emotion.

Paradise lost

Donna, a woman in her mid-thirties, came to see me in my office. Recently divorced from a man who had continually cheated on her, she had lost all trust in men. Consequently, she was very guarded when it came to relationships and was unable to fall in love with somebody new. 'You have to reclaim your innocence,' I told her. She said that was impossible after what she had gone through. 'Impossible?' I replied. 'Did you ever see what happens when you get a cut on your skin – first a scab appears, but later new skin always grows back?' The same is true of our innocence. If you allow yourself to trust again – and, yes, that involves the risk of further hurt – your innocence will always return. But if you don't, then a scab will remain and you appear permanently scarred.

Our innocence is embedded deep in our hearts. It never leaves us. All we have to do is bring it to the fore by discarding all the accumulated layers of disappointment that have made it impossible for us to feel. Connecting with someone is a mental process. Whenever you feel yourself becoming close, do not let the painful memories enter your mind; let them pass right through without a chance to linger.

As a relationships counsellor, I have watched countless singles date and date without falling in love. But men and women are made of Velcro, not Teflon: they naturally stick. So how can they for ever sow the seeds of love by dating and still watch nothing grow? The problem is that they date so many people that they become jaded and cynical about the whole experience. Soon, nobody is good enough for them, and they despair of ever finding a soul mate.

When I lived in London, the Jewish singles there told me

that there was nobody worth dating: the Jewish community in Britain was too small; there was not enough variety to find really good people. Yet, when I moved to New York, with a Jewish community fifteen times the size of London, I was still hearing the same thing. Heck, if these people lived in China they would still say that there was no one worthy enough for them!

Emotions are like human footprints on a fresh blanket of snow. They need purity in order to leave their mark. Love, for example, must be felt spontaneously and naturally. Only then can we ensure that we are actually and meaningfully carried away by the power of our emotions. But if we compromise our innocence, the next time we are overwhelmed by a tidal wave of positive emotion, we will stand our ground and not budge.

Innocence is sexy

Why is it that the really erotic jokes are always about either nuns or virgins? Why is it that most men are so attracted to virgins and women who wish after a compliment? Because nothing is more seductive in a woman than her innocence. A chaste woman is far more alluring than a seductress because she still possesses her mystery. You will never find a lonely hearts ad that reads: '*Successful businessman with yacht and private airplane seeks former prostitute for long-term relationship and possibly marriage.*'

Why don't men want to marry prostitutes? A successful prostitute should ostensibly make the best wife. She has a terrific body and is sexually astute. She is also incredibly street smart and financially secure. Moreover, if she is good enough to spend your money on, why is she not good enough to marry? The answer is that men do not marry prostitutes because, once a woman has lost her innocence, she has lost much of her allure. One of the great gifts that a woman gives a man is that she makes him feel masculine. When he pleases her, he feels strong and capable. But if he can make no original imprint because she is just too experienced, he is denied this great pleasure.

Carla was very interested in James, so I invited them both to our home for dinner. James was much taken by Carla's maturity so he invited her out to lunch. A few dates later, their relationship began to blossom. Then unexpectedly, Carla sent him some supposedly funny pornographic images by email, but James found them vulgar. Maybe she felt insecure, or she wanted to show him that she had a sense of humour. However, after receiving a cartoon image of Fred Flintstone masturbating, James called and told me that he could no longer see Carla in the same, dignified light. She had lost her innocence and James's attraction waned.

You may read this and think how sexist I sound for trumpeting the virtuous woman. But let me be democratic in my advice: the same rule applies equally to men. Innocent men are incredibly desirable, whereas men who are manipulative are the least sexy of all. The guys who try to dazzle women with their name-dropping and large bank accounts are admitting that there is nothing intrinsically attractive about them. It's the soft, open-hearted guys who aren't afraid to show emotion that women really love.

Roseanne Barr once invited me onto her show to act as matchmaker to her three daughters. I carefully selected three outstanding young men. The first two were perfect on paper. Both were Oxford scholars. One was a former officer in the Israeli army pursuing a doctorate in international relations, the other the captain of the Oxford water polo team, who was studying for a degree in advance molecular engineering. The third bachelor was more ordinary on paper. He had attended a regular college and was now working as a caterer in London. He balked at my request. 'I appreciate your faith in me, Shmuley, but I don't really want to go. People will hear about these great guys and then they'll compare me and I'll look second-class!'

But I knew that he was wrong. In fact, he had the one quality that great Oxford scholars rarely have: he did not take himself too seriously. He was thoughtful, a thoroughly decent guy who treated everybody with respect. He had an easy charm and was always prepared to laugh at himself. 'You're so wrong,' I told him. 'You're going to be the most successful of them all.'

Sure enough, as soon as we brought the three of them onto the set, Roseanne turned to me during a commercial break and said, 'I like the caterer'. Of the three attempted matches, the caterer's was the only one that immediately worked out – because of his innocence. He was simply himself, and when you are simply yourself you exude confidence and live honestly. It is no coincidence that, in survey after survey, women consistently rate confidence and humour as a man's most attractive qualities. Both are the products of innocence. Both flow naturally from a deep knowledge of self.

Flames and embers

The Bible says that women are far more sexual than men. Commenting on the verse in Genesis, 'And you shall crave after your husband', the ancient Rabbis of the Talmud said, 'This refers to exceedingly strong sexual desire.' So why do men seem to be so much more sexually driven than women? Because a man's sexuality is openly displayed, while a woman's is more hidden and private. Consider if you will the difference between the male and female genitalia: a man's protrudes, a woman's is concealed.

Furthermore, to employ the metaphor of the Jewish mystics, a woman's sexuality is like the coal hidden in a fire. If you light a barbecue, you know that the inside coals are burning embers. This internal fire lasts far longer than the flames that erupt at the surface specifically because it is hidden. Like the fire within the coals, a woman's sexuality, so much more potent than a man's, must be fanned into a flame in order to be made manifest. That is the purpose of foreplay.

In sex, men are like a triangle. They become instantly interested, on a steeply inclined plane, but immediately after achieving satisfaction, they lose all interest. The same is not true of women, who resemble an arc. It may take them a bit longer to get interested in the whole sexual endeavour, but once interested, they remain interested.

And this is the beautiful gift that a woman gives a man. She allows him to corroborate his masculinity by the extent to which he can make her femininity manifest. She gives him the unique key that can unlock her sexuality. A man wants not only to feel desired by a woman, but also to know that he transforms her from a woman who is in control to a woman who submits to her passions and instincts. In the words of the old Carole King song, he wants to be responsible for making her 'feel like a natural woman'.

This is why men do not marry prostitutes. Since the prostitute's sexuality is overt, she is unable to be transformed. She cannot go from being a woman of mystery and modesty to a voracious sexual dominatrix. She involves her body but not her soul in the sexual act. Consequently, although she can offer a certain level of gratification, she can never provide the precious feeling of desirability to her clientele.

Men also can compromise their mystery by being manipulative and insincere. Indeed, women today are especially weary of 'professional romancers', men trained in the art of getting a woman to submit to them without any desire to attach or commit.

Reclaiming our innocence

There is a Jewish belief that a person can never totally lose their innocence. There is a purity of soul that always lurks just beneath the surface, even when we sin or become artificial. Even as we grow cynical through experience, there is a pure innocent child within each of us that never ceases to believe, wonder and trust.

We can never return to that state of paradise of our infancy, to a state of being without consciousness, nor would we want to. What we must do is try, through our intellect, to attain that level of purity by being entirely honest with ourselves and others. We must peel away the layers of artifice that prevent our core being manifest. Life is too short to spend it not being genuine.

I am forever struck by the searing dichotomy of how easy young singles today find it to become physically naked, but how difficult they find it to become emotionally naked. On the first date, a man and a woman who are practically strangers are already prepared to peel off their clothes and have sex. Yet, even couples who have been dating for months or years rarely set aside their emotional baggage.

John dated Melissa for seven months and then started to get bored. 'I'm gonna terminate this relationship. I don't see the point in continuing. No matter how much time we spend together, I just don't seem to fall in love,' he told me. They were a good couple and my objective was to save their relationship. 'How can you fall in love when all you talk about is movies and your work? When is the last time you revealed to Melissa your fears, your dreams, your shortcomings? You haven't become really naked with her even once because you allow no one to penetrate your defensive layers. And then you wonder why you're not getting attached.'

The secret to regaining our innocence is to lose our agenda. If your heart is not open, you may be attractive on the outside but your inner beauty will be lost, and the relationship will not flourish. Similarly, if your intent is to gain something, you will be unable to attach yourself effectively as you will automatically cause the other's guard to go up. Manipulation only works for a limited time before a serious backlash is provoked. There is direct connection between trust and the emotions. Without trust, we cannot let our guard down. And if we cannot let our guard down, we can never get to what is real inside.

How can we always retain our innocence and never lose our sense of purity? The answer is always to avoid sin. Sin is the desecrator of innocence; it is when we do something that is unnatural. That the deepest human desire is to be decent people is evidenced by how we all want to be remembered by family and friends. Even the richest man in the world does not want to be eulogized for the buildings he owned, but for the hospitals he built; not for his commercial ruthlessness but for his philanthropic loving kindness. But sin is when we act manipulatively, placing our own agenda above the interests of others. Sin is when we feel that we can make the rules, consciously doing something wrong. The first time we regret it, the second time we rationalize it, the third time we justify it.

Remember, Adam' and Eve's great sin was not merely that they ate from the tree, but especially that they lied about what they did instead of accepting responsibility for their actions. By justifying their actions, they allowed their sin to penetrate their being. Instead of merely being people who sinned, they became *sinners*.

8

Sin

WHEN THE HEART FORGETS THE HEAD

Commit a sin twice and it will not seem a crime.
Jewish saying

All sin tends to be addictive, and the terminal point of addiction is what is called damnation.
W. H. Auden

Morrie was a pretty decent guy. A young man of only twenty-three, he was quickly climbing the ladder of success at his law firm. In an adjacent office was Toby, a woman nearly twice his age who had been married for twenty years. Being a sensitive soul, Morrie noticed how Toby seemed increasingly despondent. A woman who normally dressed very professionally, she started coming into the office looking unkempt, with dark bags under her eyes. Out of compassion, Morrie started talking to her about her troubles.

Toby's marriage was falling apart. She and her husband were spending less time together, and the children were suffering. Morrie listened sympathetically to Toby nearly every day at lunch. One thing led to another and they ended up at Morrie's apartment for a drink. Then they ended up in bed together. That was the beginning of the affair that brought much ruin to both their lives. By the time Morrie came to me for guidance, Toby's husband had sued for divorce based on her infidelity. 'My only intention was to be a good guy Shmuley, to do the right thing. I can't believe it all turned out like this.'

What Morrie did not realize was that, because the emotions are unpredictable, they need the guidance of the intellect. The mind deals with hard and objective truths; its vocabulary is limited to 'true' and 'false', 'good' and 'bad'. The heart, on the other hand, deals with subjective truths, using the words 'like' and 'dislike'. In such a situation, the mind, drawing on its value system for guidance, should weigh all the different factors and decide: bad. An extra-marital affair is wrong. You don't help a woman in distress by bringing to her life a further complication. The mind is meant to send a signal to the heart. 'Try to help, but don't draw too close. Always be on your guard.' But Morrie experienced an intellectual and emotional fissure that resulted in disaster.

In the previous chapter, we discussed how emotions clouded by intellect prevent innocence being manifest. In this chapter, we are going to posit the inverse of that statement: emotion unguided by intellect usually leads to sin. By saying this we are not, however, reversing the central premise of this book. It is my steadfast belief that the emotions are the centre of our humanity. We are human by virtue of our ability to forge ties and create relationships. But if our hearts are not guided by our minds, we have the potential rapidly to become predatory, dangerous animals.

Sinned against by sinning

In our day and age, sin is largely considered a religious subject defined as a transgression against God. After all, God teaches what is good for us. His laws were designed to safeguard our integrity, and violating those laws is certainly an offence to Him. However, the even greater offence when we sin is to ourselves because we stray from the path we know we should follow. The ultimate act of infidelity is the betrayal of self, and the greatest punishment for sin is the sin itself because it acts as a corrosive to our soul. As one person so aptly put it, 'Men are not punished for their sins, but by them.'

A case in point, the Ten Commandments teach us that

stealing and lying are sins against God. In truth, however, they are sins against ourselves because we contravene our inner will of what we truly want to be. Our inner will is certainly not to be a swindler, not to be someone for whom everyone has contempt.

When we act without considering the consequences of our actions, we become like a car without a steering wheel: we will usually crash. Similarly, when we submit to our emotions without considering our intellect, the consequence is mostly sin. It is written in the Talmud, 'The eyes see but the heart craves.' Whereas the mind is detached and objective, the heart is filled with desire. Without the proper guidance, the emotions can lead us astray from the path where we belong. There is, for example, more than a fine line between the sanctity of marriage and its transgression by adultery. Similarly, while hating injustice is good, hating your mother is not. Thus, the key to leading a successful life is to ensure that our emotions function within the proper context.

Lester was running to be a member of a local city council. Just before an important speech, his wife, who was travelling with him, was ironing his suit. In her haste, she burned a hole through the knee. Lester hit the roof. 'How could you have done this to me?', he yelled, calling her all kinds of names. Now, Lester is not a bad man. He is usually a loving and devoted husband, but in this instance he let his emotions guide his ship. Had he been able to control his temper, he would have placed the incident in perspective. Indeed, had he thought about how his marriage is far more important than this suit, how his wife does so much for him and should be forgiven for something as trivial as this, and how while the suit is easily replaced, his wife's feelings might be permanently scarred by his outburst, he probably wouldn't have shouted.

The essence of sin is forgetfulness

Why is sin so destructive? Sin occurs when we no longer weigh the consequences of our actions, when pleasure and desire so consume us that rational thought is left no room in which to operate. Sin is an act of forgetfulness wherein man exchanges his long-term objectives for short-term pleasures; success and virtue for indulgence and mediocrity – whatever provides immediate gratification.

The ancient Sages of the Mishna taught: 'Reflect upon three things and you will not come to sin: Know from where you came, and to where you are going, and before whom you are destined to give an accounting.' The essence of virtue from this point of view is to reflect on our mission in life and to have values concomitant with that mission. The essence of sin, in contrast, is to *forget* that mission and submit to temporal desire. So, if your life's desire is to be a good parent, working yourself to the bone in order to earn money is a transgression against that project.

Let's use the admittedly over-roasted chestnut of Bill Clinton's affair. So many people have wondered how such an intelligent a man as Bill Clinton could have sinned so grievously with Monica Lewinsky. 'What could he have been thinking?', they ask. The answer, of course, is that he was *not* thinking. The Talmud says that no man sins unless he is overcome by a spirit of madness, which means that no man sins if he keeps his head in front of his heart (and in front of some other organs as well). You can only sin with your eyes shut. So the best safeguard against sin is the full orchestration of mind and heart.

As mature adults, we understand that certain things in life are mutually exclusive, such as a committed marriage and infidelity. The key is to prioritize our values and keep them in clear focus. Thus, if I am Bill Clinton and I value my presidency, my legacy within history and my responsibility to the American people, I must put another desire of mine, illicit sex, at the bottom of my list. That does not mean that we have to pretend that adultery is not pleasurable. Instead, once I put it in the perspective of what I gain compared with what I lose on a simple cost-benefit scale, it is not only not pleasurable, but also downright painful! After all, does anyone believe that President Clinton does not painfully regret what he did?

But President Clinton mistakenly believed that he could have it all, that he could be an honest man, a good president, a faithful husband and still have a mistress. A moment of intelligent reflection would have illuminated the absurdity of this conclusion. This is obviously illogical but that is the nature of sin. It has to be illogical because it involves a complete shutdown of the mind.

One moment, please

Given even a few moments of rational thought, most people would willingly surrender a thrilling sexual encounter if it could permanently derail their professional and personal lives. They sin, however, because they do not even give themselves those few moments. The cry of the hedonist from time immemorial has been '*Carpe diem*' – seize the day. In stark contrast, the ancient Rabbis taught, 'Who is wise? He who always examines the outcome of his actions.' Thus, the quickest antidote to sin is even a brief instant of thoughtful reflection.

Heidi was a commissioning editor with a London publisher. She had a favourite author, every single one of whose books she had read, and lo and behold, there he was one day at a cocktail party. After introducing herself, she told him about a great idea for a book that only he could write. He said that he loved the idea and that if he decided to write it, he would hire her as his editor. About a year later, she read in a trade publication how this book was coming out from this author in two months. She couldn't believe that he had stolen her idea.

When she arrived home that evening, she immediately threw out all her cherished copies of his books. Then she called two journalists she knew to tell the story of his treachery. She wanted the fact that he was a jerk to appear in the newspapers. As neither journalist was home, she left a message on their answering machines. Afterwards, she had some time to reflect on what had transpired. 'Is this *really* what I want to do? Just because he is a louse, do I want to become one as well?' Heidi decided that her integrity was more important than her professional success. 'He stole my idea, but he won't steal my goodness.' When the journalists called back, she told them instead that she wanted to invite them to a party.

Perhaps the primary instrument of sin is our tongue. Indeed, the Rabbis identified gossip and slander as the most easily and commonly perpetrated sins. My father taught me that since most of us assume that gossip is no big deal, God ensured that guarding our tongues at all times are our lips and teeth, which must first release the tongue from its cage. The moral here is that we are given an instant to think every time we open our mouths. Make use of that precious time to ensure that you do not say something you might eternally regret.

Our emotions are incredibly important. They make us feel intensely alive. But without direction they can easily hasten our moral or actual death. We have to make certain, therefore, that they always act in conjunction with our minds. By all means act, but *think* before you act. An old Jewish aphorism declares, 'The difference between the wise man and the clever man is that the clever man can get himself out of a situation into which the wise man would never have been in in the first place.' The trick is thus to be wise rather than clever.

9

Passion

WHEN THE HEART LEADS THE HEAD

If a man is called to be a street sweeper, he should sweep streets even as Michelangelo painted, or Beethoven composed music, or Shakespeare wrote poetry. He should sweep streets so well that all the hosts of heaven and earth will pause to say, here lived a great street sweeper that did his job well.

Martin Luther King, Jr

There is no end. There is no beginning. There is only the infinite passion of life.

Frederico Fellini

As the last chapter in this section, we must discuss a key component that underlies all the emotions – passion. Passion is not an emotion but a measure of how deeply we feel each of our individual emotions. It is the foundation upon which the sturdy house of our emotional make-up is built. You may love casually, or you may love intensely. The difference is the degree of your passion.

The same is true of joy, hatred, jealousy and all the other emotions. You can even be passionately passive about something. A man who finds himself attracted to the wrong woman will appear very different in his passionate commitment to resist her charms than a man who simply wants to be passionate *about* a woman.

If the greatness of being human is our ability to experience emotions, passion is a measure of our humanity. Every human being is composed of two elements – a body and a soul – each with its single greatest need. The body needs to feel intensely *alive*, and the soul to feel intensely *understood*. The body seeks passion, the soul intimacy. The body seeks excitement while the soul seeks communion.

Simply stated, those with more passion feel more deeply and profoundly. They feel the pain of others more, they glory in their achievements more and they are able to love more. Passion, therefore, is the barometer of how intensely we lead our lives. It measures whether we blaze brightly or smoulder silently. And to live without passion is to be only half alive.

I have always been confused by those who are afraid of passion, so living in Oxford has at times been puzzling. Oxford certainly has never been a great fan of the emotions, as could probably be said of England in general. I remember when I first arrived how hard it was to listen to the news on the BBC. In the interest of objectivity, every news story was read in the same monotone. A story about a hamster crushed by a lorry would be read with the same passion, or lack thereof, as a story of London being under nuclear attack by the Russians. After the death of Princess Diana, however, I began to notice a difference – some verve – in the voices on the radio. It was as if something finally touched us all.

Passionate institution: an oxymoron?

There is nothing more hypocritical to young people than seeing institutions associated with passionate beliefs being driven by nothing more than custom. Three come immediately to mind: marriage, politics and religion. We expect people to marry because they are passionate about each other and want to spend the rest of their lives together. When we see them boring each other to death instead, we dismiss the marriage as a sham. I am convinced that this is why so many people today wait so long to brave the seemingly treacherous waters of marriage.

Next is politics, which people feel should be driven by a

mixture of patriotism and ambition. When the latter is present without the former, it is a huge turn-off to the electorate. They don't mind their elected officials aspiring to personal greatness so long as the public interest is always given precedence.

Finally, religion. Because we are meant to be passionate about beliefs, it irks us when people hang onto religious convictions purely out of custom. This is why so few kids today continue the religious traditions of their parents, who, in their minds, keep to their faith out of boredom and guilt. This was the sentiment expressed by Franz Kafka to his father in a famous letter that his father did not read before he died:

> *It would have been thinkable that we might both have found each other in Judaism or that we might have begun from there in harmony. But what sort of Judaism was it that I got from you? ... [the] few flimsy gestures you performed in the name of Judaism, and with an indifference in keeping with their flimsiness ... had meaning as little souvenirs of earlier times, and that is why you wanted to pass them on to me. But since they no longer had any intrinsic value, even for you, you could do this only through persuasion or threat.*

Conversely, seeing people passionate about their beliefs is a huge turn-on. Passionate people are the most fun to be around because their exuberance spreads and makes us all feel special and alive.

Why people fear passion

Many people fear passion, for two opposing reasons. One camp says that passion is dangerous because it is so strong that it can rage out of control. I remember the response of one of my academic friends when I first published *The Jewish Guide to Adultery*, a primer for married couples on how to bring passion into their relationship. She told me point blank that she hated it. A bit shocked by her total honesty, I asked why. She replied, 'Because passion is the most dangerous thing in the world. It's a fire that burns out of control, and a mature adult is someone who is always in control!'

To experience an emotion is to be temporarily carried away, and we are afraid of surrender. Of course, not every emotion causes us either to break down into a flood of tears or leap over tall buildings. But emotions do move us to some degree in some direction, even if the distance is only slight. Passion, however, does not only move us, it sends shock waves through our system. And not everybody wants to be shocked.

The other camp's argument is that passion is dangerous because it is weak. Because it necessarily wears off, it cannot be trusted and you are bound to end up disappointed. Just look at the generation of hippies who tried to burn the world down in the name of injustice in their twenties but settled down to comfortable lives as accountants and investment bankers in their next decade.

Whatever the arguments for or against passion, I will unequivocally state the following rule: when properly directed, there is no greater device in the quest for personal and professional success than passion. The determining factor in whether or not you will achieve something is how badly you want it and how deeply you feel it. Even if you possess a great mind, it will, if you lack passion, achieve only ordinary feats.

How can we recapture lost passion?

Larry tragically lost his wife and two of his children in a car crash. Left with two kids to raise on his own, he dated extensively in search of a new love for himself and a mother for his children. Although he admitted that some of the women he met were perfect, he could not surmount his traumatic hurdle. When he came to me for counselling, he said, 'Something of me died in that crash as well and I have never been the same person. I've lost my passion for life. I lie awake at night wishing I were in that car with my wife and kids. How can I get up the next morning and smile like I'm happy to be alive?'

How can we recapture our passion for living when life is filled with obstacles? How can we learn what real passion is, as opposed to the false passion that often gets us into trouble?

A twenty-nine-year-old woman came to see me in my office on the prodding of her parents. In the year before she had become obsessively religious, and her complete transformation was causing terrible tension within her family. She gave away her trust fund and all of her expensive clothes to the poor and spent much of her day in prayer. 'Why are you doing all this?', I asked her. 'Is your spiritual journey a case of running to the light, as you suppose, or perhaps you are simply running away from some terrible darkness.' She then told me her story. 'At sixteen I had my first sexual experience. The guy was over forty. After completing university, I joined an international community that practised free love. I've slept with over three hundred people. And I want to cleanse myself of all that. So I guess I am running from something.' I then asked, 'And why did you do all that in the first place?' 'Because', she told me, 'I wanted passion in my life. It made me feel like I was really living.'

This young woman, because of immaturity and a lack of guidance, had mistaken licence for passion. Many make the same error, thinking that passion means busting out of a mould. That is why so-called 'passionate people' have always disdained marriage; to them, passion can never co-exist alongside rules.

Passion is novelty

So what is real passion, and how can it be captured and maintained? The essence of passion is novelty. The secret of recapturing it is to approach everything as if for the first time. How can we make that which is old appear new? The answer is by using our minds. The fundamental difference between passion and emotion is that while emotion emanates from the heart, passion comes from the mind and the mind is capable of making everything appear new.

Carol works in advertising. Last year she was so bored with her job she could hardly get up in the morning. She felt she needed to do something new. However, because the job paid so well she endured the boredom.

One day she heard from behind one of the dividers that her own secretary was making a bid for her job. Alarm bells went off in Carol's head and she began to work much harder. 'It wasn't just fear,' she told me. 'I genuinely rediscovered a passion for my work. The fact that the job could be taken away from me made it new to me all over again. I was exhilarated. And now, every time I start to get bored, I just remember that at any moment this job could be lost. And there it is – brand new!'

The same is true in our marriages. Jeffrey came to me to confess that he was having an affair. I asked him why. 'My wife simply doesn't attract me any more. She undresses and I can barely bring myself to look. I'm just not interested in her.' I gave him the following advice. 'Tonight, drive with your wife to the next town where nobody knows you. Go separately into a loud and raunchy bar. No one should know you're together. She has to sit by the bar and you, like a fly on the wall, will just watch.' 'Then what?' Jeffrey asked me. 'You'll see for yourself. The ball will start rolling on its own.'

It took some cajoling, but they agreed to follow my advice. When they arrived at the club, Jeffrey's wife sat by the bar while he looked on from a distance. Within moments, men started to circle around her like bees around honey. Jeffrey was instantly beside himself with jealousy. He grabbed his wife by the hand, took her straight home, and they made the most passionate love they had in years.

Similarly, when men tell me that they have lost all interest in their wives, I tell them to persuade their wives to reveal their secret sexual fantasies about strangers. At first they are incredulous because they cannot believe that their wives fantasize. Later, however, when they learn how their wives are strongly attracted to other men, especially when they feel neglected by their husbands, these men do everything in their power to win their wives back.

The mind can make a heaven of hell

It does not take kinky and extreme devices like the nightclub scene described above in order to regain passion. Instead, it takes a mastery of our minds to rediscover our greatest blessings on a daily basis. When I first started to pray in Hebrew, I came across this beautiful prayer that praised God for being 'He who renews creation every single day.' I did not understand it: the world is just always there. I argued this with my teacher, who answered in surprise: 'Really, today isn't a new day? Didn't the sun rise anew? Isn't yesterday history and today original and exciting?'

The world around us is in flux. It takes a sensitive soul to peer beyond the surface and be alive to the novelty and nuances of the universe. With some things, it is easier than with others. Consider the miracle of a child. Because God wants us to nurture our children amid the phenomenal burden involved in doing so in their younger years, He designed them to develop rapidly so that we could never grow bored with them. At every stage they are new. After being born bald, they grow hair. Soon they offer a few sounds and then they form words. Then they start writing on the walls with crayon. Before you know it, they ask for the keys to the car. You get the picture.

Other aspects of our lives demand a far greater challenge. We wake up every day and follow a routine, so it becomes hard to sustain passion. Our spouse does not change all that much. Unfortunately, any changes we notice are almost always negative: they are getting older, fatter, more stubborn.

Such is the perspective of an insensitive soul. To over-come the boredom of routine and retain passion, the trick is to grow and evolve constantly. In *Paradise Lost*, John Milton wrote, 'The mind is its own place, and in itself can make a Heaven of Hell, a Hell of Heaven.' The key, of course, is perspective.

Actually, we do not have to convince ourselves to see the world as new because it *is* new. God could theoretically have created the world in such a way as to have one long, thousand-year day. Nor did He have to create four seasons. We could all have lived in sunny California (but who could take the traffic?). However, the world is structured in such a way that each day we start fresh in order to give us passion for life.

Opening our eyes

The same is true in our relationships. There is no such thing as an old relationship; we do not get married at the altar once and for all. On the contrary, we have to renew our commitment to our partner every single day. When I first got married, I wanted to be totally in love and devoted to my wife. I was horrified, therefore, when I awoke the day after my wedding and discovered that I still noticed an attractive woman in the street. Later I understood that this innocent attraction had its merits because God wanted me to choose my bride anew every single day. Amid our attraction to strangers, all of us choose to come home to our spouse and this is what renews our commitment and prevents our relationships growing stale.

Even couples who have lost passion in their marriage often experience a completely new buzz after a geographical separation. Their lovemaking becomes more intense because their bodies are new to each other. Why are men and women who are not passionate about each other passionate about strangers? It is because these strangers represent the exciting possibilities of new flesh.

Judaism well understands the nature of passion and has for this reason instituted a period of sexual separation, the Laws of Family Purity which mandate that husband and wife abstain from sexual relations for the five days of menstruation and seven days thereafter. There are several reasons for this custom, the most important being to cultivate passion by separating a husband and wife for several days each month. The hope is that when they embrace after a period of separation, the spark of their wedding night will be reignited. When we have everything whenever we want it, we lose interest fast, just like small children lose interest in their toys. But any seasoned parent knows that the way to cultivate interest in old toys is to take them away for a while and then reintroduce them at an opportune moment.

In short, passion is contingent upon newness, and newness is contingent upon choice. If we are like sailboats pushed by the wind, we will lose our passion. We must choose to live our lives passionately and purposefully every single day. We must be constantly reminded of our blessings so that we never grow bored of them. As a marriage counsellor, I have discovered that simply reminding a man how special his wife is, or vice versa, is enough to restore appreciation and passion in a relationship, to cause the person to choose anew their participation in the relationship.

Herein lies the ultimate role of friendship. A good friend helps us see that to which we have become blind. This is why it is so important for friends to compliment each other. Compliments not only make us feel special; they also remind us of our blessings. They reintroduce us to key elements of our lives that we have begun to take for granted.

Here again, we see how dependent emotions are on an external other. Our emotions not only link us to people outside ourselves, but are even dependent on those outside ourselves in order for them to be more passionate. So we are caught up in a large web in which we have to help one another re-engender passion by constantly reminding one another of our blessings. My friend Cory Brooker always reminds me of what Martin Luther King said so eloquently, 'We are all caught in an inescapable network of mutuality, tied in a common garment of destiny.'

PART THREE

Understanding the Individual Emotions

10

Depression

THE ABSENCE OF ALL EMOTION

I am in that temper that if I were under water I would scarcely kick to come to the top.

John Keats

This is my depressed stance. When you're depressed, it makes a lot of difference how you stand. The worst thing you can do is straighten up and hold your head high because then you'll start to feel better. If you're going to get any joy out of being depressed, you've got to stand like this.

Charlie Brown

Without a doubt, ours is the most prosperous generation of all time. We live longer and have more money and are healthier than any age the world has ever known. Yet while certainly characterized by access and mobility, it would not be too off the mark to say that the most defining aspect of our generation is depression. A recent poll showed that one in every five Americans currently takes Prozac or some other antidepressant (the other four being on Viagra), and that one in three Americans has sought therapeutic relief from depression at some point in their lives. Even those who are not clinically depressed still consume inordinate amounts of meaningless distraction such as television and frivolous magazines about the rich and famous. This begs the question, if we are so happy with our lives, why are we constantly trying to escape? And if we are satisfied with who we are, why are we always talking about someone else?

One reason that civilization is discontent is because we all seem to be plagued with feelings of inadequacy. We never feel fulfilled because we chase elusive goals that are always just beyond our reach. They say that this is Generation X, a generation of anonymity; on the contrary, this is the generation that carries everybody else's name. We are the generation who feel more comfortable wearing Calvin Klein's name on our behinds than parading our own. We seem to feel more comfortable talking about the people in *People* than about those in our own lives. We love reading about the shenanigans of the rich and famous because it excuses our own mediocrity. We value movie stars and sports heroes so highly that we pay them the highest salaries in the world.

Another symptom of this cultural dis-ease is that we take pride in the people we know rather than the people we are. I often do this myself. Through the L'Chaim Society, I have come to meet many famous people, and it truly bothers me that I can occasionally be a namedropper in order to curry favour with somebody important. But we all have our insecurities, and it seems that human insecurity just keeps growing.

These feelings of inadequacy are partially the result of living in the entrepreneurial era. The tremendous opportunity available to all segments of society has caused us to compare ourselves to others in order to determine our own self-worth. Because nobody feels good enough with how they are, they constantly try to become something else. It is a very sad commentary on our culture that young girls starve themselves in an effort to resemble waif models in magazines. It is no wonder that plastic surgery is now big business. If you don't like your nose, get a new one. If you are bald, get implants. The sky is the limit.

On one level, the issue is economic because hypercompetition undermines the innate value of human beings by equating it with what we produce. That is why motherhood as a profession has become so devalued in the West. Although the mother provides invaluable and unmatchable resources for her children, her time is not worth money. The nanny, on the other hand, is valued because she brings an income for her own family. In sum, taking care of another's children is considered OK but taking care of your own is not.

It is a very sad fact that Western man has ceased to judge himself on his character and the impact that he makes on others, focusing instead on the content of his bank account. This criterion, however, is bound to push man over the precipice. As he can never find satisfaction watching his peers outperform him, he ends up wallowing in bitterness and jealousy. And when these negative feelings completely consume him, he finds himself depressed.

Unexplained melancholy

Feeling inadequate and suspecting that we are not making the most of our lives is just one factor that leads to depression, others being broken relationships, financial difficulties and serious illness. These causes are, however, situational and are often remedied with time and change. But there are other times when we are depressed for what seems to be no reason at all.

Abby was a highly intelligent student who won a Marshall scholarship. She was conscientious in her work and even volunteered much of her time to the L'Chaim Society. In addition, she was involved in a good relationship and had many friends. Nevertheless, there seemed to be something missing in her life. She was always unhappy and had developed complaining into an advanced art form. I asked her what was wrong.

'Shmuley, I feel I am wasting my life. My studies are not fulfilling and I feel like I am not maximizing my potential. Maybe my time as a student has come to an end.' So she dropped out of university and immediately landed an outstanding position with a management consultant. Yet she didn't look any happier. I asked her, 'What's wrong now? You did exactly what you wanted to do.' 'Well, maybe I made a mistake. I acted in haste.' So she quit her job and resumed her studies. She was happy for about a month, but shortly afterwards reverted to her old melancholic self.

Abby's story is certainly not an isolated incident. Many people seem to search and search yet never really find what they are looking for, leaving them despondent and unfulfilled. When I ask friends and acquaintances what percentage of their time they would say they were happy, they usually tell me that it is about fifty per cent, maybe less. Fifty per cent of the time! What a way to live a life. Success requires exuberance and joy. Nobody likes to be around someone who mopes. Trust me on this because I mope all the time and my friends tell me that I am so much more pleasant when I look happy, rare as that may be.

The essence of depression

Jonah, a mathematics student, seemed prone to manic depression. Although he worked very hard, he spent most of his time complaining about everything and everyone. After a psychiatrist advised him to take lithium, he asked me for my advice. I told him there was nothing wrong with antidepressants – provided that they are truly needed. 'Well, how can I tell if I need this or not?', he asked. I replied that medication should be taken only after two conditions have been met: first, that you really understand what depression is; and second, that you have made repeated efforts to combat it but have ultimately met with failure. 'So what is depression?', I asked. 'Well, it's an emotion that makes you feel sad.' I told him that his answer was totally incorrect: 'So how can you know if you need Prozac before you have even properly diagnosed your condition?'

Contrary to popular belief, depression is not an emotion at all. You cannot *feel* depressed because depression is, by definition, the absence of feeling. Indeed, depression is not about feeling down; it is about beating yourself so down that you cease to feel.

Some of the confusion over depression comes from the wide array of pop psychology available to the thirsting public. In the classic self-help manual *The Road Less*

Traveled, by M. Scott Peck, the author actually advises that depression can be a good thing. 'Since mentally healthy human beings must grow, and since giving up or losing the old self is an integral part of the process of mental and spiritual growth, depression is a normal and basically healthy phenomenon.'

Much as I loved the book, I could not disagree more with this outrageous claim. Saying that depression is beneficial is entirely illogical, like saying that thin air is good, or nothingness is life-affirming. How can nothingness be a positive thing? It is simply the absence of presence. By the same token, depression is not an emotion, but the absence of all emotion.

I do agree, though, with the general thrust of Peck's argument. One of life's most painful features is having to let go. Had he said that losing the old self can lead to bitterness, I would have completely agreed. Bitterness and regret over past misdeeds can be very productive by serving as a springboard to higher levels of achievement, but depression leads to nowhere but a funk.

How does somebody feel when depressed? Numb. Strike a man when he is depressed, and he barely feels the sting. Have you ever tried to cheer up a depressed friend? It probably went something like this: 'Come on Johnny. Cheer up. Why don't we go out and have a drink? You'll feel better.' 'Nah, you go on without me. I don't feel like a drink. I'll stay home.' 'OK, then let's go and see a movie. It would be good for you. Get your mind off things.' 'Look, I appreciate the offer, but no thanks. I just want to stay here by myself.' You feel like slugging him because he is so unresponsive. You want to scream, 'What's wrong with you? Don't you feel *anything*?' But Johnny is so far gone that he cannot muster the strength to offer any emotional response.

The death of the soul

It is the premise of this book that what makes us most human is our ability to feel and thereby be moved to action. Our heart is our most precious organ because it is the life force within us. Indeed, holiness is associated with everything that is alive. God is described in the Bible as 'the living God', and the Torah is called 'the fountain (or tree) of life'. When our heart pulses we can be moved to great heights, but once it stops beating we die. Depression causes just such a death, turning our most beautiful organ into an unfeeling stone.

I previously stated that depression is the most destructive of all the emotions because it robs us of our ability to feel. However, I will go a step further and say that depression is the most degrading of all emotions because it robs us of our very humanity. Lacking the energy to accomplish even the most menial tasks, we feel no inner compunction to act. We don't even want to be left alone because we just don't want anything. Depression is the human transformation from the animate to the inanimate, from person to thing, from personality to object.

Depression is heinous because it robs us of life itself. Depression is the breathing equivalent of death, like existing in a waking coma, feeling neither pain nor love. And this is precisely why Judaism dismisses it as the most unholy of all emotions, much more unholy than hatred. At least with hatred you can turn it, as you can love itself. Every kind of energy, whether constructive or destructive, can be directed and redirected. The energy is neutral; its application is not.

But what can you do with energy that does not exist? How can you turn emptiness into something positive? When you are depressed, all your possessions can be taken from you in front of your very eyes and there is nothing you want to do about it. You are like a vacuum, possessing no ego or will. Depression involves the disintegration and evaporation of the self. You have ceased to live and now only exist. The ego has atrophied and your will to be or do has imploded.

Depression and gender

Men are more prone to depression than women, and in my experience, depression is one of the leading causes of marital discord and divorce. Wives can put up with a lot. They can deal with husbands who are angry or jealous. However, they cannot cope with being married to a man who is so unresponsive and caught up in his own melancholy that he shows no emotion.

Depressed men rarely reach out for help in the way that women do. Instead, in most cases they try to escape their misery by alcohol or suicide. Why do they avoid confronting their problems? Why don't they talk it out like women do? Because men view depression as a sign of weakness. Indeed, 43 per cent of Americans in a Gallup poll said they believed that depression is not an illness but a sign of 'personal weakness'. Sadly enough, in the past four years alone, more than 120,000 Americans have committed suicide, mostly because of untreated depression.

The future does not look bright with regard to these statistics. The World Health Organization and the Harvard School of Public Health have now predicted that within twenty years, acute depression – rather than war, hunger or global warming – will be the world's leading cause of death and disability, second only to heart disease, a staggering figure.

Solly had high ambitions to be one of the world's great Rabbis. When he procured his first pulpit in San Diego at the tender age of 25, he felt the sky was the limit. He worked tirelessly for the community, and they loved him. Unfortunately, the emeritus Rabbi who was forced into retirement did not leave the community, choosing instead to take a more than active role in his former congregation. Apparently jealous of Solly's immense popularity, he undermined him at every turn, even going so far as to suggest that Solly was more interested in popularity and money than in Judaism and God.

Slowly but surely, the whispering campaign against Solly started to work. He soon found himself on the defensive for every project he proposed. The straw that broke the camel's back was when Solly suggested a massive carnival for the children of the community. In a tone that was both insulting and disrespectful, one of the board members piped up in the midst of a large synagogue meeting and said, 'Why; so you can be photographed with the mayor?'

Publicly humiliated, Solly resigned his post and sank into a deep depression. Usually full of life and energy, he could now barely muster the strength to get out of bed. When I called him, he refused to come to the phone, but his wife insisted. 'I feel like all my dreams have been destroyed. My first pulpit and it went down in flames', he said.

This is the essence of depression. It is when we feel that we have been defeated by life and have lost the will to fight another day.

What made Solly's depression so much more acute was that he felt ashamed of being depressed. Had he not been embarrassed, he would have confided in his friends.

Battling depression

When I had just turned twenty-two, I arrived in Oxford to serve as Rabbi to the students. I quickly set up the L'Chaim Society to cater for their needs. We started to procure some important speakers, and the organization was really taking off. I had just read former President Ronald Reagan's autobiography, *An American Life*, in which he wrote that he had attended a simple university called Eureka College. Although, as president, he had visited all of the greatest universities in the world, he said he would never have traded his experience at Eureka because of how friendly it was. So I wrote him a letter saying how wonderful it would be if he could bring some of that humour and warmth to a place as cold and proper as Oxford.

To my great surprise, he wrote that he would be honoured to deliver our lecture. We were ecstatic. Two years into our organization's existence and we had secured a former American president to speak for us. Moreover, he was kind enough to waive any expenses for his travel.

We worked our guts out organizing the event. The costs were astronomical, and, in addition, we were simultaneously opening a new student centre smack in the middle of Oxford. It was beautiful, but equally expensive, and I began to despair at being able to afford it. We asked President Reagan to open the new centre, and he agreed. I then approached the publisher Robert Maxwell, an Oxford resident, and asked him to cover the centre's expenses for its first year. Maxwell agreed, and in turn, we agreed to name the centre after his relatives who were murdered in the Holocaust. It was all happening.

Just a week before President Reagan was to arrive, I flew to New York to obtain a blessing for the event from my spiritual leader, the Lubavitcher Rebbe, Rabbi Menachem Schneerson. I was sitting in a kosher restaurant watching CNN when a newsflash suddenly came up: 'Publishing magnate Robert Maxwell missing at sea.' I was both shocked and saddened by the news that Mr Maxwell might have met with a terrible tragedy. This also spelt the ruin of our plans.

When I arrived at Heathrow the next day, I saw the headlines. Maxwell's body had been found, drowned. I tried to place a call to his wife to express my condolences. I also feared that President Reagan's visit might be in jeopardy. Then, a few days later, the controversy over pension funds started to appear in the press. During the Sukkoth celebration, Judaism's most joyous holiday, we received the dreaded phone call from President Reagan's office: 'Due to an unforeseen scheduling conflict, the President will not be able to deliver the lecture.' My heart sank.

First we had to clear up the mess of the cancellation. We were not only tens of thousands of pounds out of pocket, but also humiliated. Whereas for months we had been known as the dynamic student organization that booked President Reagan, we were now known as the organization that Reagan had forsaken. Far worse, we did not have enough money to pay for the fitting out of the new centre, let alone its rent. I had never been so depressed.

When I came into the office, I would see the workmen who at this point could not be cancelled and my despondency would deepen. Although I had always prided myself on my energy and activity, I felt that I could not cope. Gloom pervaded my psyche. I would put my head on the table and keep it there for an hour, too listless to do anything to lift myself out of my problems.

My friends told me, 'Don't worry; it's going to be all right', but I felt they were just being naïve. As I saw it, my career was over and nothing could help. We had no money and our creditors would soon be pressing to be paid. Then my friend Sandy called me. 'What's the matter with you?' he said. 'Something this small has broken you? Stop feeling sorry for yourself. Get up and fight back.' Those simple words served as a spur for me to extricate myself from this mess. Why wasn't I fighting? After all, I was engaged in a struggle for financial survival. When God had endowed me with health and talent, why did I assume defeat? In translating my own negative thoughts from the potential into the actual, I was being the architect of my own nightmare.

Depression is based on a false idea that humans are meant to have only victories, that life is meant to be smooth. But the essence of life is struggle. All good things are worth fighting for, and life itself is a good thing. Defeats are just part of the ongoing battle. The greatest blessing of all is life, and so long as you have breath in your lungs and blood pumping through your veins, you can still rise to see another day. But the moment you cannot pick yourself up to fight back, depression has claimed another victim.

The solution to depression

Many people insist that they have to take medication for their depression, which may be so. Certainly, long bouts of depression must be referred to a proper mental health expert. But before doing so, Judaism insists that there is a solution to depression. Unhappiness must be battled with joy, depression must be fought with action, nothingness must be countered with presence.

Since depression is based on the lie that the battle is lost, you have got to pick yourself up and just start doing again. Don't reason with your depression. Don't dignify it by giving it the pretence of authenticity. Simply act, and the darkness will disappear. You are battling a mirage, so stop thinking, stop worrying and just start doing.

In Judaism, we are commanded to perform a mitzvah (commandment) even when we do not feel motivated to do so. A man is, for example, commanded to pray three times a day. There are certainly days when we do not feel up to this. Yet, the logic is that once you act, your heart will follow suit. If we wait to pray until the urge grabs us, we may end up waiting a lifetime. But action has the power to create the corresponding emotion.

The same is true of depression. If you passively wait for the urge to recover, you may wallow forever. Once you act, the chances are that your heart will kick in feeling where it was previously frozen. Indeed, the more heat you can generate in the form of action, the more the depression will thaw. Soon you will know that you are alive again.

Every week, we have guests at our home for the Sabbath meal. As the host, I do most of the entertaining, but after a difficult week, I often do not feel like talking. What I really want is to hibernate. But forced to be hospitable, I start talking, and, lo and behold, the conversation begins to animate me. Soon I am swigging whisky, dancing on the tables and swinging from the chandeliers (slight exaggeration)!

Through my limited bout of depression over the Reagan saga, I discovered that the quickest road to recovery was to forget my own self-absorption and direct my actions towards helping others. That big centre that we could not afford was soon filled with students. After hearing our plight, Israel's Housing Minister at the time, the legendary war hero Ariel Sharon, agreed to open it for us. Soon, Friday night Shabbat dinners were buzzing with excitement as both Jewish and non-Jewish students came to enjoy each other's company. The office's new central location made it much easier for students to stop by during the day to speak to me about their problems over a falafel or tea. And slowly I began to discover my own inner strength to make the centre work. Funders who were impressed with the quality and quantity of students stepped forward and slowly the debts were all paid.

Loss of purpose

There is a strong correlation between depression and self-absorption. It is not coincidental that studies show that single men and women who live on their own are those most prone to depression. Because they only have to take care of themselves, they have extra time on their hands, which makes it easy for boredom to set in; this is certainly also the case with many of the graduate students at Oxford researching for theses. Doing little for others and sharing minimal human interaction can lead to deep depression.

We rarely find busy people depressed, although being busy does not prove that our lives are meaningful. Depression sets in when we lose our sense of purpose. We have no map, no engine, no stars. I have also counselled many of the students' mothers too: when their kids leave home, they lose their sense of purpose and begin to flounder.

In order to nip depression in the bud I used to encourage students to volunteer some of their time to the L'Chaim Society or other worthy causes even during the intense build-up towards their final exams. They thought I was crazy. One student said, 'Why do you want me to help now of all times when I need every spare minute to study?' 'In order to keep your spirits up and your energy levels high,' I said. 'Helping others will give you the all-important realization that even if your exams don't go so smoothly, there are people out there who depend on, appreciate and love you.' Purpose in life is the strongest bulwark against depression.

A final word: the power of the human smile

There is nothing that brings out our humanity as much as a smile. One night, I came home late gloomy over some problems I felt could not easily be resolved. Everyone in the house was asleep except for my four-year-old daughter, Shaina. Rather than scold her for getting out of bed, I let her climb on top of me as I sat to sulk.

She immediately ran to get her tzedakah box – her charity-box – and insisted that I put some coins in. I put one in, but she insisted on more. Two, but she still wanted more. 'Tatty, I want all of your coins. Hand them over.' After we thought she had cleaned me out, she stuck her tiny hand in my pocket and found another five pence. Upon discovering the treasure, she looked up at me with the most devious little smile. That smile shot a wave of joy through my heart. Despite all the troubles, life was great; my kids were healthy and smiling; I just had to see it.

Do you know why God wants us to be happy? Because He wants to know that we know how to appreciate, that we know how to say thank you, that we are cognizant of the countless blessings He showers upon us daily. To be depressed is to be ungrateful. It is to say to God, 'What about all the things you *haven't* given me?' Reminding ourselves of our blessings will help to lift us up again.

Since we are not naturally good at counting our blessings, we need to have a friend count and recount them for us. Never be afraid to rely on friends in your moments of great depression. The more you interact with people, and the more they make you do everyday things, the faster you will rejoin the ranks of the living.

Finally, when you go out with people, ask them about *their* problems. You will quickly realize that everybody has troubles and that your own problems are not intractable. You will also take joy from your ability to offer comfort. By offering to help others with their problems, you will also begin to feel valuable. The low self-esteem you feel from your depression must be countered by feeling how much other people depend on you.

11

Loneliness

THE MOST UNPLEASANT EMOTION

The most terrible poverty is loneliness and the feeling of being unloved.

Mother Teresa

On stage I make love to twenty five thousand people; and then I go home alone.

Janis Joplin

In the previous chapter, I argued that perhaps the most defining characteristic of our generation is depression. By the same token, I would argue that our generation is also the loneliest of all time. For all the noise of television, the sold-out stadium concerts and sporting events, I believe that a great crisis of intimacy inflicts our world. People may join together *en masse* to salute their favourite rock star, but once the event ends, they go home to their anonymous existences. One of the striking icons of our generation is that of someone coming home to an empty apartment and dining alone on a microwave meal in front of the television. Indeed, solitary pursuits like television, computers, shopping and video games are the defining hobbies of the modern man and woman.

Even the Internet, which theoretically has the potential to unite humanity in its worldwide web, reinforces loneliness and isolation. How do we communicate in the Age of Information? By writing on a computer screen instead of meeting face to face. We buy, sell, chat, date, even have 'safe sex' online. There is now hardly a reason to see a person, let alone speak with someone. Sadly enough, people these days have more interchange with people they have never met than with their own neighbours, whom they may not know even after living in a place for years.

The same is true in marriage. Some of the loneliest people I meet are married men and women who have long since ceased to communicate deeply and affectionately. They talk only about the functional side of their relationship – picking up the kids from school, having the boss for dinner on Thursday night and paying the mortgage. They no longer reveal their fears and dreams to each other.

My single friends joke that you can always tell whether a man and woman sitting together in a restaurant are married or dating. If they just stare blankly around the room and hardly exchange a word, they are married. Because they have long since run out of subjects to talk about, each sinks into their own world of loneliness. The mystery and curiosity are gone from their relationship and each treats the other as a known quantity.

Why has loneliness become such a pronounced pheno-menon? The global society is characterized by two features: the scientific rejection of God and the promotion of capital-istic values. Both lead us to suffer an abysmal void that cannot be filled. Consequently, man defines himself in terms of his productivity rather than his intrinsic self-worth. Feeling unconnected to a Divine Being, he is permanently on his own.

In my eleven years in Oxford, I noticed how students began life very innocently, choosing their friends on love and mutual sharing. But as they left university and entered the workforce, they quickly lost that innocence. Friendships became entirely symbiotic: You do for me, and I'll do for you. Each endeavoured to know the 'right' people and revolve in the 'right' circles. When you exchange meaningful relationships for the functional variety, however, the inevit-able result is loneliness.

Lonely is as lonely does

As John Milton noted in *Tetrachordon*, 'Loneliness was the first thing which God's eye named not good.' From the time that man first trod the earth, God determined that it was harmful for a person to be alone. Even God Himself, as it were, appeared to demonstrate the features of loneliness at the beginning of time. After all, why else did He form Adam? And one might further ask why He felt duty bound to reveal Himself at Sinai and declare, 'I am the Lord your God who brought you out of Egypt.'

In his masterly work *Naked Nomads*, a study of single males, George Gilder repeatedly demonstrates why the Biblical verse concerning the negative consequences of loneliness should be understood literally. It is truly not good, and certainly not healthy, for a man to be unattached and unmarried. Among the amazing statistics that Gilder cites are the fact that the death rate of late-middle-aged single men is more than twice that of married men; that bachelors are twenty-two times more likely to be committed for mental illness and three times more likely to suffer from insomnia; and that single men are far more likely to commit suicide.

Nor does society as a whole benefit from a man's decision to remain unattached. While single men comprise only about thirteen per cent of the population over the age of fourteen, they commit about ninety per cent of major and violent crimes because they are not distracted by the concerns of their wives, who attempt to keep them on the straight and narrow. While a man's conscience may not always influence him, a wife who wants her man to be home with the children instead of in prison with convicts often serves as a far greater impediment to crime.

Three levels of loneliness

Unlike depression, which is a black hole of feelings, loneliness is a true emotion because it drives us to eradicate its negative impact. Simply stated, we seek to alleviate our loneliness either by running out to meet people or, at the very least, calling and complaining to a friend. There are nevertheless different degrees of loneliness, some of which can impede action and ultimately lead to depression. The three levels I identify here are aloneness, lack of recognition (existential loneliness) and not feeling understood.

Aloneness is the simplest type of loneliness, occurring when someone is isolated in an unpopulated area. Solitude would be the more positive way of looking at aloneness, when we voluntarily go off on our own to reflect on our lives and regroup. In the eighteenth century, Robinson Crusoe left the bustle of London in order to discover peace of mind on his own deserted island. Today, like Henry David Thoreau, we all need to go to Walden Pond once in a while both to commune with nature and to remind us of the importance of self-reliance.

In essence, solitude means that we enjoy being by and with ourselves. Like all matters of life, however, self-reliance taken to the extreme is unhealthy. The novel *Robinson Crusoe* can also be seen as an allegory of urban isolation, the island serving as the ultimate metaphor of human detachment. The narrator himself repeatedly questions whether the shipwreck secures his reign or his captivity.

Aloneness, on the other hand, is not a state of being we elect and therefore we have difficulty coping with it. Aloneness means that we do not enjoy our own company but are easily bored. We attempt to deflect its impact by escaping through media such as television and junk novels. Statistics show that American children watch an average of four hours of television a day, and most homes have as many as one hundred channels hooked up. Why do we try to escape from our reality? Because time alone with ourselves can be frightening. Introspection must be avoided because it makes us confront those aspects of ourselves we dislike; it can make us face how empty our lives might really be. Witness how people today are never alone with themselves. As soon as we walk into the home after work we inevitably turn on the radio or TV, or light a cigarette. Frenetic activity and external noise quickly cover over the black hole of solitude.

Nevertheless, aloneness is easily remedied: all one needs to do is go to a pub and exchange pleasantries with animate souls, even with the bartender, or go to Wembley Stadium and sit in the presence of hundreds of screaming fans. Even Thoreau eventually rejoined civilization because he was lonely by himself in the woods.

We all have experiences of aloneness, especially in this technologically dominated age. A recent study by Carnegie-Mellon University showed that those who spend more than five hours a week surfing the Internet are ten times more prone to depression. I know how I feel when I need to finish writing a book. As the deadline looms and I spend large amounts of time in front of my computer, I begin more and more to crave human company. When I finally finish, it's like a horse breaking out of its stall at the beginning of a race. I indulge myself in others, to the great dread of all those around me. My wife tells me that when we have guests over for dinner after I finish a book, I positively talk them to death. Such is the danger of taking aloneness and isolation to an extreme.

Existential loneliness

The second level is existential loneliness – feeling lonely even while in the company of others. We all know that you do not have to be alone to feel lonely. I have spoken with far too many wives who, despite the presence of a husband and children, still feel themselves to be the loneliest people in the world. To believe that simply being in a relationship or in the company of others is a cure for loneliness is wildly mistaken.

Existential loneliness comes when a person no longer feels special because nobody recognizes their distinction. Adam experienced this kind of loneliness because he received no attention from any kindred spirit. Indeed, while he had the company of all the other creatures of the earth, he still felt terribly incomplete. Whoever said that a dog is a man's best friend was in error because no animal could ever fully alleviate human loneliness. Because animals are not our equals, they cannot confer upon us any meaningful distinction.

In order to alleviate existential loneliness, we must be around people who appreciate our distinctiveness. Above all, this comes in marriage because only in marriage is there the choosing of one individual and the non-selection of all others. In contrast to just 'being involved' with someone, we establish in marriage a relationship of exclusivity, demonstrating that the person we love is the most special in the entire world. Suddenly there is also someone who needs us so strongly and feels so satisfied with our presence in their life that they have foresworn romantic possibilities with every other person on the planet.

But not being appreciated for his uniqueness was not Adam's major dilemma: it was the fact that Adam desired to give to someone else but was initially denied this privilege. According to Midrashic literature, having been the handi-work of the Almighty Himself, Adam was possessed of supernal knowledge and able to communicate with the angels. So if he had billions of angels to hang out with, why was he so lonely?

The ancient Rabbis explain that loneliness results from not feeling needed. The angels were perfect and therefore did not need Adam. Sure, he could go to a local bar and have a beer with them, but no angel ever came to Adam for a loan or for comfort after being bereaved. Loneliness is not when there is no one around with whom to share human company. It is when there are twenty million people sur-rounding you but none acknowledges your existence by making you feel necessary and unique.

It was not until Eve was fashioned that Adam felt com-plete. Here was someone who was *not* an angel. Eve was like Adam. Alone, vulnerable and in need of a hug, she made Adam feel profoundly necessary. Finally, there was a flawed creature, just like Adam himself, who made him feel alive. It was Eve's vulnerability and dependency that made Adam feel he belonged. She not only appreciated him, but needed him. In Eve, he finally met the soul mate to whom he would dedicate his love and his life. This is a great lesson to all those who complain about their spouse's imperfections. If your spouse were perfect, they would not need you, and you would have no permanent role in the marriage. You would feel useless and ordinary.

Thus, existential loneliness comes not when we lack someone who loves us, but when we lack someone upon whom to bestow our love. Every human being is special. When someone needs our love and attention, it reinforces that feeling of uniqueness. It makes us feel like we possess a unique spiritual gift that only we can offer. On the other hand, when the recipient of our gift rejects us, we experience terrible loneliness because we feel mundane and redundant.

For example, we all feel terrible when we are fired from a job. The same is true, and much more so, when, God forbid, we discover that our spouse has been unfaithful. Here, even the closest human contact has been betrayed. The person who has pledged to affirm our uniqueness forever has replaced us with a substitute. Women who are cheated against often describe the emotion as feeling as if they were bereaved of themselves, present at their own funerals, which is especially appropriate because the betrayal has caused their specialness to die.

Arguably the most popular author on the topic of relationships is John Gray. In what may be the best-selling self-help book of the last century, *Men Are from Mars, Women Are from Venus*, Gray advocates that it is advantageous to marry at an older age because each partner is more complete and better empowered to offer something meaningful to the relationship. But it may be that the very opposite is true. When we marry in our mid-thirties rather than mid-twenties, we may already have become too independent to truly lean on each other. And when you marry someone who loves you but does not really need you, you are bound to feel lonely even in the relationship.

The loneliness of not feeling understood

The third and deepest level of loneliness is the most troublesome because in some ways it can never be overcome. This deepest level is the understanding that, even within a relationship, we will never ever be fully understood. As unique and distinct individuals, no other human being – not our parents, not even our spouse and children – will ever be able to enter into our head or soul and understand exactly who we are.

To be sure, our spouse can hold us in their arms and dull the pain of existence for a time, but they cannot remove that pain as it is inextricably linked to the phenomenon of existence itself. Herein lies the paradox, and ultimately the tragedy, of human existence. On the one hand, what makes us special is that we are individuals, that we have a spiritual gift to give to the world that no other person in any generation has. We are mentally, emotionally and spiritually unique, and the loss of one individual can never be supplanted by the presence of another. Indeed, our immortality is established not by the future generations of our children, but rather in our own lifetime through the idea that no one can ever be like us.

On the other hand, this uniqueness must by definition result in our isolation and loneliness: since I am unique, no one can truly understand me. A medieval Jewish thinker said concerning God, 'If I knew Him, I would be Him', meaning that to know another being is to become that being. And since we are not someone else, we can never really understand someone else or truly fathom their pain. So all of us are trapped in what can only be described as existential loneliness, the loneliness necessitated by existence itself.

The role of God and prayer

It is only God, in His role as Creator, who can ultimately understand our deepest loneliness. Because He created us, He is the only one that can fathom that unique part of us that no one else could ever understand. And just as we need

Him to relieve our loneliness, so too does He desire to be a living reality in our lives.

Herein lies the purpose of prayer. Real prayer is where man calls out to God from the depths of his being, knowing that only God can understand his loneliness. God is ultimately the only being that can be one with man. Prayer, far from being merely a religious rite, is thus a deep psychological need. This daily conversation with God is necessary if we are to unburden ourselves of the feeling of isolation and abandonment.

Abraham Joshua Heschel wrote, 'Dark for me is the world for all its bright cities and shiny stars, if not for the knowledge that God listens to me when I cry.' Prayer is like a bright ray of sun that penetrates a gloomy day. Indeed, if not for the knowledge that we can expose the wounds of our hearts to the One above, who could tolerate being immersed into such a cruel world? Each of us is God's beloved, and He listens intently to our voice.

Here also is the reason that religions have the rite of confession. In the Catholic faith, you confess to a priest. In the Jewish religion, you confess directly to God through the medium of prayer. But confession is characteristic not only of monotheistic faiths. Across the globe and throughout the ages, most creeds and civilizations have sought the same vehicle in order to relieve loneliness. Indeed, there is a distinct and universal human need to pour out our fears, to unburden ourselves of the accumulated scars of living. And the only Being who can truly understand our torment is the Creator Himself. Without a God, we are once again lost in the maelstrom of loneliness.

When Orthodox Jews pray in the synagogue, men and women sit in separate sections divided by a partition. Why do we do this? Wouldn't it be more comforting to sit next to one's spouse when trying to communicate with God? The answer is that we remain separate in order to engender a sense of total dependency on God. Ultimately, no matter how necessary our spouse, it is God alone who can bring comfort to his children. Prayer is about facing the abyss of human despair and latching on to God as the sole source of our redemption. In our comfortable pews in today's churches and synagogues lined as they are with wall-to-wall carpeting, we often do not feel the terrifying experience of what prayer really is, in which we raise ourselves from the prison of total isolation and abandonment.

In another paradox, it is specifically because we are individuals whom no one else can understand that we enter into relationships at all. If others could fathom us in our entirety, they would quickly tire of us. But because each of us represents an infinite enigma, others want to try to penetrate our mystery. I have long maintained that curiosity is the soul of every relationship. It is for this reason that modesty too is the cornerstone of every relationship. Modesty means that an individual protects that part of themself which is unique, rather than, so to speak, exposing themselves in public.

In sum, to remedy all three levels of loneliness we need community, the loving companionship of marriage and an ongoing relationship with God. Immersed in a modern world in which real communities have been replaced by 'virtual' communities, fifty per cent of all marriages end in divorce, and everyone has time to watch television but nobody has time to pray, it is no wonder that we all feel so desperately alone.

The extreme of loneliness

In its most extreme manifestation, loneliness leads to suicide. Suicide becomes logical when someone feels that they have no contribution to make to the world, that they are of no value. When you arrive at the conclusion that the world can go on just fine without you because no one seems to need you or notice you anyway, it suddenly becomes perversely logical to confirm in action what everyone harbours in thought.

Although as a Rabbi, I twice had to help students whose parents had committed suicide, I never expected it to happen in my own family, so I was shaken to my very core when my brother rang me in the middle of the night to tell me that my uncle in Israel had taken his life. About five years earlier, my uncle had suffered a serious financial loss. He tried in vain to recover the money from someone he felt had short-changed him, but his obsession led him to alienate many of his family.

I had felt very close to this uncle because I lived in Israel for two years as a student, where he served as a surrogate father to me. When I visited him six months prior to his death, he seemed despondent and detached. To my great shame, I must confess that, although I saw him in pain, I did not give him the time that could have made a difference. His depression was pulling me down and I wanted to have a good time on my vacation. My selfish attitude, like the attitude of many of the family, said that I was not going to be a party to his self-pity, that it was about time that he got over this once and for all. Feeling alone and abandoned in his pain, my uncle took the only step that seemed logical to him.

Contrary to all the psychobabble about the need to love oneself, we even more need others to love us. Indeed, we are only as alive as others make us feel. Because no one, including myself, made my uncle feel alive, he was in his mind already dead. Thus, suicide is not an insane undertaking but the confirmation of a pre-existing condition.

It is not difficult to prevent this kind of horror, when someone feels they have no worth. The key is to simply be there for each other, to tune in when those we know are in need. Loneliness is the most unpleasant of all human emotions, something so terrible that God Himself labelled it as bad. Our first mission as human beings must be to end the loneliness of others, learning how to listen to and value their words. When Adam experienced loneliness, God responded by creating Eve to take it away, so we must emulate this. Indeed, we must always keep in mind that the very purpose of our existence is to ensure that no one else ever has to inhabit this planet on their own, or feel lonely even as they share it with others.

12

Grief

A TOUCHSTONE FOR OUR HUMANITY

There is a time for everything, and a season for every activity under heaven . . . a time to weep and a time to laugh, a time to mourn and a time to dance.

Ecclesiastes

Man could not live if he were entirely impervious to sadness. Many sorrows can be endured only by being embraced, and the pleasure taken in them naturally has a somewhat melancholy character. So, melancholy is morbid only when it occupies too much place in life; but it is equally morbid for it to be wholly excluded from life.

Emile Durkheim

If, as we just said, the first human obligation is to put an end to each other's loneliness, it is certainly also our obligation to help others in their grief. But unlike loneliness, which isolates and draws us inwards, grief is one of our most humanizing attributes. Sadness, unlike depression, means that we are alive, that we feel for other human beings enough to mourn for them. Indeed, only by experiencing pain as the result of loss can we ever value that which is lost. Moreover, if we can get over any loss, why should we try to improve the world by curing cancer or preventing war? Our grief thus serves as a touchstone for our humanity.

A mother once came to a lecture series I delivered on the subject of suffering. She sat in the corner all by herself throughout the eight-week course. When it was over, she told me she had wasted her time. 'I came to your lecture series because a year ago, my 28-year-old daughter had a brain haemorrhage and collapsed into a coma. A month later she died. I have been looking for comfort ever since and hoped that you would provide it. But you haven't.' I first apologized to her for letting her down. Then I said, 'But think about it. How precious could your daughter possibly have been if, after being grief-stricken by her loss, you could suddenly hear a lecture and feel fine again? It is because human life is infinitely precious that it is so difficult to recover from its loss. People can't be replaced with words.'

We should not mourn and grieve excessively because by doing so we enter the land of the dead ourselves, but when we are not attuned to grief, we become worse than animals. Humans are the only creatures on this earth that will in large numbers annihilate members of their own species, but the only way to do this is by becoming desensitized to tragedy. The Nazis desensitized themselves by believing their victims were subhuman. Killing a Jew was ridding the world of a rodent, of a parasite. The irony, of course, is that in their beastly effort to dehumanize their victims, their own humanity was destroyed.

The bottom line is that if we cannot feel grief, this shows that we lack the moral sensibility to differentiate between right and wrong. An inability to experience loss betrays an inability to appreciate gain. Paradoxically, therefore, grief is the ultimate measure of how much we appreciate our blessings. And one of the great challenges of life is to learn to embrace and appreciate our blessings *before* they are taken away from us.

Grief in the secular world

Grief is one of the most difficult emotions to express today, certainly one of the least encouraged. We tell our little girls that 'Big girls don't cry', and we have little tolerance for boys who cry because it is considered a sign of weakness.

When women cry, we label them 'sentimental', and when men cry, which is a rarity, we do not know how to react. Consequently, when loss affects people who seem to be inarticulate in the language of grief, they become emotional cripples, not really knowing how to respond.

After his mother Virginia Kelley died, President Clinton went to Russia only hours after her funeral to meet with President Yeltsin at a major summit. Was this the proper way to mourn the woman to whom he owed his very life? To be sure, he has tremendous public responsibilities, but some private obligations outweigh them. As a leader of a great and humanitarian nation, should he not have set an example on how to show respect for a parent? It was almost like pretending that his mother's death had not occurred. Moreover, was it healthy for *him* to continue with his obligations and not afford himself some way to express his grief?

Although I was stunned by Clinton's decision to proceed with his trip, I cannot really fault him for his behaviour because, culturally, we do not have rituals in place that help us respond to loss. Although we put on elaborate funerals with flowers and eulogies, most people do not understand what it means to mourn. They know about moments of silence because this is how we respond collectively to loss, but that's about all. Following the funeral of a loved one, most people, like President Clinton, are back at work the very next day.

George lost his mother the day before an important business meeting in Bucharest and actually asked the Rabbi to hurry the funeral so that he could make the last flight out of London and not miss his deal. When he returned, I told him that whatever profit he could have possibly gained from his recent journey, it could never equal his loss. 'I don't refer to the loss of your mother, but the loss of your own psychological well being. Because if you think that you can lose the woman who brought you into this world without making any accommodation in order to absorb that loss, you are sorely mistaken.'

It is not only the mourners who respond awkwardly, but all those who attempt to comfort them. We do not usually know what to say. We offer a quick condolence – 'I'm sorry about your loss' – and maybe take it easy on them for a few days, but we basically treat them as normal. So the difficulty with grief lies at a collective level too. Indeed, grief affects the entire public health.

Part of the reason we run back to our normal activities is because our society measures how well we do in grief in terms of how quickly we get on with our lives. From a secular point of view, the purpose of mourning is to help us get over the loss and move on. It is entirely a means to an end. We are not meant to dwell on our sadness because, in our culture, we desperately try to rid ourselves of all pain. We are commonly told that time heals all wounds, so if we are still hurting we just have to wait. Most people do not offer much support for those who feel grief months or years later because they see it as a sign of weakness and poor resolve. We are the 'Don't worry, be happy' generation and we just do not know how to handle grief.

Mourning from a Jewish perspective

In contrast, Judaism demonstrates a deep and profound understanding of the nature of human loss. Indeed, it understands that we cannot just go back to business as usual after losing a loved one; we need time to make the necessary transition from living with them to living without them. The period of time taken off is not designed to return us to our previous state of productivity. It is not about recovering, but about *adjusting*. How does one reintegrate oneself into the world when one has been made an orphan? Can one put someone else in place who will provide love and guidance? Thus, the Jewish period of mourning consists of concentric ripples of intensity, beginning with the immediate aftermath of the death and diminishing onward for a year.

Just after the death of a loved one, there are the seven days of mourning, known as shiva (meaning seven). This is the worst time, accompanied by the greatest sadness. Although many people mistakenly believe that shiva is a time to pay respect to the deceased, it was instituted for the living. The mourner sits on the ground or a low stool wearing torn clothes. He does not shave, bathe or look in the mirror because his vanity is supposed to be the thing farthest from his mind. He is not trying to 'get over' his loss; for seven days, he just tries to cope with the fact of the loss. Moreover, his dishevelled state reflects the fact that he is not trying to impress anyone. He is only trying to come to terms with the terrible pain that he has just experienced.

During this period, the House of Mourning is open for friends, relatives and members of the community to pay their respects to the deceased and show their sympathy to the living. The purpose of shiva is to show the mourners that they are not alone in their grief. Indeed, grief is something that cannot and should not be experienced alone. There is a basic need to share one's pain with people who care because the essence of grief is a feeling of abandonment and isolation; its underlying theme is one of loneliness.

There is a need to have these feelings of abandonment countered by warm displays of affection from one's own community. Visitors usually bring food so that the mourners do not have to preoccupy themselves with the mundane. They sit and listen or talk according to the mourner's mood. The law is that a visitor is not allowed to initiate conversation with the mourner. Maybe the mourner does not yet feel like talking, and why pressure him to respond?

Because there are no words to truly express either grief or what we feel for those who are grieving, it is customary to say upon leaving the house, 'God is a righteous judge' and 'May you be comforted among the mourners of Zion.' Critics may object that such a universal gesture sounds too contrived, but it helps both the bereaved and the visitors to have a ritual in place so that we realize we are neither the first nor the last to suffer loss. The ritual gives us our much-needed sense of community at a time when we feel terribly abandoned.

Shiva is meant to give the mourner the time and space to recover their basic humanity and strength. The total outpouring of caring one receives through this week helps to ease the transition back to regular activities. The concern that is shown is of immeasurable help in enabling the mourner to begin the long process of emotional reconstruction.

As time moves on, however, the sadness itself must diminish, and the living must return to the land of the living. As the crowds go away, we have to confront our loss more privately and less intensely. So, following the shiva period are the thirty days of less intense mourning, known as the shloshim (which means thirty). During this, one does not cut one's hair or attend joyous events. Instead, the mourner attempts to return to normal activities, but it is recognized that he or she is still deeply grieved.

The shloshim stage is followed by a year of less intense mourning during which the mourner must attend synagogue every day in order to recite the kaddish, a prayer that extols the greatness of God and is said in the memory of the departed relative. Indeed, while one may usually pray alone without a minyan – a quorum of ten – this is not the case during the year of mourning. The sense of isolation and loss must be countered by total immersion within a community.

It is not an arbitrary dictum that the *kaddish* must be recited in the company of others. In secular society, psychologists and sociologists have recently begun to form support groups for mourners to deal with their losses. Attending daily services to say the *kaddish* has, since early times, enabled Jews to have the support of such groups. In the year following the death of a loved one, attending daily services serves as a prescribed time for channelling grief so that it does not become repressed and suddenly overwhelming. Moreover, we have the opportunity to meet others who are also saying kaddish for a loved one, and thus form immediate bonds of commonality with them.

After the year of mourning, individuals must nurse themselves back to full health. Judaism maintains that we cannot allow ourselves to grow too sad; we have an obligation to be fully alive. Even when a relative dies we cannot allow a part of ourselves to die with them.

The conservation of spiritual energy

The question may be asked, how is time a remedy for loss? Is it that the loss can never be made up but that time simply causes us to forget it and the pain it engenders? Or is it that time actually restores all things?

The first law of thermodynamics, the most tested law in all of science, states that all energy in the universe remains constant. Energy can be neither created nor lost; it is just constantly converted into different forms. The same is true of every other area of life. When you love someone, you can hold them and hug them in physical form. When their eternal soul departs their ephemeral body, you can experience them in another form; they are never completely lost.

That is another reason why we recite the *kaddish*. It affords the mourner a sense of the eternity of the departed one. It is not true that all of the individual dies and is buried in the grave. The spirit is eternal and, to an extent, those who have died can be spiritually closer to us once their spirit is no longer constrained by the confines of the flesh.

Time is a critical factor in mourning not because we need time in order to forget the pain. What parent could possibly forget the pain of having lost a child? What time does is to allow us gradually to make the transition. We have to learn how to rediscover that which we have lost on a newer, more spiritual plane, but it takes time to make the ascent.

Take Moses, the greatest Jewish prophet. The Bible speaks very movingly about his death, how he died alone 'and none know his burial place until this very day'. The children of Israel who were encamped in the desert cried bitterly at his loss and mourned his passing for thirty days. But was he truly gone? Every week when I go to synagogue and read about Moses in the Bible, I experience his presence leading me as one of his flock, as if he were alive today.

The patriarch Jacob never died

Another Biblical example is the death of our patriarch Jacob. Interestingly, the Torah never actually uses the words 'He died', but 'He gathered up his feet into the bed; and he departed this life, and was gathered to his people.' Because the word 'death' is not used, the Talmud makes the spectacular pronouncement that our forefather Jacob never actually died. But if he did not die, what are we to make of the lengthy description in the Torah of his burial, which ends with the words, 'For his sons carried him into the land of Canaan, and buried him in the cave of the field of Machpelah which Abraham bought with the field for a possession of a burying place' (Genesis 50:13)? Did they really bury a live man? 'Of course not', responds the Talmud. The statement is meant to be taken not literally but metaphorically: 'Since his children were alive, he lived on through his children.'

The Talmud is saying that Jacob was the last in a tradition of three great men who gave the world monotheism, the most radical and important concept ever set out before humanity. Abraham was the originator of monotheism, but when he died, only one of his two principal children carried it forward. It was as though half of Abraham had died, the other half living on through his son Isaac in the doctrine that he gave the world.

Isaac also had two sons. As with his father, only one proved true to Isaac's principles of holiness. Half of Isaac died when he departed the world, but half of him remained alive, so everything he stood for was carried on nobly by his son Jacob.

But Jacob had thirteen children, all of whom remained loyal to the God of Israel and His commandments. Since his children were all alive and carried on their lives according to the traditions he had imparted to them, he lived on forever through them.

Time cannot heal all wounds

A little while ago, I was on a television show debating the pros and cons of a new drug that supposedly enhances memory. The implications are, of course, far reaching. We can teach students to remember their mathematics better, parents to remember their kids' names, and politicians to remember their campaign promises. But is enhanced memory truly a good thing? What if prisoners of war suddenly cannot forget the pain of their experiences? What if the ordinary man cannot forget the large sum of money he lost on Wall Street?

Remembrance is, of course, both a blessing and a curse, but the real meaning of forgetfulness is not that we forget pain but that we learn to forget our boundaries. Spatial–temporal limitations, which are the main terms of reference employed by humans, begin to dissolve as we embrace higher and more infinite coordinates of existence.

Sadness is what we feel as we make the transition across borders. All transitions are painful. It's like growing wisdom teeth: when they break through the surface, it hurts. As we continually break through the surface to ever higher planes of experience and consciousness, we are bound to endure the pain of growth as well as the pain of loss. We think we are losing something only until we discover that we are actually gaining.

Ultimately, time cannot heal all wounds because the people whom we love are not replaceable. Therefore the purpose of mourning is to readjust our lives to accommodate the loss that will be permanent, while actually opening up new possibilities for experiencing closeness with the one lost.

In Judaism we commemorate the anniversary of our loved one's death by lighting a special candle, called a yahrtzeit candle. That yahrtzeit candle is lit every year for the rest of our lives. It is a sign that, although our relative has gone, he or she still possesses the capacity to illuminate our lives and inspire us out of our darkness. We are never meant to forget our loved one. By the same token, it is customary among Jews to name our children after the deceased to say that even death holds forth the promise of new and exciting life.

When grief paralyses us

Grief is appropriate at the right times and in the proper quantity. When taken to an extreme, however, grief ceases to demonstrate our humanity but begins to quell it. Grief is meant to be therapeutic rather than crippling. Excessive grief draws us inwards and leads to depression, which takes away our humanity by making us numb to others.

Elayne had been married to Arthur for fifty-five years. When Arthur died, Elayne could not face the prospect of continuing her life without him. Although Elayne's children and grandchildren adored Arthur, they found it easier to get on with their lives as the months passed after his death. Elayne, however, was unable to cope effectively with her loss even though her family made every attempt to comfort her. The grief eventually turned into depression and Elayne had to seek medical intervention in order to lift her mind from constant thoughts of her husband. Four years later, she was still unable to face the morning in good cheer.

Although the grief was genuine, it became her life's purpose. Her home became a morgue, her bedroom a roomy coffin. Unfortunately, when we grieve excessively, it tunes out our other emotions. Elayne lost most of her capacity for compassion because she felt that no misfortune was greater than her own. In addition, she lost all capacity for happiness because she wallowed in self-pity. When her only granddaughter got married a year later, she could not muster true joy for the occasion. Even after her first great-grandchild was born and named after her husband, Elayne was unable to feel happiness because her self-absorption was so heightened.

This kind of self-absorption is precisely what the Creator did not have in mind for us because it is debilitating. Grief is, after all, meant to be temporary and transitional. If we are unable to shake off grief, we become stuck with sensory perception as our only frame of reference and thereby limit the possibility of experiencing our loved one on a higher spiritual plane, of accepting the infinite quality of the soul or the human personality.

When we do not allow time to mourn

At the other end of the spectrum, and far more common in my experience, are the people who grieve too little. If we do not allow ourselves the time to mourn properly, we do ourselves a great disservice.

One terrible day, Todd was summoned into the room of his head of college at Oxford to be told compassionately but as a matter of fact that his father had died of a heart attack. Todd was obviously stricken with grief but had a major examination two days later, which would decide his continued presence at the university. He had to choose whether he should go to the funeral in America or take the exam. The college was adamant that while they would allow him to sit the papers later in the year, they would have to be taken alongside his final examinations. This would make it impossible for him to prepare for, or succeed at, both.

There are certain things in life that can never be compromised. Respect for a deceased parent is one of these, and I told Todd there was no possible way that he could miss the funeral and sit for an exam during the *shiva*. For his part, he insisted that his father, who had been so proud that Todd had been admitted to Oxford on a scholarship, would have objected to his son observing a period of mourning at such a crucial juncture in his academic career.

That may be, I told him, and that is how a father executes his duties as a loving parent. But a child also has duties, one of which is respect for a parent even when the parent refuses to accept it, and this is especially necessary where the final respect one can show a parent is concerned. 'Your father can tell you many things that you are obliged to obey and hold precious, but he cannot tell you that he is not your father or to behave towards him in a fashion that contradicts the obligations inherent in the parent–child relationship.'

Todd did not heed my advice. He sat the exam with his mother's consent and obtained one of the best results at the university, but success had its price. A few months later, terrible guilt set in. His self-reproach deepened when he finally arrived home and friends could not believe what he had done. When he returned to Oxford, he became 'numb'. He was unable to do any work and began dating a succession of girls whom even he knew to be unsuitable.

Todd's life reached crisis point, and his college thought he should be expelled. It was now many months since his father had passed away. I sat and spoke to him, telling him that there was no reason to feel such a weight of guilt and that he had to pull his life together again. His father's *yahrtzeit* was rapidly approaching, so I asked him to undertake to put together a *minyan* for the three prayer services and to say *kaddish*. He was not very observant of Jewish ritual yet I told him that he must be observant of his father's *yahrtzeit*. Saying *kaddish* faithfully, lighting a candle and trying to arrange a meal for fellow worshippers at the synagogue would be his atonement.

Presence in absence

In the Bible, there is the story of how the jealous king Saul sets out to take the life of his son-in-law David, whom he fears will be his successor rather than his son Jonathan. But Jonathan and David are the best of friends, and the former warns the latter that he must flee his father's wrath. Jonathan tells David, 'Tomorrow is the first day of the month when all the king's household gather at the king's table for the festive meal. And your presence will be noticed through your absence.'

There are moments when someone is better remembered through their absence than their presence. A yahrtzeit is such a time. Although a father may be deceased, his absence is noted and he comes back to life, as it were, through the actions of his children.

If on a *yahrtzeit* a family just goes about its normal business as if nothing has happened, their father has died an eternal death. But if they mark the occasion by visiting his tomb and performing and dedicating good deeds in his honour, they cause their father to live on eternally. He is still influencing and affecting their lives in death as he did while alive.

It may come as a surprise to know that this ancient way of describing life is also the most basic definition of life that we have today. Professor Velvl Greene, former director of NASA's Life-Science Research Center, once gave a lecture at the L'Chaim Society in Oxford. He described how he and a team of specialists were charged with immunizing the Viking Lander in preparation for its landing on Mars in search of life. This was done to ensure that no microbes from earth were present on the Lander that could mistakenly be attributed to life indigenous to Mars. The most important question that arose in the mission's quest for life was this: supposing they did find life on Mars; how would they identify it as being alive? Perhaps a life form could be so radically different that the instruments would fail to recognize its significance. It suddenly became essential to postulate a universal definition of life equally binding on all planets.

It is uncanny that the approach they adopted resembles the Jewish definition. They decided that anything found on Mars that somehow changed its environment was alive. By the same token plants on earth are considered to be alive because they oxygenate the air; animals are alive because they constantly change the environment around them.

In Judaism, life is defined as the positive impact that one leaves on one's environment. The Talmud states with some confidence that 'the righteous, even in death, are said to be alive, while the wicked, even in life, are said to be dead.' So it follows that something continues to live as long as it is affecting its environment, even long after it has lost that principle which we commonly call life that distinguishes a vital and functional being from a dead body. However, once you stop affecting lives – even while you still walk this earth – you may exist but you are no longer alive. As long as someone's memory serves to bring the world another step forward, they are still alive, even though they may have walked the earth centuries earlier.

13

Hatred

THE MOST INTENSE NEGATIVE EMOTION

*I have always hated that damn James Bond. I'd
like to kill him.*

Sean Connery

*Love blinds us to faults, but hatred blinds us to
virtues.*

Iba Ezra

You cannot shake hands with a clenched fist.

Indira Gandhi

———————————

Hatred is the complete inversion of the human heart and its
most noble emotion, love. God created love as a vehicle for
the comprehensive embrace of all things. To love is to desire
to be one with the object of our love, to feel that our
completion hinges on embracing it. When a man loves a
woman, he feels incomplete without her. He thinks about
her all the time and longs for the moment when he can hold
her in his arms. He devotes his life to her happiness because
on it is contingent his own.

Hatred is, in contrast, when our happiness – our feeling
of completion – is contingent on someone else's pain and
suffering. Rabbi Samson Raphael Hirsch went one step
further by defining hatred as the feeling that the very existence of some other being is a hindrance to our own. From
this point of view, it is only through their destruction or
their misery that our own existence becomes more meaningful and complete. We cannot be happy unless they are sad.

We cannot move forward in our own life until we know that theirs is moving backward.

Hate groups will tell their followers that hatred empowers, but this is of course a lie. Hatred debilitates by making our existence contingent on someone else's non-existence. It imprisons the spirit and suffocates the senses. Rather than being free to get on with my life, I am attached to the object of my hatred, and I can have no happiness unless I control his or her destiny. Hitler blamed the Jews for the ills of Nazi Germany, but in so doing he simultaneously conceded that a few Jews were more powerful than all the Germans combined.

Hatred is an act of alienation

Goodness is, by definition, when we become sensitive to the presence of God in the world, when we recognize the image of the Creator that is implanted on every human face. This heightened sensitivity reaches its apogee in the fraternity of all mankind, whereby total strangers treat each other with compassion and respect because they are aware of their ultimate connection. Love is an act of unification, a statement of oneness with all creation.

In hatred, however, we distance ourselves from the object of our hatred. Indeed, to hate is to treat the object of one's hatred as a stranger or enemy with whom one shares nothing of substance in common. Moreover, because it rejects the common origin of humanity, hatred is in essence the denial of the existence of God Himself, and a rejection of the unity that underlies all that is. Since one cannot truly hate oneself, every act of hatred must first be preceded by an act of alienation.

According to the Talmud, gratuitous hatred is the most vicious form of hatred, and the Rabbis denounce it in the most extreme terms. In their view, the Second Temple was destroyed not by the Romans but by the Jews themselves because of their sin of unjustified hatred, when, instead of working together, the Jews conspired against one another.

Hatred is always other-oriented

Note that the object of our hatred is never ourselves because hatred, by definition, cannot be directed inwards. We may be angry at ourselves, but we are incapable of real self-hatred. The proof is this: the next time one of your friends says, 'I hate myself so much. I can't believe I did something so stupid', agree with him. Then see how your friend reacts. He will probably take great offence at your having agreed with his self-disparagement. This is because he does not really have such a lowly opinion of himself; he is just blowing off steam for having made a mistake. Indeed, hating oneself contradicts the human survival instinct, which dictates that we must always feel that we are necessary and essentially good.

Since we cannot hate ourselves, every act of hatred is directed towards 'the other'. Indeed, only when you consider someone an 'other' can you truly hate them. Morris became so exasperated with his rebellious teenage son Patrick that he lost his temper and struck him hard in the face. Blood gushed from Patrick's nose. At that moment, the person who was in the most pain was not Patrick but Morris. Seeing the blood come from his son's nostrils immediately awoke his paternal instinct. He was reminded that this was his son, not some stranger off the street with whom he was having an argument. Overcome by the gravity of his action, Morris broke down and begged his son's forgiveness.

This story is an extreme example of what it sometimes takes to be reminded that the person you hate is actually your own flesh and blood, and you certainly cannot hate your own flesh and blood. A far healthier approach is to try never to lose sight of that fact in the first place by having your intellect intercede on behalf of your emotions. You must keep in mind your inner will – to sustain a lasting and loving relationship with all those who surround you. In marriage especially, this can sometimes be forgotten as we often tend to take the ones who love us most for granted.

No husband can truly hate his wife, and no wife her husband, as long as they truly comprehend that the marital bond has rendered them one flesh. No matter how much anger they may feel in a given moment, they may argue but they can never hate. A husband and a wife are one flesh, and that bond transcends momentary feelings.

The only way a man can hate his wife is if he has convinced himself at that moment that she is not his wife, but a foreigner or, worse, an enemy intent on harming rather than helping him. When God created Eve He said, 'I shall make for Adam a helpmate *against* him.' The words 'against him', in Hebrew *kenegdo*, can be translated either as 'opposite' or 'against'. Husbands can see their wives either as helpmates or antagonists. When a man yells at his wife, it is because he sees her as the latter.

Similarly, a woman can hate her husband only if at that moment she considers him to be a stranger. Indeed, every wife I have ever spoken to who has been devastated to discover her husband's infidelity has said, 'The man I thought I knew was really a stranger.' So the quickest way to overcome a feeling of hatred towards someone is to remind yourself of your relationship to them, be they your parent, your spouse or your fellow man or woman, for all members of the human race are brothers and sisters.

The seven types of hatred

All hatred can be divided into seven basic categories. Although an in-depth study is beyond the scope of this book, we will examine several of these categories in this and subsequent chapters. If we can learn to classify our negative feelings, it may be possible to purge ourselves of them:

1. Envy and jealousy: the desire to put down those who out-do us
2. Racism and prejudice: inbred and passed down in families, being either taught to small children directly or picked up passively through the social environment
3. Revenge: the desire to strike back at someone who has wronged or hurt us

4. Irrational, instant dislike: like love at first sight, some people hate at first sight with no provocation or cause. Often due to a feeling of inferiority on the part of the one who hates
5. Judgementalism: hating people whom you think are evil or in other ways beneath you
6. Collective hatred between nations that result from territorial disputes and the like, which are not due to racism. The Arab–Israeli conflict is a good example. Here two Semitic nations are fighting a battle largely over land, albeit with religious overtones
7. Hatred of those closest to us whom we once loved the most, that is, best friends, husbands and wives, parents and children, a highly intense hatred that cannot be included in the previous categories

Racism

Racism is, perhaps, the ultimate form of estrangement. The racist views another person not just as fundamentally and irreconcilably 'other' but as categorically inferior. In the land where all men were supposedly created equal, for example, American slave owners considered their slaves to be sub-human chattel to be abused at will. The slave owners dehumanized their 'property' by denying them not just their freedom, but also their dignity.

Slavery is the ultimate act of human alienation. It is one thing to feel alienated from another human being and to hate them by denying the kinship that exists between you, but quite another to deny one's kinship by denying that someone is even part of the same species, by reducing them to an animal to be owned and whipped. In perhaps the darkest era of American history, human beings were, on the basis of their colour alone, denied the most funda-mental human rights to selfhood, marriage and family. In order to sever familial attachments, slaves were cruelly and deliberately bought, sold, raped and abused; infants were systematically taken from their mothers' breasts and delivered to unrelated Mammies for care.

The one who is ultimately dehumanized by acts of racism is, of course, the racist himself. Slave owners became worse than beasts for their crimes. Besides the cruelty inherent in slave-owning, the masters in many instances ended up whipping or selling off their own progeny, products of relations with their slave mistresses. The irony is, of course, that while the owners tried to destroy the families of their slaves, they ended up destroying their own in the process. Similarly, the Nazis, who created their death camps in the name of civilization and progress, will go down in world history as the most sadistic savages of all time for their unspeakable crimes against God and humanity.

What the slave owners, the Nazis and all other racists have in common is the failure to understand that both they and the 'other' they demonize are members of the same human family, and that the bonds that unite a family are infinitely stronger than any issues that might ever divide them. Had they understood this, it would have been impossible to hate despite the difference in colour or faith. Every time we feel a kinship with another human being, it becomes impossible to despise them. This is because the common denominator for humanity is that we are all created in the image of God. Indeed, the belief in the equality of all people can only be justified if we believe that God is the father of all creation.

If we do not believe that we all emanate from the same source, or if we consciously deny God's existence, blatant inequality is most evident. Some are certainly born more intelligent, more gifted, wealthier than others. It is because of this undeniable disparity that the West has come to define equality as equality of opportunity. In the Bible, however, equality means simply, yet profoundly, that every human being is God's child and that there is a spark of the Infinite Divine in each of us. In the eyes of God, therefore, we are all equal.

The Bible's famous imperative in Leviticus (19:18) to 'love one's fellow as oneself' is based on the idea that one's fellow *is* oneself. Hatred is such a strong emotion that it cannot be countered by fighting it within our breast but only by training our minds always to focus on that oneness. There must be a cognitive appreciation for the fact that we are all cast from the same image, products of one indivisible flesh. One cannot be good to God, observing all ritual, and bad to one's fellow man.

The terrible abuse of religion throughout the ages that has justified maiming and killing in the name of God is predicated on the misguided belief that God desires us to be closer to Him than to our fellow man. However, just as the easiest way to flatter a parent is to practise kindness with his or her children, so the easiest way to please God is to practise kindness with all of His creatures.

Epiphany atop a mountain

Growing up in sunny Los Angeles and Miami did not afford me the opportunity to master the art of skiing. In fact, until I was twenty-five years old, I had never even been on a ski slope. When my wife and I took a trip to Switzerland a few years after we were married, I knew the time had finally come. We drove to one of the many beautiful ski resorts perched atop the high Alpine peaks that surround Geneva. With only minor apprehension, I put on my gear, went up the lift and found myself slowly making my way down the slopes, falling every fifteen feet or so to be buried in the fine white powder and terrifying my wife in the process. Slowly but surely I persevered until I gradually learned to navigate a slope all by myself.

Because we were at the resort for only four days, I insisted on the last day, obviously forgetting my desire for a long life, on putting on my skis and heading outside, even though there was a terrible blizzard. For my final day, I decided to go for broke. I was going to ski down the very highest peak at well over three thousand metres – alone. I mustered the courage to get on the huge gondola that moments later disappeared into the clouds.

I felt a bit uneasy when I realized that there was absolutely no one on the ski lift but me, and I mean *no one*. As I ascended to the summit, I saw that virtually all the other lifts had been closed. The higher the elevation, the more I felt the deafening howl of the wind. At about two thousand metres, the fog became so dense that I could not even see my own hand in front of my eyes. But still the gondola climbed.

Thoughts of basic survival occupied my mind as I alighted from the lift and started my descent. I yelled and hollered hoping that someone would hear me, but not even my own echo responded. The whole experience was so frightening that I began to wonder whether this was just a bad dream.

But this was no laughing matter. With zero visibility, I could not see the markers that prevent skiers going off the cliff, and I could not find a path. Shivering with cold and fear, I decided to halt rather than choose the wrong route, which would be the shortcut back to Geneva. With my meagre skiing ability, I couldn't take chances. I stayed put and waited for thirty minutes on top of the mountain, but no one appeared.

This experience was to serve for me as a deep lesson of the bonds that unite humanity. The only thing I could think of was how it was the loneliest, most frightening experience of my life. I was positively desperate for any form of human company and kept hoping that someone would come down off that ski lift. For the very first time in my life, I did not care who it was who joined me, just as long as they were human. They could have been male or female, young or even very, very old and incapacitated. It could have been someone who was a better or worse skier than me (preferably better), someone who liked me or someone who hated me. I remember thinking that it could even have been someone who didn't like Jews too much – a skinhead, perhaps. I just wanted to see another human face so that I was not completely alone on that forlorn mountain.

After about an hour, as the frostbite was just beginning to set in, a school of young Swiss Alpine skiers (in my mind a band of angels) came and inadvertently rescued me. I felt not only gratitude for my own life but, even more importantly, added wisdom and love for all humanity. Henceforth that mountain would serve for me as a metaphor for our lonely planet.

Through my experience, I came to understand that the problem of the inhabitants of the earth is that we rarely view each other as being stranded atop a mountain. We hate because we think that we can afford to hate. We reason that if we hate all of the Africans and Asians, so what?; there are still hundreds of millions of Europeans with whom to fraternize. And if we also hate the European Jews, we still have all of Europe's Catholics and Protestants.

Because we all too often surround ourselves with people who are just like us, we do not feel enough of a dependency on those beyond our immediate circle and thus fail to embrace a truly transcendent philosophy of mutual and complete dependence and tolerance. No, not tolerance because to tolerate someone is to stomach their differences. What we must recognize is the interdependency that connects and unites all humanity. Only when we become honest enough to experience and admit our inner, existential loneliness will we understand how we all need each other. Then and only then will we finally overcome every form of racism.

Universal brotherhood

In my third year at Oxford, I had the privilege of meeting the man who subsequently became one of my very closest friends, Cory Booker. An African-American Rhodes scholar, he was the first non-Jew to serve as president of the L'Chaim Society. Ours is the story of two people who, despite tremendous differences in race, religion and upbringing, found deep friendship and connection through daily acts of kindness.

I share one instance of Cory's kindness here. The Jewish custom is that the night before a baby boy is circumcised, the father stays awake the entire night and studies mystical texts in order to protect the child from unseen malevolent forces. We usually do this with someone else so that we do not fall asleep. When my son Mendy was born, it was during

Oxford's exam period, when students are assessed on three years of work in a single week of tests. The students needed their rest, and I could not persuade any of the Jewish students to stay up and study with me. So Cory volunteered to do so, even though he was not Jewish and was utterly exhausted after studying for weeks. Our love for each other allowed us to feel like we were true brothers even though we were, on paper, divided by so much.

If I have been given one overall blessing by the Almighty that allowed me to appreciate Cory's friendship, it is that from my earliest childhood I felt myself to be atop that mountain. A child of divorced parents, I truly understood the loneliness of the human condition. I watched two lonely people who had everything in common, including children, religion, and a committed marriage, fail in their relationship because they neglected to show each other everyday acts of kindness. I thus came to understand that man shares brotherhood not necessarily with members of his own peer group but with anyone who shows him love and respect. Indeed, the love of humanity transcends the boundaries of race, class and gender. The best way to uproot hatred between human beings is simply to realize how much we *need* each other.

Hatred is born of smugness and arrogance. You can only hate someone when you believe that you no longer need them. In *The Ethics of the Fathers*, the Jewish sages wrote, 'Never be arrogant to anyone or anything, for there is no person who doesn't have his time, and there is no thing which doesn't have its place.' My friend Marty, with his very practical approach to life, put it this way: 'Shmuley, never fall out with anyone. You never know when you might need to use them again.'

When hatred is a valid emotion

Exhortations to hate all manner of evil abound in the Bible, and God Himself hates every form of immorality because of its harm to mankind. As we read in Proverbs, 'The fear of the Lord is to hate evil.' By the same token, in The Book of

Ecclesiastes, King Solomon wrote that there is 'a time to love, and a time to hate; a time for war, and a time for peace', thereby affirming that at certain times hatred is a valid emotion.

Thus, unlike depression which has no beneficial value, hatred is a legitimate emotion and an appropriate response when directed at the truly evil – those who have gone beyond the pale of human decency by committing acts that unweave the basic fabric of civilized living. Contrary to Christianity, which advocates turning the other cheek and loving the wicked, Judaism obligates us to despise and resist the truly wicked at all costs. Hating Hitler becomes as great a moral imperative as loving Mother Teresa.

About a year ago, I appeared on one of my favourite radio shows, the Nicki Campbell Show on BBC Radio 5 Live. We were discussing the terrible wave of racist bombings in Britain, in particular the bomb that had killed three people at a gay pub. Nicki told me that, moments before the show, he had spoken to President Clinton's spiritual adviser, Pastor Tony Campalo, who said that we had to love the perpetrator in the spirit of compassion and forgiveness. Similarly, I have heard many victims of IRA terrorist attacks who lost relatives immediately go on air to announce their forgiveness for the murderers in the spirit of peace and reconciliation.

To love the terrorist who bombs a school or the white supremacist who drags a black man three miles tied to the back of his car is not just inane but downright sinful. *To love the evil is evil itself.* By deliberately choosing to murder innocent victims for no reason at all except hate, the wicked person has forfeited the image of God and removed himself from the human family.

Contrary to those religious figures who preach that religion is about unconditional love and forgiveness for all of God's creatures, I believe there is a point of no return for the Hitlers of this world. The Talmud certainly teaches that the true object of proper hatred is the sin, not the sinner, whose life must be respected and whose repentance effected. The Talmud also teaches that it is forbidden to rejoice at the downfall of even those sinners whom it is proper to hate: 'Rejoice not when thine enemy falleth.' However, this attitude does not apply to impenitent and inveterate sinners who pay no heed to correction. For us to extend forgiveness and compassion to them in the name of religion is not just insidious, but it is to mock God who has mercy for all yet demands justice for the innocent.

A Christian artist friend showed me a picture he painted of Jesus embracing Hitler. I told him that the picture was obscene. 'How can you have Jesus holding Hitler?' 'That's the whole point,' he told me. 'That even Hitler can be loved by Jesus. That's how far Jesus' love extends.' 'Well, that's way too far', I responded. 'And that isn't even love anyhow, it's hatred. If you love Hitler, than you are showing contempt for the good and decent people who were his victims. The only way to react to the incorrigible evil is to wage an incessant war against it.' In the interest of justice, the appropriate response is to hate the evil person with every fibre of our being and to hope they find no rest, in this world or in the next.

The pacifist will challenge that fighting hatred with hatred accomplishes nothing, that, as in the old Bob Dylan song, if we take an eye for an eye, we all just end up blind. But in order for an emotion to be a true and beneficial emotion, it must lead to action. In this case, our valid hatred – which is a response to the invalid hatred of others – must be directed towards ensuring justice, and combating those who trample on civility and decency.

To this end, I wholeheartedly embrace the example of Simon Wiesenthal, one of the great men of the twentieth century, who has devoted his life to the pursuit of justice by not letting Nazi murderers go to their graves in peace. Once again I emphasize the word 'justice'. We do not pursue Nazis in order to take revenge, nor for the Jewish people's desire for retribution. Instead, we chase them on behalf of all humanity so that all the world should know that apologizing for genocide is not enough, and no mass-murderers will ever escape culpability.

And justice for all

Just consider how the world would be if we all embraced a 'forgive-all' philosophy. What lesson would this teach our children? That we can commit a crime as long as we apologize in the end? That we can hate all we want and still be received in love? No, the just society demands that we all bear the consequences of our actions.

Justice is not a cultural construct, not a human invention that society imposes on its members in order that they treat each other with decency and respect. Instead, justice, like goodness, is *intrinsic* to human nature. We do not tell our children not to steal or cheat because they might get caught; we teach them that stealing and cheating are intrinsically wrong. End of story. Even if the kid asks for an explanation, we simply tell him this is wrong. It is a law of the Universe.

Two years ago, I participated in a live forum about the South African Truth and Reconciliation Commission on Robyn Island, where Nelson Mandela was incarcerated for eighteen years. On the panel, there were three men who had actually been imprisoned with Mandela, but also a fourth man, a white police officer who had given the order to have two houses burned in the black townships in retaliation for a riot. Seven adults and five children were brutally murdered as a result of this order, but because he confessed his sin to the commission, he was let off scot free. As he told his story at the forum, lamenting how much he regretted his action, the members of the audience began to weep for him. They were moved by the beauty of his repentance and gave him a standing ovation.

I, on the other hand, was completely aghast. I stood up and said, 'I'm sorry but this is ridiculous. Real life isn't a television talk show where you can get up and say how much you regret killing children and actually get applause for it. You can't sadistically murder twelve innocent people by burning them alive and then just apologize!' One of the other panellists immediately attacked me with this outburst: 'That's because you Jews don't know how to forgive. In the

141

Hebrew language, there isn't even a word for forgiveness.' 'Nonsense', I responded. 'There are three words for forgiveness and atonement: *selicha*, *mechila* and *kapparah*. But because we respect and value these concepts so highly, we cannot allow someone to simply cry remorse in public and thereby get away with murder. The bottom line is that there are some offences for which there is no forgiveness; there are some borders whose transgression society cannot tolerate in any circumstances whatsoever. Murder of the innocent is foremost among them.

I know that the death penalty is a very complicated issue, fraught with danger because we might end up killing a person for a crime they did not commit. In theory, however, if we could ascertain *beyond any shadow of doubt* the people responsible for perpetrating, for example, a terrible series of racist bombings, I would support their being put to death – just as Timothy McVeigh, responsible for the Oklahoma City bombing, is now sitting on death row.

Two things I certainly would never do, however, is to forgive them on my own or call on the community that I serve to forgive them. If we do not hate those who are truly evil, we will not summon the passion and determination to fight them. Odd and uncomfortable as it may seem, hatred has its place. Although referring to a different era in history, the words of Martin Luther King Jr still ring true today: 'We will have to repent in this generation not merely for the vitriolic words and actions of the bad people, but for the appalling silence of the good people.'

But amid asserting our hatred of the truly wicked, we must always ensure that this loathing is built upon the solid foundation of justice rather than the equally horrible grindstone of revenge, retribution and anger. For anger is an entirely negative emotion, as we shall explore in the next chapter.

14

Anger

THE MOST DESTRUCTIVE EMOTION

Anger is never without an argument, but seldom with a good one.

Horace

There are two things a person should never be angry at, what they can help, and what they cannot.

Proverb

Like hatred, anger is one of our strongest emotions and one of our most destructive. However, unlike hatred, which when directed against wickedness and injustice has its place in the palette of human emotions, anger has no redeeming value whatsoever. This is why, after acknowledging that each emotion had its place and should be exercised in moderation, Maimonides made one exception: he said that anger should never be entertained because it can only worsen a situation, never improve it. Furthermore, anger is nothing more than a sign of human frailty and weakness. It is fundamentally about losing control.

Mike, a bright law student, became engaged to Melanie. Mike was passionate about everything in life, but his passion sometimes spilled over into anger. Because of his insecurity, he was so jealous of Melanie that he would explode whenever she talked to other men. Because Mike's rage was so unpredictable, Melanie's life became a living hell. One moment he would be the perfect romantic, picking her flowers and taking her for long walks along the river; the next moment he would be verbally abusive, calling her offensive names and threatening to lock her out of their house.

At first the diatribes occurred in private; Mike would pull Melanie over to one side at parties and deliver his abuse. But after a while he lost control and berated her even in public. This public humiliation did it for Melanie. With tears in her eyes that rolled onto her notepaper, Melanie wrote to Mike that she could not continue to stay with him and suffer.

Although Mike was devastated by the break-up, six months later he was dating again. He knew that his new girlfriend, Caroline, possessed a far gentler disposition than Melanie, would never be able to handle his outbursts, so he began to see a professional counsellor. Four months went by and he hadn't lost his temper even once. But then at a Halloween party, Caroline, in costume as a Swedish milk maid, was chatted up by a handsome Count Dracula. Mike totally lost his composure. He thundered at Caroline in front of all the revellers, accusing her of dressing provocatively to attract men: 'You're a whore, you're a slut. I'm ashamed to even know you.' The next day, she stormed out of his life. Five years later, Melanie is happily married to another man while Mike continues to be angry at the world, feeling victimized at every turn.

Anger is, without a doubt, a true emotion, one of the truest because it almost always leads to action. However, the action it inspires is purely negative. What do we do when angry? We yell and scream at others in a display that makes us look at best comical, at worst ugly. The transformation takes place on a physiological level too: our heart rate increases, our blood pressure rises, and our face becomes flushed as we feel the kettle boiling inside us.

The heart of darkness

In *Dr Jekyll and Mr Hyde*, Robert Louis Stevenson allegorized the inner beast that lurks within every human being. That beast is anger, and it has the power to transform us from kind and well-respected citizens (and who more respectable than a doctor?) into raging monsters. As Stevenson so brilliantly illustrated, losing one's temper is the equivalent of lowering the cage to let the animal escape. And just as wild animals know no boundaries, so too does our anger which, when released, wreaks all kinds of havoc on its environs.

Also fascinated with the beast that lurks within us, Joseph Conrad explored the duality of human nature in his masterpiece novella, *Heart of Darkness*. Although the reader is led to believe that the heart of darkness lies in the African Congo, Conrad shows unequivocally that the dark side of the human personality is universal. We know that had Kurtz not gone to Africa, he would have shown his rage at home in England. It was the *idea* of Africa that allowed him to peel off his civilized mask and reveal the 'horror' of his primitive instincts in their most unbridled form. Such is clearly the case with anger too: it rears its ugly head only when we dismiss all pretension of civil behaviour.

While great literature has attempted to penetrate the heart of darkness, Hollywood loves to glorify it. Consider the film *Braveheart*. Mel Gibson's anger and revenge make this a movie about courage and justice. Similarly, in the classic *On the Waterfront*, Marlon Brando's anger at the mob causes him to lose control and singlehandedly take them on fist to fist. Brando is the unequivocal hero of the film because, after the big fight, the weak union members no longer kowtow to the mob. In real life, however, anger is never heroic. It demonstrates human weakness rather than strength.

Anger is also ugly. I remember how I first came to realize how downright silly I looked when I got mad. When I was twelve years old, there was a girl named Shirley who said she liked me. She decided to leave her current boyfriend Bernard, who was twice my size, for little old me. Bernard picked a fight to prove he was the better man, a fight that took place in front of all the buses after school. Shirley watched the two gladiators compete for her hand just outside her bus. Bernard hit me right in the forehead causing a big red bump. 'OK, that's it. Now I'm *really* mad,' I thought, as I began swinging wildly with my fists, hitting nothing but air.

Even though Bernard beat me to a pulp, I was still proud of my intense display of passion. I felt I was heroic, like David, because I did not run away from the giant Goliath. But this did not impress Shirley. 'You looked really funny when you got angry,' she told me, giggling. Shirley was right. I wasn't a hero; I was a clown and I was provided with a valuable lesson.

Righteous indignation

Anger is always accompanied by righteous indignation: we do not get angry unless we first pass judgement. If someone steps on my toes, there are two possible responses. I can either get angry or I can feel pain but not get angry. My response depends on why I believe the perpetrator stepped on my toes. If I think he did it on purpose (or even negligently), I will respond by getting angry, but if I believe that it was purely accidental, I might be annoyed, but I won't lose my temper.

Righteous indignation has its pros and cons. On the one hand, it is positive because it invokes a person's deep-seated feeling of justice. Indignation leaves us feeling that we have been hard done-by, mistreated, exploited. It is the feeling that we are not respected and treated equally. And when we are treated unjustly, we have the right to feel righteous indignation.

But indignation is rarely righteous. And it is usually thoroughly harmful. First of all, it often leads to self-pity and self-righteousness. Second, it fails to leave room for simple human error. When we lose our temper, we believe that we, rather than God, are the judge of the world. The ancient Rabbis thus stated that losing one's temper is an act of idolatry because we then believe there is no higher moral authority than ourselves. We assume the right to become mind-readers and assess people's motives, even though we are poorly equipped to do so. This is the ultimate act of rebellion. There is no God. There are no rules. There is only me. But our mission on this earth is to be compassionate angels of mercy not judges.

By the same token, the Rabbis said that every loss of temper is a denial of God's providence. After all, if we believe that God controls the world and everything happens to us for a purpose, our anger is a sign that we question God's plan. So rather than blame the messenger, we should think to ourselves, 'What lesson is there to be learned from this incident, however painful it may be?' In order to be righteous, we must first rid ourselves of judgementalism and indignation.

Understanding the six stages of anger

There is nothing in the world uglier than anger. When we lose our temper, we humiliate ourselves and compromise the image of God that should be on our countenance at all times. Because I have wrestled with the topic of anger since I was a child, I have given the subject much thought.

Although there are many metaphors to describe anger, the one I find personally most compelling is that of a wave on the ocean. Just as a wave builds up until it reaches its crescendo and crashes to shore, so too anger swells up inside us until it finally breaks. With this in mind, I have divided the throes of anger into the following six stages:

1. Swelling of the wave: incipient anger
2. Rising of the crest: moral indignation
3. Riding of the wave: justification
4. Sustaining of the wave: finding similar justifications
5. Blowing of the stack: blindness and forgetfulness
6. Plateau: regret and humiliation.

Swelling of the wave: incipient anger

Let me illustrate the six stages by looking at a day in my office. Because I usually do not get enough sleep, I am, when I arrive, *a priori* irritated. The first thing I see on my desk is the urgent fax that I had put in my out tray the day before, the one that said 'This positively must please be sent TODAY.' This is stage one: I feel the swell of anger begin to take root inside me. 'Why is this fax still on my desk? I made it clear that it could not wait to be sent. Now, the person I promised it to will think ill of me, all because of some forgetfulness by a member of my staff,' I think to myself.

Next, I begin to feel the rising of the crest. Although I think that my assistant has been negligent and the fax was of critical importance to my career, I nevertheless tell myself not to get angry. I tell myself that if I get angry, I will say things I will regret, and only end up apologizing. I am familiar with the sagacious words of Benjamin Franklin, 'Whatever is begun in anger, ends in shame.' Anyhow, I know that I will calm down soon if I keep quiet, so I try to distract myself until the wave passes.

Rising of the crest: moral indignation

But how can I distract myself, the other voice comes back, before I even hear the explanation of why the fax is still on my desk? So I camouflage my anger; I pretend that I am going to talk about the situation in order to rectify it. Like most bosses, I feel it would be irresponsible if I did not at least find out what went wrong. I continue to ride the crest of my anger because I have not only neutralized its harmful effects in my mind, but also actually made it into something positive. Forget the logical response that I should simply send the fax now by myself, call to apologize for the delay and explain the mistake. No, I am a crusader on a mission from God. I am out to promote justice. The justification of my anger begins stage three.

Riding of the wave: justification

I call my assistant in; I try to speak calmly but the effort is abortive. 'Cheryl, please tell me, why is this fax still on my desk?' Silence. She is embarrassed because she forgot. 'Look, I'll repeat the question. Would you perhaps know why this fax is still on my desk when I expressly asked – ABOUT TEN TIMES – that it be sent yesterday? Do you realize how important this is? Mr Bucketloadsofmoney waited for this all night and now he'll never speak to me again. My reputation is ruined.' (Anger, incidentally, always involves exaggeration.) My words only add fuel to the fire. Cheryl begins to respond, 'Oh, I'm so sorry. I was just about to do it when I went out to get a coffee, and I must have forgotten.'

'Forgotten?' I reply. 'This is my life and reputation we're talking about.' (You see, we only get angry over big issues, never petty ones, so we take the most insignificant trifle and distort it all out of proportion.) 'Do you realize', I say, 'what Mr Bucketloadsofmoney is going to think of me now that I have broken my word to him?' The truth is of course that Mr Bucketloadsofmoney would be easily appeased if I just called him and explained the situation. But anger is interested not in repair, only in destruction.

Taken aback over my zeal for a minute human error, Cheryl gets flustered. She desperately wants to correct her mistake by sending the fax now. But while I am in stage three, I can only entertain egocentric delusions. I can think only of the prospect of my shattered reputation. I now enter the next phase of anger, the horizontal spread.

Sustaining of the wave: finding similar justifications

You see, when we are angry, we have not taken complete leave of our senses because we still have a conscience that nags at us. There are two ways to react to this intrusion of conscience. We can either gain control of ourselves or, most probably, continue to justify our egregious behaviour. At this point, our anger is like a war: it is hard to surrender once we have marched in so far.

So we start looking for similar instances that can further

justify our right to be angry. So I tell Cheryl, 'You know, I wouldn't make such a big deal about this if it was just this one instance. But don't you remember that time in 53 BCE when you did the same thing? You were supposed to decipher those Egyptian hieroglyphics for me and send them to King Tut, but you forgot that as well. And then there was the time when you promised to bring me coffee, but you totally forgot and I had to suffer the pain of living without a beverage for a full forty minutes. I mean, these aren't just little things you know!'

Cheryl looks at me and says, 'Look, I'm sorry, but I don't see the point of talking about it endlessly.' She picks up the fax and heads to send it off. Enter the plateau stage. You can now leave the matter alone and let the wave subside or you can urge it on further. So what are you going to do?

Every anger wave has a breaking point just before it crashes. If you let the wave subside, Cheryl will send the fax and you can go with your tail between your legs and apologize. But if you do not get off the wave, you are going to follow her out of the room nagging, wreaking havoc in your wake. This is stage five, by far the worst stage of anger, where your top blows and the volcano erupts.

Blowing of the stack: blindness and forgetfulness

So you were not smart enough to quell the rising quest, nor did you move aside and try to be forgiving and flexible so that the wave would not pick you up. Nor did you invoke your intelligence to counteract the justification. Then you found more and more reasons to justify your outrage.

Finally, you arrived at stage five, where all the emotion built up and exploded. You could not see past your current state because the fifth and worst stage of anger, where you are so completely absorbed in your own self-righteousness, your own sense of moral outrage, is always associated with blindness. Stage five is when you do not care how much your anger hurts others. It is when your ego is so inflated that you cannot see beyond the border of your own self and, like Samson in the temple of the Philistines, are prepared to take everyone and everything down, whatever the repercussions. Here verbal abuse can become the expression of anger.

Plateau: regret and humiliation

After the volcano erupts, there is the period of plateau and regret, when the boiling lava begins to cool down. In this stage, you begin to feel bad about having blown your stack. You cool down and now witness with your own eyes the destruction your actions have wrought. You feel embarrassed at your immature behaviour. You try to pick up the broken fragments of your relationships. If you have the courage and decency, you will beg forgiveness for the damage you have caused. More often than not, however, you will grasp onto tiny straws of justification. 'I shouldn't have gotten mad. But I was provoked.'

Anger is an act of forgetfulness

So what changed? Just a moment ago you were flinging verbal arrows at people and now you regret it? It is my staunch opinion that every act of anger is an act of *forget-fulness*. You forget God, you forget the people you love, you forget your own innermost desire, to be a good and decent person. Anger involves a complete suspension of our higher rational faculties.

The way to ensure that your anger never consumes you and those you love is simply to remember. I mentioned earlier how my father always told me that God made three physical processes (that we must move our tongues, open our jaws and curve our lips) prerequisite to speech in order to give us that extra split second to contemplate what we are about to say. Similarly, Seneca said, 'the greatest remedy for anger is delay'. If in that precious time of delay you simply try and remember, you will not lose your cool. So if you are about to shout at your employees, remember how much you need them. And if you are about to strike your kid, remember that this is your very flesh and blood and that hurting him ultimately hurts yourself.

The next time you let your anger rumble like an earthquake, remember that, once broken, certain valuable items can never be repaired or replaced. It is for this reason that we must strive to treat the feelings of our loved ones like diamonds. Just as we would not throw diamonds into a fire, so too must we take extra special care not to throw our most precious gems – our priceless relationships – into the coals. We must never allow our anger to burn the most important bridges of our lives – those which connect us to others. Try, try, try, the next time you get angry, simply to remember all that is precious to you and how you risk losing it by blowing your stack.

Giving the benefit of the doubt

I once read a story about a man who was travelling on the subway with his four children. He was sitting down, oblivious to his kids, who were annoying the other passengers. A man who was observing the bad behaviour finally got up and said, 'Sir, can you please control your children. They're bothering everybody.' The father, who was day-dreaming, suddenly came to life and said, 'Oh, I'm sorry, you're right. Please, please forgive me. I wasn't paying attention to the children. I'll round them up and get them out of the way. You see, we just came from the hospital where their mother died after a long bout with cancer, and I guess I was just thinking about her for a minute.' You can imagine how awful the passenger felt for rebuking the man.

Anger is at its essence primarily about selfishness, about putting our own needs before anybody else's. How do we know what other people are going through? Sure, we can judge a person's *actions*, but to judge the person when we have no idea what is going on in their life and what spurs them on . . .? Jewish law requires us always to try to put ourselves in someone else's shoes. If we keep this very simple concept in mind, we will very rarely get angry. It is not easy to achieve, but with practice and discipline, it eventually becomes intuitive. Giving the benefit of the doubt is much, much easier than picking up the pieces after an angry outburst.

Can people change?

The question asked from time immemorial has been whether human beings have the potential to change. Are we victims of our nature or products of our nurture? My response is this: that people rarely change their fundamental natures, only the application thereof. People with bad tempers rarely, if ever, completely overcome their fiery temperaments. And it might not necessarily be a good thing if they did change because they would become less passionate people. They would lose not only the destructive fire of anger, but also the productive fire that their passion engenders.

In order to extinguish the raging fire without destroying the igniting spark, we must immerse ourselves in an *environment* of change, and then we will change incrementally. We must learn to control our tempers by speaking to a good friend or counsellor every single week. The mistake that Mike from my earlier example made was that he believed that he had been cured of his temper from a few short months of therapy. However, had the fire that burned inside him been extinguished, he would be dead. What he needed was to vent his frustration not on his girlfriends, innocent bystanders, but with someone whom he trusted completely who was prepared to listen and help him cope in the long term. The listening ear need not necessarily be a professional counsellor; it can be a good friend who cares and is not inhibited in speaking honestly. The important thing is to immerse oneself in a regular and ongoing schedule and environment of change.

Does such a project sound futile? After all, if I'm not sure that I will ever be completely healed, then why undergo the therapy at all? In Jewish thought, struggling to do right is superior to righteousness because struggling is about process and change. God is never looking for those who are perfect, but rather those who always wish to grow and better themselves. For those who have a bad temper, life can be a great struggle. They can feel the damage they cause almost every day of their lives. But that struggle can also prove just how precious their relationships are because they are prepared to work at improving them. Moreover, God loves those who struggle because it means that goodness is so important to them that they never cease to conquer their inner demons.

15

Guilt

A WASTED EMOTION

Let other pens dwell on guilt and misery. I quit such odious subjects as soon as I can.

Jane Austen

True guilt is guilt at the obligation one owes to oneself to be oneself. False guilt is guilt felt at not being what other people feel one ought to be or assume that one is.

R. D. Laing

A Jewish son complains, 'Mom, you lay too much guilt on me,' to which the mother responds, astonished, 'How can I possibly lay too much guilt on you, my dear son? I DON'T SEE YOU ENOUGH TO LAY GUILT ON YOU!'

If there is one emotion that seems universally associated with being Jewish, it is guilt. Jews are the most guilty people in the world, apart from Catholics, that is. Didn't visit your mother recently; feel guilty. Shot your landlord in the back when he came for the rent; don't worry, you can always feel bad about it. Irrational guilt consumes man at every turn.

Jewish mothers in particular, as the joke above illustrates, seem to be born with a world-class instinct to lay guilt. Every year in October I watch impressive young Jewish men and women arrive confidently in Oxford to launch their three-year quest for a degree. When they first disembark from their parents' cars, they are radiant. But as the cars drive off, their mothers impart one final glance that says, 'I hope you feel awful about abandoning your parents as you live it up. Don't worry, we'll probably die at home while you're enjoying yourself in the pub.'

This poor innocent kid walks around for the next three years with this three-hundred pound weight of guilt tied around his neck like an albatross. All the other students wonder why he is staggering around as if he were drunk. Not being Jewish, they are unable to see the unbearable burden of guilt he carries.

Being good without doing good

Is guilt a productive emotion? Many people think so. After all, isn't it good to feel bad about the bad things we do? I mean, if you only call your grandmother twice a day, shouldn't you feel guilty about it when you know that you could have called a third time? Especially when you know that her other grandchildren never call her? And especially since every further phone call gets you another mention in her will?

Having identified depression as the most destructive of all human emotions, I now want to identify guilt as the second most destructive. Guilt is an emotion that allows people to do bad things and still feel like they are good people. It is the ultimate escape clause from the human obligation to do the right thing. Indeed, guilt becomes the justification for bad behaviour because it tells us that we are still good just as long as we feel remorseful.

Consider this: a man knocks on your door and tells you he is hungry. He asks for something to eat. 'Come back when you really look emaciated,' you tell him. At first, you feel good, really proud of yourself: 'There, I didn't give in to that parasite. Let him go and get a job like the rest of us.' But a few minutes later you are, suddenly and unexpectedly, racked with guilt. So why do you suddenly feel bad about what you have done when, a few moments earlier, you had no qualms whatsoever?

Because this way you can avoid giving money and still

feel like you are a good person. If you had simply turned the guy away and not felt any pangs of conscience, that would be proof you are selfish and unsympathetic. But now, since you feel guilty, you can get away with not giving and still be good. After all, you felt bad when you turned him away, right? Doesn't that show that, deep inside, you are a caring person? With guilt you get the best of all possible worlds: you can be stingy and caring at the same time.

In this way, guilt actually serves as a barrier between you and your ugliness. It dresses up your selfishness and painlessly converts it to goodness. What guilt does is, in effect, to assuage the conscience. Because it is goodness without sacrifice, being good without *doing* good, guilt is the ultimate form of hypocrisy.

Guilty as charged

Sharon had a very overprotective mother. A Holocaust survivor and only child, Sharon's mother had a real difficulty in granting her daughter's independence. Soon after Sharon arrived at Oxford, her mother called her nearly every day, treating her like a little child and driving her batty. She was so concerned for her daughter's welfare that she even asked me, as her Rabbi, to keep an eye on her.

Because Sharon had an inclination to date the wrong kind of man, her mother asked me to report back if I had any information. I told her that I could not exactly do that because I was a Rabbi, not a secret service agent. So one Friday night, she suddenly turned up for the L'Chaim Society dinner. Our Sabbath dinners drew about a hundred students, and everyone was welcome, including parents. Sharon, however, did not take kindly to seeing her mother arrive unannounced. Trying to assert her independence, she felt truly uncomfortable introducing her mother to her friends.

But there was also something deeper. Sharon was the upwardly mobile type who always wanted to have the 'right' friends, and I sensed that, deep down, Sharon was embarrassed. An immigrant from Eastern Europe, her mother had a strong Yiddish accent. In addition, her parents did not have much money. Add to that her mother's very simple dress sense, and Sharon did not exactly want to be seen with her.

So Sharon did something that must have been out of character: she publicly confronted her mother and accused her of prying. Everybody watched as Sharon shrieked, 'You're ruining my life! Why don't you just leave me alone?' It was as if Sharon were trying publicly to distance herself from her own mother. Utterly humiliated, her mother ran to her car and drove off.

I was flabbergasted. Sure, we all have issues with our parents, but there is a time and place for everything. In an attempt to salvage the spirit of the Sabbath meal, I acted as if nothing had happened, trying to distract everyone with an impromptu story. A few minutes later, Sharon asked to speak to me in my office.

'I feel terrible, Shmuley. I feel so guilty about what I just did.' I knew what Sharon was trying to do – trying to regain my respect. She was saying, 'Sure, Shmuley. I have publicly humiliated my mother and broken the fourth commandment. But I want you to know that I feel really bad about it. I feel guilty. I'm remorseful. So don't think ill of me.'

'You know, Sharon,' I said, 'I believe that if you want to be selfish at least take pride in it! All this guilt stuff just robs you of the deep satisfaction that selfishness can engender. Guilt is for cowards. You're way too tough for that. Why are you robbing yourself of the pleasure of having socked your mother in the solar plexus? She has been a pest and you belted her publicly. I can guarantee that you won't be hearing much from *her* in the near future. Just be proud of how much you loathe your Mom. After all, she deserves it.'

Well, truth be told, this isn't what I did say. But it was what I *wanted* to say. I wanted to demonstrate to Sharon the uselessness of her guilt. So what that she felt bad about what she had done? Did that change anything? The only proper response was for Sharon immediately to beg her mother's forgiveness. Feeling guilty about her behaviour was actually impeding that process, and I wanted to tell her so.

Guilt as vacillation

So guilt means you can walk all over your parents like a doormat and still be a good person afterwards. You do not even have to apologize. Thus, guilt is destructive because it seeks to counteract any corrective action you might have taken.

I think that the average person understands just how unimpressive guilt is. In the popular imagination, guilt is associated with indecision and a lack of resolve. You do one thing, then regret it a moment later. You do another thing, and the same thing happens again. If you are going to be selfish and callous, 'just do it', as the Nike commercial says, but don't drive everyone else crazy with vacillation.

At the famous showdown between Elijah and the four hundred prophets of Baal that took place on Mount Carmel, Elijah first addressed the idolatrous masses of the Jewish nation who had come to witness the historic event: 'How long will you go limping with two different opinions? If the Lord is God, follow him; but if Baal, then follow him.' In response, we learn, 'The people did not answer him a word' (1 Kings 18:21). Because they understood the mediocre nature of their vacillation, they had nothing to say for themselves.

In essence, guilt represents indecisiveness. Pathetic and weak minded, guilt-ridden people want to have their cake and eat it too. In the process, they end up losing on all fronts. The only reason people are selfish and self-absorbed is because it is superficially more pleasurable to feed yourself than it is to feed the stranger. The guilty person denies himself even this pleasure.

The difference between guilt and conscience

As I said earlier, the opposite of guilt is not innocence, except in the legal sense; it is conscience. Conscience is the safety net that prevents us descending into the abyss of evil and spitefulness. When we do something wrong, we can suffer from either guilt or pangs of conscience. The radical difference between the two is that while the former leads us to idleness, the latter impels us to self-improvement.

Guilt addresses the weakness in our character and tells us, 'Don't feel so bad about doing the wrong thing. You're weak. So is everybody else.' But success in life requires determination and resolve. Guilt accomplishes absolutely nothing, so the determined individual simply has no time for it. It is a parasite that sucks up our energy and renders it useless. It has no power to transform us into someone better.

Conscience, on the contrary, occurs when we refuse to make peace with our weakness. It is where our higher selves force us to try to act in accordance with what we know to be right, in accordance with our inner will.

Unlike guilt, conscience is not an emotion and is therefore not subject to manipulation. Conscience is a dictator that issues commands the individual must obey. That is why so many people can live with guilt but few can tolerate their conscience. While guilt is unpleasant, it is never unpopular, but conscience is neither pleasant nor popular because while guilt liberates, conscience obligates. Conscience is the part of us that cries and beckons to us in these terms: 'You know you're better than this. This is never what you wanted to be. So pick yourself up by your bootstraps and change. This is wrong and there are *no* excuses. So don't feel bad about doing bad. Do good instead.'

So how do you know if what you are feeling is guilt or conscience? If you sit and feel sorry about what you have done, making yourself miserable and utterly immobile, you possess guilt. But if something inside you says, 'Stop feeling bad and do the right thing', you have a conscience.

What about all those people who object, 'Hey, so are you saying that a person should not feel bad about the bad things they do? Is there no room for remorse in life?' The answer is that of course you should feel bad for the bad things you do, but the proper emotion for regretting the bad things is not guilt, but shame, as we will explore in the next chapter.

16

Shame

THE SAFEGUARD OF OUR DIGNITY

Shame arises from the fear of men, conscience from the fear of God.

Samuel Johnson

Whilst shame keeps its watch, virtue is not wholly extinguished in the heart; nor will moderation be utterly exiled from the minds of tyrants.

Edmund Burke

Radically different from guilt is shame. While shame can certainly be a very negative emotion, it can also lead us to radical self-improvement. In order to understand shame, however, we must first consider its underlying cause, the loss of human dignity.

I first saw former Soviet President, Mikhail Gorbachev, when he came to the United Nations as all-powerful head of the Soviet Union. I remember the day because it was the same day that I left the USA for Oxford. There were six thousand New York policemen lining the streets to protect Gorbachev, and all the world's cameras were watching his every move. I was standing in the crowd when his motorcade of approximately sixty cars drove by. When his Zil limousine passed, I caught a glimpse of him surrounded by humongous KGB agents. It was all very impressive.

Little did I know then that, only four years later, I would have the honour of serving as his host as he addressed a crowd of approximately two thousand Oxford students on behalf of the L'Chaim Society. For a man of his stature, he was unusually warm and had a terrific sense of humour. It was therefore with some sadness that, after hugging good-bye, I watched him drive off to the neighbouring town of Milton Keynes to open a new mobile phone shop. Three years after that, he appeared on a Pizza Hut commercial in Russia. Although I completely understand a man's need to earn a living, all I could think was, 'Oh, how the mighty have fallen.' Later, when he ran for president of his country, he took only one per cent of the vote.

Now don't get me wrong. I think that Gorbachev is a truly great man, a man to whom every human being currently alive owes a debt of gratitude. But how does someone restore their sense of dignity when they are running half the world one day and throwing pizzas up in the air the next?

Shame and ignominy are now certainly big business in the media, often the first stories that make the news. There are entire programmes devoted to humiliating people. Even reputable news programmes like *Sixty Minutes* seem to find great verve in broadcasting the stories of disgraced public figures.

Examples of our obsession with disgrace are everywhere. In a recent edition of an international newspaper, the three major headlines all centred upon shame. The first was of an Olympic Gold medallist who had failed a drug test. The second alleged an affair between Hillary Clinton and an old Arkansas colleague. And the third was about an ordinary man who was arrested after his own fifteen-year-old daughter had reported him to the police for locking her in the house. (He did so, incidentally, in order to prevent her staying out the whole night with her thirty-year-old boy-friend.) This father spoke of his total humiliation before all who knew him, as he was arrested by the authorities.

The greatest human need

What brings about shame, and how can it be overcome? Unlike animals, which require only food and shelter to survive, human beings require something far more subtle but equally necessary, namely dignity. Hegel was right on the mark when he said that the greatest human desire is to have our humanity and uniqueness recognized by others. While a dolphin at Sea World jumps in the air and does impressive tricks that make the audience roar, that's not why he does it. His only motivation is to get the treat of fish after the performance.

A human being will, in stark contrast, risk even his survival in order to gain respect. Indeed, throughout the ages, men have gone to war, risking their lives, in order to obtain glory. Today, in order to attain prestige in the eyes of their peers, people will donate large sums of money just to receive some little plaque with their name on it.

Many laws in Judaism have been legislated for the sole purpose of preserving dignity, so critical is it to our existence. The main altar in the holy Temple in Jerusalem, for example, had a ramp rather than stairs in order not to uncover the nakedness of the priests working there. Also, when soldiers go to the field of battle, they are commanded to keep a shovel for when they relieve themselves. Even during wartime, a man must preserve his dignity and distinguish himself from the animals that defecate where they will.

If the laws to preserve human dignity are stringent in war, how much more so are they during times of peace? The sages, for example, said that charity involves not just supplying a person in need with the basics of food, clothing and shelter, but restoring to that person his chariot and horses if such was his previous standard of living. The sages understood that to be stripped of one's social station is more than humiliating, it is palpably painful, and we are obligated to do whatever we can to alleviate someone's pain.

The word for charity in Hebrew is *tzedakah*, but what *tzedakah* actually means is justice, so when we give to the needy, what they receive is not charity, which could be humiliating, but justice. The Jewish laws of charity are painstaking in their emphasis on never causing those who are dependent on other's generosity to lose their dignity or sense of worth. Thus, the Talmud describes the two highest forms of charity as first, giving someone a trade so that they can earn their own living, and second, giving in such a way that the benefactor does not know to whom he is giving, and the recipient does not know from whom he is taking.

Loss of dignity can lead to desperation

Isaac owned a large shoe factory that exported its goods to five countries. A survivor of the Holocaust, he had transformed himself from a penniless refugee to a man of considerable wealth who became one of his community's chief providers. Although a frugal man who despised extravagance, he nevertheless took great pleasure in entertaining guests in his large home on the Sabbath. However, after some unfortunate investment decisions, the business went bad and he became bankrupt.

When the bank foreclosed on his house, Isaac became a different man. People in the community started to invite him and his family for the Sabbath to make sure that they had enough to eat. I never saw Isaac smile again. Slowly he began to deteriorate and a year later died of a heart attack, a broken man with a shattered ego.

It is no surprise that loss of dignity is the world's number one cause of suicide. However, as Isaac's case attests, it is not the loss of money that causes people to go over the precipice but rather the humiliation of losing their station and their ability to support their family. I believe that if Isaac had been responsible only for himself, he would have subsisted on a few loans until he got back on his entrepreneurial feet. Or moved somewhere new and started again. There was, however, so much more at stake in his life.

Similarly, no woman kills herself because she has lost a man's love. Anna Karenina, although a fictional character, took her own life not because she could not survive without Vronsky, but because she could not cope with the humiliation of rejection. Indeed, once Vronsky discarded her, she could not bear to wear the mark of Cain – the mark of a woman scorned – for the rest of her life. Dignity is not a luxury but a necessity.

In Japan, losing one's dignity is so grave that *hara kiri* – suicide – used to be commanded by the government for disgraced officials. In Judaism, however, suicide is absolutely forbidden. One is, on the contrary, commanded to do whatever one can to save a human life because, as the ancient rabbis of the Talmud proclaimed, saving one life is the equivalent of saving an entire world. Even martyrdom is viewed as something that has been forced upon us. It is thus easy to understand why the quintessential Jewish toast is L'Chaim, to life.

The reason we abhor death is because, more than anything else, it robs man of his dignity. In death, a man who was loved by his family and respected by his community becomes fodder for worms. As the Talmud says, 'While a man is alive large beasts like elephants fear him and run from him. But the moment he is dead, even a mouse does not fear him.'

Finally, so important is our dignity that the Talmud declares the public humiliation of a fellow human being to be tantamount to murder, since it makes him wish he were dead. Some rabbinical commentators have even said that humiliating someone in public is worse than murder because by humiliating him, you make him want to take his own life, to bury himself in a hole in the ground. And the cruellest sin is to make someone into their own murderer.

Becoming the one and only

The Bible says that every human being is created in the image of God, born with an aura of dignity, an invisible cloak that bestows upon them the majesty of self-esteem. To strip a man or woman of their dignity is to leave them naked and bare. It was this Godly aura that was taken from Cain after he killed his brother Abel. Hence he immediately complained to the Almighty, 'I will be a restless wanderer on the earth, and whoever finds me will kill me'; whoever loses his human dignity is helplessly exposed to the elements and is as if half dead.

As part of the Jewish morning prayers, we recite the following blessing: 'Thank you, O Lord, for having allowed us to walk erect.' Unlike the animals, human beings walk on two legs with head held high, a princely posture reserved only for our species. When a man loses his dignity, he no longer walks erect; he becomes stooped. He feels beaten by life and has lost his magisterial countenance. He trudges along, bent, cynical and broken.

What does it mean that man was created in the image of God? Some have interpreted the verse in a purely legal sense, that like a shadow must ape its image-maker, man must always obey the will of God. And like a shadow, if man leaves the image of God to pursue his own agenda, he is immediately cast off and ceases to exist.

Others have interpreted the verse to mean that, like God but unlike the animals or even the angels, man has freedom of choice. Unrestricted by fate, he is the arbiter of his own destiny. Like God Himself, for whom the possibilities are limitless, man is infinitely capable of being whatever he desires.

I believe, however, that the true meaning of this verse is that each and every one of us is the one and only. In the same way that God is utterly unique, so are we. A great Rabbi once said that God's infinite power is manifest in the fact that no two snowflakes are alike. But an even greater demonstration of His power is that no two individuals are alike, which is precisely why they are *individuals*.

There are three uniquely human privileges that flow from this lofty Biblical description. As Rabbi Yitz Greenberg writes, every human being is endowed with infinite value, equality and uniqueness, independent of any factor such as heritage, status or background. Since God is the source of all human importance, and we are made equally in His image, no human being can ever be more valuable than another.

In this light, we can understand the gravity of murder. I

said before that the Talmud teaches that saving one life is equivalent to saving an entire world. By the same token, taking a life is equivalent to destroying an entire world. Murder is terrible because the murderer has created a *cosmic* imbalance, upsetting not only the lives of the murdered and his loved ones, but the entire universe.

Denial of dignity is the source of human misery

Tyrants have long understood that if you wish to control a man, you must destroy his dignity by invalidating his individuality. The Nazis were certainly no strangers to this. Among the various degradations they inflicted on the Jews, the most critical from their point of view was substituting names with numbers. Once they taught their victims to cease thinking in terms of their own dignified selves, all resistance would vanish.

In his book *If This is Man*, Primo Levi details how the Nazis branded numbers on the arms of the inmates in the same way that ranchers brand their cattle. The result was that the prisoner became a *Muselmann*, concentration camp slang for a skin-and-bone walking corpse. Indeed, as Levi described it, the prisoners became an 'anonymous mass, continuously renewed and always identical. Of non-men, already too empty really to suffer. One hesitates to call them living. One hesitates to call their death death.'

The denial of our human dignity is without doubt the primary source of all human misery. Janine worked two jobs to support her four children. She came home just before the Sabbath with tears in her eyes. Her children could see that she was not her usual ebullient self. 'They fired me', Janine said. Janine worked as a bank teller and had made an error that cost the bank a thousand dollars. She apologized profusely and begged for the money to be deducted from her wages but her employers refused. 'I have children to support', she pleaded. 'Well, you'll have to find work somewhere else.' 'But I know the systems and the customers better than anyone. How will you manage without me?'

'We'll get someone else who knows it just as well or better.'

What ultimately caused Janine so much pain was not being told that she had made too many errors, but the idea that she was not special, that they could so easily discard her, that she was so easily replaced.

The origin of shame

It is significant that the very first emotion ascribed to humanity in the Bible is shame. Before eating from the Tree of Knowledge of Good and Evil, Adam and Eve 'were both naked, and were not ashamed' (Genesis 2:25). Thus their nakedness was never the source of their shame, as a Puritan reading of this critical passage would have us believe. They felt shame only after they acted against the Divine will and indulged their animal appetites. They felt shame because, in contradicting God, they compromised their previously un-adulterated human nobility. Consequently, their shame caused them to hide from God: 'But the Lord God called to the man, and said to him, "Where are you?" He said, "I heard the sound of you in the garden, and I was afraid, because I was naked; and I hid myself" ' (Genesis 3:9–10).

When Adam and Eve sinned, they needed to cover them-selves up because they felt emotionally exposed. Rather than feeling confident, they now had something to hide. Because they had lost their inner dignity, they now depended on external, material things for security and self-assurance.

Today's Adam is the man who tries to impress a woman with the car he drives instead of the person he is, who prefers to flaunt the initials of others such as BMW rather than his own. Similarly, today's Eve is the woman who feels insecure unless she is wearing Gucci or Donna Karan's name on her behind. And we are all modern-day Adams and Eves when we seek to impress others with what we have rather than who we are, when in the words of psychologist Warren Farrel we become *'human doings'* rather than *human beings.*

But there was also a positive outcome from Adam' and Eve's disobedience – that the inner mechanism of shame was born. Indeed, we know that shame is valuable because it is something God Himself breathed into us and wanted us to have. Furthermore, it is God Himself who actively helped the first couple to cover their nakedness by making them clothing. Why did God play such an active role in trying to remedy their sin? Because He wanted to provide his children with a mechanism to recapture and preserve their innocence.

The value of shame

Shame is horrific when it is caused by an outside party, especially when it occurs in public. When it comes from within, however, shame is beneficial, acting as the guardian of our human nobility. Rabbi Samson Raphael Hirsch said that what differentiates humans from animals is our cognisance of a higher reality. But what happens when we act in contravention to that knowledge and blindly submit to our passions? What happens when we betray our own inner convictions?

Whenever we betray our Divine calling, we feel shame. Animals never feel shame or guilt even though they publicly fornicate, steal from and kill each other. Indeed, the preservation of dignity never even enters an animal's mind because humiliation is a uniquely human emotion designed by our Creator to safeguard our virtue.

Carolyn came to me for counselling about having an abortion. I could barely understand her words through the muffled sobs. 'I'm in such trouble because I have no one to turn to. I'm so ashamed of myself. Although I can usually tell my mother anything, I don't know how to tell her this. You see, I'm just not that kind of girl. My mother raised me to respect myself, not to be used by a guy who said he loved me but then promptly discarded me as soon as I became pregnant.'

Although Carolyn's mother should have been available to

her daughter in any circumstance, Carolyn's point was that she was better than this. She knew that what she did was wrong as she understood that making love is higher than having sex. She knew that real love is judged by caring and commitment and that being true to the values her mother raised her with was superior to discarding them in favour of a man with little character.

What Sharon experienced was an inner alarm bell telling her she was better than her behaviour at the time suggested. Indeed, this inborn security system told her that she needed to realign herself with her deepest desire to be a decent, ethical human being.

God has endowed each of us with this same power to protect our nobility – shame. When we cut our finger and it bleeds, we instinctively feel pain. The same is true when we cut into our inner nobility of spirit. It hurts. We feel the need to heal, and to regain control of our lives. This feeling of inadequacy, of having to recapture our innocence, is what shame is all about.

From this point of view, shame is not just another emotion but one of our most important. It is aroused as soon as our animal side gains victory over our spirit. It steps forward everywhere, even in the most abandoned and utter reproaches, declaring that man has a nobler mission in life than the rest of creation. It is the critical last barrier that protects us from descending to the level of the beast.

Sacrifice the beast within

Many students ask me why the Bible focuses so much attention on animal sacrifice and whether the practice has any relevance today, either practically or allegorically. My response is that since it was such a sacred rite, indeed the primary function of the Holy Temple in Jerusalem, it certainly existed to teach us a great lesson. God wanted us to sacrifice not just the animal without but, even more importantly, the animal within. The great lesson we are meant to derive here is that we must sacrifice that lowly part of us and devote it to a higher purpose, turn our beastly passions into beautiful actions.

The purpose of our animal passion is, therefore, to feel invigorated whenever the opportunity for a good deed presents itself. The purpose of a man's lust is not to yearn for strangers but rather to make his wife feel like the most desirable woman in the world. And the purpose of our physical desire to eat, drink and be merry is not to live hedonistically but to enjoy our blessings so that we might wish to praise and give thanks to our Creator and to share our comforts with all members of the human family. If we forget these objectives and behave like animals, shame makes us aware of how we have acted contrary to the majesty of our spirit.

On a personal note

All of us have, I am sure, had some experience of shame and humiliation. I personally, as a Rabbi who often writes on controversial subjects, have had more than my fair share. I would like to share just one recent example here as I palpably recall the dread of facing national and even global humiliation.

I had arrived in Israel for the Hebrew launch of my book, *Kosher Sex*. My publisher had arranged for me to appear on Israel's leading television talk show, watched by fifty per cent of the Israeli public. *This* show, however, was going to be watched by even more people since Labour Party leader Ehud Barak, the front-runner to become Israel's next Prime Minister, was also going to appear, just weeks before the election. The programme's format involves seven guests sitting around presenter Dan Shilon.

As soon as the show began, Dan erroneously announced to the television audience that *Kosher Sex* was my ninth book on the subject of conjugal relations (actually, it was my first). Initially, the questions were predictable and inno-cuous (What gave you the idea to write this book? What makes you such an expert? How have your friends and family reacted to the book?), but, as I expected, the conversation suddenly took a different tone: 'You are a Rabbi, how can you write about sex? Especially such explicit statements like what couples can do in bed to enhance their erotic attraction? Don't you think that you should have stuck to religious themes rather than writing the Jewish Kama Sutra?'

A word of explanation is in order. In Israel, secular Israeli Jews perceive Rabbis as ultra-pious people who do not participate in contemporary culture. So whatever surprise my book *Kosher Sex* elicited elsewhere, it was in Israel ten times as controversial. While I had suspected that the ultra-orthodox might be puzzled, my publisher and I had assumed that secular Jews would embrace it with open arms. Major Israeli newspaper articles had already extolled the book with a 'finally a Rabbi who writes for the people' attitude, and I myself felt confident that the book would rightfully be seen as an attempt to bring the beauty of Jewish religious teachings about marital intimacy to a wide readership. I thought that secular Jews would embrace a Rabbi who showed how open-minded, forward-looking and wise religion was and encouraged married couples to expand their sexual repertoire in the name of marital sanctity and exclusivity. But as the programme continued, these illusions quickly began to fade.

First, Dan Shilon challenged an assertion in my previous book, *The Jewish Guide to Adultery*, that husbands should have affairs with their wives. 'Are you trying to say that husbands and wives should do kinky things, like make love on an airplane in the lavatory?' 'Well,' I said, half-humorously, 'it's better than the husband fantasizing about the stewardesses or the wife fantasizing about the pilot!' Shilon then turned to Barak's wife and, on national television, asked her if she and her husband, Israel's Prime Minister-to-be, had ever had sex in an airplane bathroom. 'No,' she said shyly.

Shilon next brought in the other members of the panel to comment. Anastasia, one of Israel's leading models, immediately broke into the conversation and said that I should be ashamed. Didn't I know that the woman on my left, a famous Israeli singer, was also the mother of two children? Was I not humiliated discussing this subject in the company of a mother?

Next, Israel's most famous football star chimed in. 'I also have to admit', he said, 'to feeling very uncomfortable hearing the Rabbi talk about this subject. Rabbis are meant to be holy, not to sully themselves by speaking about so lowly a subject.'

Only Ehud Barak rose to my defence, saying that books like mine were important. He even went so far as to call my book holy. But Barak's rush to my defence did not lend me much credibility because aligning himself with the Rabbi was interpreted as his deferring to the religious constituency only weeks before his election. His support was seen as a shrewd political gesture, rather than a genuine vote of support.

Although I have endured sharp criticism throughout my professional career, I was entirely shocked by what happened that night. I was not prepared to be attacked for penning my book on sex by a fashion model who models clothes that are anything but modest. Even more shockingly, it seemed that everyone agreed with her. I really did not know what to do. I assumed that this view must fairly represent the secular Israeli public who were watching the programme.

Afterwards, I felt like a national laughing stock. In a country where Rabbis pride themselves above all else on their respectability, I was left with none. Like Adam and Eve before me, I felt naked, stripped of all dignity. I walked through the hotel lobby with my head down in order to avoid all stares. I called my wife and told her that I was contemplating leaving Israel and rushing back to the UK, where I could at least escape the controversy, but I then decided that running away was not the proper response.

Miraculously, I survived and even flourished. As it turned out, the panel reaction was created deliberately for television – a bit of spice, a bit of controversy. My views had actually gone down really well with the Israeli public. The interview sent *Kosher Sex* in Hebrew selling all over the country, and it was the talk of the town on all the radio shows, but I will still never forget those initial feelings of shame and humiliation.

Real dignity comes from the notion that we are a child of God

All of us are special not because we are senators, or computer programmers or even parents; our dignity comes from the fact that we are all God's children. The supreme Ruler of the universe has called forth our existence as an act of special creation in His special plan, and nothing we achieve in life will ever exceed that amazing fact. Fortunately for us, neither can anything diminish it.

Shame, therefore, is an immensely positive emotion because it reminds us at all times of our royal status. And it guides us to steer clear of actions that are unbecoming to princes and princesses.

When I first started studying to be a Rabbi, I felt confused about the meaning of religion. Was it about being a good person, or being close to God, or refraining from sin, or all these? While I was in Rabbinical College in Jerusalem, I watched a poor and elderly Rabbi who had been a refusenik in Russia, a man whose courage I greatly admired, walking down the street.

It was an odd day, snowing in Jerusalem, which is a most rare occurrence. The Rabbi trudged through the snow with shoes that were hopelessly inadequate to protect him from the terrible cold, the only thing affording him any measure of protection being a scarf wrapped tightly around his neck. I watched from a distance as he chanced upon an old woman beggar in the street. She stuck out her hand for money, and he reached into his pocket and gave her a few coins. But because she was shivering, she could not hold her hand out long enough to take them, and they fell on the floor. The Rabbi picked them up and put them in her pocket. Then he took off his scarf, wrapped it around her neck and continued on his way.

Two weeks later, I found myself in the same synagogue as the pious Rabbi. I recounted the story and asked him why he had risked his own health for her. 'You did it because of charity, right? Because you wanted to do a good deed, no?' 'No', he said to me, in his thickly accented Hebrew. 'I did it because I saw a princess on the street who wasn't wearing her usual royal garb. So I lent her mine instead.'

It was in that moment that I came to understand the purpose of religion. Religion teaches us to recognize the noble and princely quality of every human being and enjoins us to treat them according to their noble standing. While religion teaches us to recognize that in every other human being, shame teaches us to see it in ourselves, because there are times when we forget, times when we cannot see the Divine image within ourselves because we stray off course.

Some moral Darwinists, for example, tell us it is okay to cheat on our spouses because we are like animals and have an evolutionary compulsion to spread our seed. Since it is natural, it can't be wrong. They also tell us that it is predictable that people will be less than honest in their business dealings because it's a dog-eat-dog world out there and everybody must undercut and outdo the other in order to survive in a world of limited resources. When we begin to be persuaded by this logic, and the spark of the Divine within us is in danger of blowing out, our shame alarm rears its head and says: 'Don't disgrace yourself for you are of noble birth. Great things are expected of you and it is within your power to make them happen. All you need is to see and believe.'

17

Fear

THE MOST DEBILITATING EMOTION

He who is afraid of a thing gives it power over him.

Moorish Proverb

Fear defeats more people than any other one thing in the world.

Ralph Waldo Emerson

Shakespeare said, 'Of all base passions, fear is the most accursed.' There are few emotions that make life as unpleasant as does fear. Indeed, fear and joy are inversely proportional such that the more fear, the less joy – and the more anxiety. Those who live in fear witness the gradual diminishment of their humanity, becoming less adventurous, less truthful, and ultimately less alive. They also become deeply cynical.

When I was ten years old, I went to a Hasidic sleep-away camp in Florida. Unlike most summer camps, where the counsellors tell the kids ghost stories, at ours they used to tell us stories about Rabbi Israel Baal Shem Tov, the founder of the Hasidic movement and a great Jewish folk hero. On Friday nights, my bunkmates and I would take long walks together on the highway outside the camp. It was pitch dark and hardly a sound could be heard. For a boy of ten, the experience was terrifying. I remember begging my counsellor to return to the safety of the camp because I was so frightened. In response, he told me a Baal Shem Tov story.

He said that the great spiritual master began his pious

journey at eight years old when he was orphaned with no one to raise him. Terrified at the prospect of being all alone, he resolved to conquer his fear. He made a point of walking alone through the forests in the dead of night. With haunting shadows and blood-curling howls at every turn, he continued to walk until he became part of the forest. Instead of him fearing the beasts of prey, they learned to fear him. Walking upright through the darkness, he would not allow fear to stoop his posture or deny him his dignity. He later wrote that he undertook these exercises so that he might learn to fear none but God alone.

There was something immensely noble in this action, which even a boy of ten could appreciate. Personally, I have lived with many fears. When I was a child I hated my parents' frequent shouting matches that would keep me awake at night. As we never had a lot of money, I always feared being poor. Most of all, however, I feared being alone. I feared that my parents would be so consumed by their own pain that they would sink inward and leave us children to fend for ourselves.

Later, when I became a Rabbi, I discovered the immense fear that came with the position. As a religious leader, you are part of a large organization in which many are determined to preserve the *status quo*, but as a young Rabbi, you are equally determined to address the needs of your constituents, the two postures often conflicting. So when you go out on a limb and state things that others find objectionable, you put your job and your reputation on the line. What you fear then is isolation from your community: being branded a revolutionary or even an outcast. Few lay people can understand how great is the clergy's fear that they will be rejected for saying something that is deemed heretical or too controversial.

Although the battle against all my fears has not yet been entirely won, I have tried to understand and conquer them because I believe that fear is the most degrading and humiliating of all human emotions. It exposes our inadequacy and vulnerability like no other emotion. Worst of all, it holds us back from being ourselves. It teaches us to cover ourselves in increasingly thick layers until our goodness is totally obscured. Our fear makes us freeze and panic, debilitating us and rendering us hopelessly inadequate to meet the great challenges of existence.

But isn't fear good?

A close friend of mine proposed that fear is actually a positive emotion. 'After all', he said, 'isn't it important that human beings experience their vulnerabilities so that they do not begin to believe that they are gods? Isn't it through fear that we come to acknowledge our dependency on others? And if we didn't fear retribution, might we not care whether we hurt people? Doesn't this show the positive side of fear?'

I can take his argument even one step further, to the global level. Isn't it a fear of sickness that builds the whole apparatus of a nation's health and welfare system? Isn't it a fear of war that erected the machinery of *détente* and peace, however creaky it was during the Cold War and still is? Isn't it a fear of the possible destruction of our beautiful planet by pollution that has produced environmentalists and a new ecological awareness?

Although the argument is convincing, I told my friend that he was mistaken, because while fear undoubtedly serves as one of the principal engines of human advance, any scenario could easily be accomplished by love instead of fear. If we loved health and desired it for all of the world's citizens, we would not content ourselves with curative medicine; we would search for preventative medicine. If our government loved democracy rather than feared communism, we would never have supported fascist dictators with deplorable human rights records, such as Marcos, Pinochet and Rhee.

So even at its best, I responded, fear cannot be affirmative but only defensive; neither innovative nor creative, but reactive. Fear and the emotions it conjures up are inherently limited in their productive capacity. We should learn to protect our reputations because goodness is wonderful and sin is terrible. We should learn to respect others because all people are our brothers and sisters, not because they are potential enemies who will avenge slights.

In contrast, internal fear – when you refrain from harmful acts only because you are entirely focused on yourself – is always selfish and narcissistic. Internal fears betray insecurities, weaknesses and a mediocre self-centredness. Internal fear, like depression, takes us inside ourselves. When it paralyses us to the point of inaction, we call it a phobia.

But there is healthy fear: the fear of being cut off from the people we love. The fear of heaven does not mean that God will punish us for our sins but that we will be distanced and alienated from our Father because we transgress His will. As the prophet said, 'For your sins have created a barrier between you and the Lord.' This healthy fear can have a positive effect on our lives. We fear insulting God by being reckless with the precious life He bequeathed us. We fear gossiping about our friends because it will get back to them and people who love us a lot will now love us less.

The greatest human fear

Our fears usually change as we enter different stages of life. Some small children fear that they will be eaten by a monster or become lost in the darkness and never re-emerge. Because they feel neglected by their parents, they fear that no one will protect them or come looking for them should they get lost.

When I was a child, I had a recurring nightmare that a monster with eyes on the back of his head was chasing me around the house because I had taken shampoo and rubbed it into the hair on his back. Then I hid in the dryer so he couldn't find me. When he asked my family members where I was, to my surprise they all turned me in. So the monster would come to the dryer, turn it on, and I would go round and round. Then, when I was sufficiently disoriented, he would pull me out of the dryer and eat me. (Boy, would

Freud have a field day with this one.)

As we get older, our fears change. The fear of not being special is manifested in men in the form of a fear of failure in their various business undertakings. Because they think their importance lies in the money they make and the positions they reach, they fear they will become instant nobodies the moment they lose their job. Men try to combat the fear of nothingness through productivity, running from the fear of failure like it is death.

By the same token, a big movie star may fear being forgotten, waking up one morning and discovering that the world no longer cares about her. One day the paparazzi are following her everywhere, denying her even a moment of peace; the next, there is no one to take her picture. A celebrity has a shelf-life. She is like a balloon with a slow leak, needing constantly to be pumped up with helium. There is actually a clinical condition called PDS – publicity deficiency syndrome – that is experienced by people who have achieved celebrity and recognition and have subsequently lost it. This clinical disease chronicles the depression and loneliness that so many celebrities feel when the public moves on and leaves them behind.

At root, all of these fears are the fear of losing one's dignity and ceasing to matter. As I said in the previous chapter, the greatest human fear is that we might lose our uniqueness, that we are ordinary and unimpressive, that ultimately nobody loves us because we are not worthy of love.

Remember that really powerful point in the movie *Indecent Proposal*? Demi Moore and Woody Harrelson have agreed to divorce. The unravelling of the marriage began when Harrelson allowed his wife to spend a night with Robert Redford in exchange for one million dollars. As he signs the divorce papers, Harrelson says to Moore: 'I was afraid to say no to the proposition because I thought you wanted it. And I thought you were right in wanting it because he was the better man. But I have since learned that he is not a better man than me, he simply has more money.' That fear that someone else is better than us and that we are therefore not distinguished is something that plagues us throughout life.

This accounts for why death is the primal human fear, greater than all the rest. Why is the fear of death innate within the human condition? Sure, fear of the unknown is a part of it. We do not know if we are going to heaven or hell, or if we are not going anywhere at all, which might be even more frightening. But fear of the unknown is not enough to account for how much we abhor the eventuality of death. The reason why death is the number one fear is because in death we cease to be; death means that one day the world will wake up and we won't.

Moreover, the world will continue without us. Sure, a few people will miss us; they may even shed a tear or two, and if we are lucky they may even grieve for us longer than a few days. Nevertheless, even our family will return to their own lives and get along just fine. Death is the seeming ultimate confirmation that we are not special, not unique, not irreplaceable. One day we will exit the planet, and yet it will continue to spin without us.

Overcoming the fear of nothingness

How do we overcome the trepidation of nothingness? Many attempt to counteract it through professional achievement. They assume that if they distinguish themselves by earning a lot of money or becoming famous, their existence will matter much more. If you become a famous model, cameras will flash their bulbs at you. If you become president, all the country's citizens will salute your speeding motorcade. Crowds will part as you pass by because you are more important than everybody else.

Many successful businessmen attempt to combat the fear of nothingness by dumping their wives and marrying younger women. They reason that the further they stay from the grave, the more important they become. It seems incredible that they are blind to what everyone else sees as patently obvious: a trophy wife who is interested only in their money is the demonstration *par excellence* that *they* do not matter – only their money does.

Professional achievement offers at best only a temporary solution to the problem. When you distinguish yourself in others' eyes, you become a slave to public opinion. Because you have placed the focus of your importance outside yourself, you have empowered others to determine your value. You are like a dog at the pound who hopes to be taken home by some nice family.

Deficient by comparison

The key to counteracting this deepest of human fears is to first identify its root cause. The Kabbalists explain that insecurity is the natural consequence of humans feeling the weight of the infinite pressing against them at all times. Job said, 'Bold as a lion you hunt me; you repeat your exploits against me' (10:16). God pursues us at every moment and we subconsciously feel the weight of His presence, feeling deficient in comparison.

The cause of this feeling is that God is significant and we are insignificant; God is eternal and we are mortal; God is all good, and we are flawed. When we look at ourselves in comparison to this eternal model of perfection, we cannot help but feel grossly inadequate. Fear suddenly grips us. We go from focusing on our deficiencies to fearing that we are perhaps just one big joke, less worthy than nearly every other person on the planet. Comparing what we are to what we could be is bound to make us feel inadequate.

Fortunately, this insecurity can be countered and controlled. Since the cause of our feeling unimportant is directly related to God's absolute importance, we must seek to connect ourselves with God. Real security is found by linking up with the infinite and leading a virtuous life. If we attach ourselves to His greatness, we ourselves become great. By submerging our will to the greatest of all wills, we raise our being to the highest heights.

When we do good deeds and make a positive impact on other people's lives, we feel profoundly worthwhile, and our insecurities subside. When we call out to God in prayer, we feel that our being and essential self-worth are something more than just the figures on our last balance sheet. This explains why so many ordinary men and women have been capable of such extraordinary acts of faith and courage throughout the ages. Because they tapped into something infinite, nothing temporal could break them. Paradoxically, only by losing ourselves in the face of God's all-encompassing unity do we learn to find ourselves. In God's infinity, we overcome our finite nature. In God's ultimate uniqueness, we overcome our own insignificance.

We are all members of the royal family

What gives human beings true value is not the appreciation that others show them, because that can waver. Instead, we are all special by virtue of the fact that we are God's children. The only effective way to counter the fear that we are perhaps not adequate is to focus on the fact that, having been created in God's image, each of us is part of the infinite. Created in the image of God, we are eternally significant.

The bottom line is that this is the only basis of human dignity. It is not how much money we have – that can come and go in a flash, just ask any day trader. It is not how clever or smart we are. It is not our capacity to make other people laugh – after all, what would happen if we became depressed? What makes us all special and dignified is that we are all princes and princesses, sons and daughters of the King of Kings.

Therefore, as the Baal Shem Tov taught, the only fear that we should allow to dominate our lives is the fear of being severed from God. Many people wrongly think that fear of God is synonymous with fear of punishment, but there is nothing spiritual about fear of punishment. Indeed, refraining from sin for fear of punishment is the most cynical of all insurance policies. Instead, we must refrain from acting in contravention to Divine will because we love God and fear disfavour. The Talmud teaches, 'Act out of love, for the Torah makes a distinction between one who acts out of love and one who acts out of fear . . . In the former case his reward is doubled and redoubled' (Sifra Deuteronomy 32).

Impacting the lives of others

The second way we counteract the fear of nothingness is by impacting on others' lives. If the greatest human fear is the fear that you will one day cease to matter, by all means make sure that you *do* matter. How do we make ourselves matter? In the eloquent words of Ralph Waldo Emerson, one must make every attempt 'to give of one's self, to leave the world a bit better, whether by a healthy child, a garden patch or a redeemed social condition.'

In an obscure and mysterious passage that precedes Emerson by a few thousand years, the Bible commands the Priest to go before the Israelite army on the eve of war and order three different groups of people to return home:

> *Then the Priests shall address the troops, saying, 'Has anyone built a new house but not dedicated it? He should go back to his house, or he might die in the battle and another will dedicate it. Has anyone planted a vineyard but not yet enjoyed its fruit? He should go back to his house, or he might die in the battle and another will be first to enjoy its fruit. Has anyone become engaged to a woman but not yet married her? He should go back to his house, or he might die in the battle and another will marry her.' The officials shall continue to address the troops, saying, 'Is anyone afraid or disheartened? He should go back to his house, or he might cause the heart of his comrades to melt like his own.'*

Here the Bible addresses three different kinds of fear. Anyone who had experienced any of them could not go forward and fight the battle of life for it is too disheartening. The first is someone who has built a new house but not dedicated it. How does one dedicate a new home? By sharing it with others. When it becomes a house of hospitality, it becomes a sanctuary for the Divine. He who has a home that has not been consecrated is riddled with fear because he has made no mark on his community. Since he lives only for himself, he lives with the fear that his life is transitory and meaningless. When he dies, he will die an eternal death; because he has touched no hearts during his lifetime, no one will truly miss him.

Next is the man who planted a vineyard but did not enjoy its fruits. How does one enjoy the fruits of a vineyard? Again, by sharing it with others. God created wine so that people could toast each other. (There is a reason they sell beer and wine coolers in six packs.) What fun is it having a drink alone anyway? But when you live an isolated and lonely existence, you not only deny yourself the pleasures of human company, but also live in fear that your life does not matter. You fear that if you do not wake up the next morning, no one will even notice. How can you go and fight a battle when you are convinced of your own inconsequence?

Finally, someone who has not yet married must similarly not go to battle. He or she who has not found that special someone who places them at the centre of their universe is bound to be riddled with fear. With such anxiety facing them at every turn, how could they possibly go forth into the struggle for existence and the battle of life? If no one will miss you if you die, how can you have the incentive to live?

On the other hand, he or she who has found someone who always puts them first can never really know fear for they can never really know loneliness. When you have a significant other, a person who has given up all others, your specialness is corroborated. You are now strong and invincible. You can now go out into the struggle for life. To be sure, you'll come home one day looking sad and dejected when your boss won't give you a raise because there are others who are better than you at work. But then your wife will turn to you and say, 'What does he know, that boss of yours, that *shmendrick*? I know how special you are.' And all the bumps will come out of your macerated ego.

In the final analysis, we fear abandonment. We fear that, in our day of need, no one will come to our aid because we're *not worth it*. We fear that, one day, all who care for us will cease to care. This is the mother of all fears. When other people are around, we do not feel afraid as we know that we cannot be harmed in a group. The value of our lives is determined by the quality of our relationships and the impact we make on other people's lives. So, by filling our house with people, and most importantly by having one principal relationship that we place above all others, we are not only guaranteed the pleasures of human company but are assured that we will never have to lead even one day in fear. Friendship is, therefore, not a luxury but a necessity.

18

Jealousy

THE MOST INTENSE HUMAN EMOTION

*My wife's jealousy is getting ridiculous. The other
day she looked at my calendar and wanted to
know who May was.*

Rodney Dangerfield

Jealousy is the jaundice of the soul.

John Dryden

Jealousy is the most intense of all human emotions and, like
most others, embodies a very antithetical quality. On the
one hand, it is a positive emotion. Because it presupposes
the existence of an external other, it binds us to people like
no other emotion. After all, we can never be jealous of
ourselves. As a result, our lives are guarded from isolation.
Jealousy is probably the one emotion that Robinson Crusoe
did not experience all alone on his island (unless, of course,
if he was jealous of people who weren't marooned on an
island).

In *The Jewish Guide to Adultery: How to Turn Your
Marriage into an Affair*, I argued at length that without
some measure of jealousy, there can be no passion in
marriage. Indeed, jealousy does for our marriage what ambition does for our careers: it prevents complacency and
boredom. It can further be compared to water on fire: a
little kindles the fire of our romance and prevents us taking
our spouse for granted; a lot is certain to extinguish the
relationship entirely.

Furthermore, although Christianity denigrates it as one

of the seven deadly sins, jealousy nevertheless serves as perhaps the principal engine of human advance. Without it, we would most probably still be in the Dark Ages. Jealousy makes us desire to achieve someone else's good fortune. The Talmud says, 'Were it not for jealousy no one would marry or build a house' (Mid. Psalms 37:1)

Finally, jealousy is beneficial because it prevents human indifference. Because we are all to some extent naturally jealous, we care about what people around us do. Jealousy is what guarantees that no man becomes an island.

Nevertheless, and herein lies the paradox, although jealousy connects us to each other, it also undoes the knot that binds humankind. Jealousy is not about cooperation but about competition, not empathy but envy. Instead of promoting brotherhood, jealousy pits human beings against each other in a dog-eat-dog adversarial relationship, demonstrating the interconnectedness of all people in an almost purely negative fashion.

Jealousy is fuelled by insecurity

In Hebrew, the word for jealousy derives from the word *kan*, or nest, thus meaning the desire to occupy someone else's nest. Why would we desire this? Because our own nest is somehow inadequate to serve our needs. In other words, like most negative human emotions, jealousy is fuelled by our feelings of insecurity and insatiability. The more insignificant we feel ourselves to be, the greater the envy we feel for what others possess and achieve. Jealousy makes us more envious of someone else's possessions than satisfied with our own.

Not unsurprisingly, jealous individuals are profoundly unhappy with who they are. Because their own identity is inadequate, they desire someone else's to compensate for what they lack. When they feel that their own horizons are limited, they begin to look to their neighbour's. Like a radar tower, they continuously ascertain everyone else's co-ordinates in their own progressively narrowing universe.

Furthermore, jealousy places all human beings in an inversely proportional relationship wherein someone else's success indicates our own failure. It is for this reason that the jealous man is more interested in the destruction of his peers than his own personal success. When he becomes jealous of a colleague who is dating a beautiful woman, for example, he prefers to see them split up rather than find a girlfriend of his own. At its essence, jealousy is profoundly possessive; it involves taking, or at least wanting to take, that which belongs to another instead of earning one's keep for oneself.

One of the most public examples of such jealousy in recent times is that of Tonya Harding and Nancy Kerrigan. Although both women were world-class US skaters, Harding felt consumed by jealousy of her team-mate. In her mind, Kerrigan was better, more graceful, more beautiful. But instead of working on her own performance, Harding attempted to remove Kerrigan from the spotlight by having her injured. In the supercompetitive world of the Olympics, Harding felt that the only chance she had to win the gold medal was by eliminating her rival.

It is a curious dimension of jealousy that it makes us profoundly other-person oriented. It is, therefore, not only harmful in the sense that it causes friction between human beings, but also doubly destructive because it gets in the way of our own self-development.

Finally, jealousy is ugly because it reveals a false and predatory sense of entitlement. The ancient Rabbis said in their profound wisdom that a person is never jealous of anything that is not his. Nor is he jealous of that which is beyond his realm of possibility. When we are jealous of our neighbour's success, it is because we think that we work so much harder than he does and that *we* deserve to be rich instead of him. In a curious way, you cannot be jealous of someone until you first consider yourself their superior and you subliminally believe that what they possess should really belong to you. Hence, in your mind, you are really being envious of *your own* possession, or at least of what by right should be yours.

Jealousy is a denial of God

Consider the Bible's first instance of sibling rivalry, the story of Cain and Abel. Although the Bible does not explicitly say so, we may infer that the two brothers started life with the same bonds of affection that all brothers share, but their brotherly love could not survive the deep jealousy that engulfed them when one was favoured by God and the other scorned.

When Cain saw that Abel was chosen amidst his own rejection, he began to view his sibling as an adversary instead. And herein lies the reason why I say that jealousy is the *most intense* of all human emotions: because it is so potent that it can even undermine filial love. Jealousy has the awesome power actually to undo the genetic links that connect us with our kin, making us view them instead as total strangers.

Like anger, jealousy is profoundly unGodly because it means that we ultimately deny God's abundance and bounty. It means that we have no gratitude for what we have been given. By being jealous, we cry out that God is unjust in what He gives different people. Jealousy results from feelings of deprivation, born of the belief that there is not enough to go around, so when someone succeeds, he has stolen our success. And since everyone else poses a threat to our own fortune, we consequently find ourselves jealous instead of joyful at their good fortune.

If we believe in a never-ending supply of blessings, however, we cannot possibly be jealous. If our neighbour earns a million dollars, we have no reason to be jealous because we know that there is an endless supply of money available for us as well. We have just yet to figure out how to earn it. Jealousy only thrives in a world that is inherently limited, which is why it is almost always accompanied by pettiness and narrow-mindedness.

Finally, jealousy is unGodly because it always presupposes judgement. We are only jealous once we have decreed our neighbour to be inadequate. Estelle applied for a tenured position at Oxford in the history faculty. To her great annoyance, her colleague Ruth received the post instead. 'This is an injustice', Estelle told me. 'I have been with the University twice as long, and I have far better references.' Estelle was not only saying that she deserved the job: in the same breath, she was saying that Ruth did not deserve it. If we believe that God runs the world, however, we cannot be jealous because we have no right to judge.

Jealous of our own flesh and blood

Since all of us are naturally jealous, does this mean that none of us is satisfied with who we are? If not, why? And were those who are not jealous born that way or do they constantly fight their naturally jealous disposition?

The Talmud says that a man is jealous of every other man except his own son. Is this because he is your very flesh and blood? No, because you can be jealous of your brother who, on the face of it, is even more your flesh. After all, because you have the same parents, you and your brother swim in the same gene pool. Your son, on the other hand, swims in a different pool because he possesses your spouse's genes too.

The nature of a brother's jealousy can be so destructive that the Bible relates several examples of it, Cain and Abel being the most prominent because Cain's jealousy led him to murder his brother in cold blood. But jealousy inflicts even the righteous: although Joseph's brothers were holy enough to progenitor eleven of the twelve Tribes of Israel, they were also consumed by jealousy to such an extent that they sold their brother into slavery.

So why can we be jealous of a brother but not of a son? As I said, jealousy results from feeling that each person in this world is our rival. Two brothers reared in the same household feel love but also the need to compete for the best place at the dinner table, achievements at school and, most of all, their parents' affection. They have inherited the same mantle and been given the same start in life. But what will they do with it? The more pronounced the adversarial relationship between them, the more they feel they are at each other's throats.

Hence, many siblings fall out when they are charged with dividing their parents' inheritance. I know a world-renowned industrialist who specifically sold his business upon retiring because he was afraid that his three sons would fight over who would manage it. 'It was easier to divide the proceeds into three equal parts', he told me, 'than to watch the business divide my three boys into enemies.'

But a man is never jealous of his son because he never sees him as his rival. On the contrary, far from being someone who *undermines* his success, his son guarantees his success. He is his continuity, the heir to his mantle. Anything his son does brings glory to his name.

Sure, there may be some glitches in the father–son relationship. A man may sometimes see his son outperforming him and feel jealous of his achievements, but when push comes to shove, he will always protect his son's interests because *his son's success is his own*. In ancient Israel, a man was not even referred to by his first name but as 'the son of so and so': in nearly all the ancient rabbinic literature, the great prophet Moses is referred to as 'the son of Amram'.

The same, however, cannot be said of a brother, who maintains his own separate identity. If your brother vastly outperforms you, this can show you up as being inadequate. Here you are, both emanating from the same source, recipients of the same genes, yet your brother has achieved so much more than you. Look at all the comparisons that were made between Jimmy and Billy Carter, and the current comparisons between Bill and Roger Clinton (nobody understands how Roger turned out to be such a success – just kidding!). Isn't your brother's success proof that he is the better man?

The objective in overcoming jealousy is to *cease seeing others as our rivals*. We must train our minds to see others as partners who enhance us rather than enemies who detract from us. This takes a great amount of discipline, but as the world is enhanced by people doing well, when other people win, we all win.

Without healthy competition and rivalry, some of our best qualities would never develop in the first place. We would be trapped in a hopeless morass of mediocrity. In such a world, we would have no jealousy but neither would we show any progress. Polio would never have been cured; for goodness sake, we would have no sports to watch on television. But, like most things in life, this is far easier said than done.

When jealousy is a virtue

How do we turn jealousy into a virtue? First, we must have healthy competition. The difference between healthy and unhealthy competition is that in healthy competition we want to be successful, but in unhealthy competition, we have the insatiable desire to be *more* successful. We want success not for success's sake, but to beat all our friends to the mountain summit. Enough is never enough.

The second way to make jealousy a virtue is to be jealous of the right things. The ancient Rabbis said that while it is forbidden to covet or be jealous of another man's possessions, it is fitting and proper to be jealous of his spiritual possessions, his virtue. One Biblical commentator even says that had Rachel not envied the good deeds of her sister, she would not have borne children (Genesis R. 71:6). Therefore, if your neighbour is generous, you should be jealous of his generosity and seek to emulate, or even outdo, him.

In fact, the Talmud even says that jealousy between scholars is a positive emotion. According to Talmudic law, if one teacher of Judaic studies is already in a city, a new one is permitted to move into his territory to teach children the Torah, even if this will encroach upon the business of the first. The reason given is simple: the Jewish people need the best possible Torah teachers and 'jealousy amongst scholars increases wisdom'.

If we harness the positive aspects of jealousy, it can spur us to ever higher acts of altruism. After all, if someone else's curing cancer makes me want to cure AIDS, don't we all benefit? By the same token, if someone else's giving $1,000 to a cause makes me want to give $2,000, aren't we all better off?

But to be jealous of someone's money? How is that going to make us into better people? And to be jealous of the fact that they found love and we did not? Go out and find yourself some great person to love. Being jealous in situations like these will not only not spur you on to higher action, but also prevent you progressing in your own right.

Yossele the tailor came complaining to the village Rabbi: 'Rabbi, that new tailor Isaac, who opened a store across the street from me, is stealing all my business. Everyone is going to him. And you know what, for every inch I put in six stitches while he only puts in four. And I use 100 per cent worsted wool, while he uses a synthetic blend.' On and on he went about Isaac until the Rabbi stopped him and said, 'You know Yossele, it seems to me that if you knew as much about your own business as you do about Isaac's, you wouldn't have lost your clients in the first place.'

In sum, the main problem with jealousy is that in wasting our energies on what the Joneses next door are doing, we cease to examine and improve ourselves.

Surmounting jealousy

The ancient Rabbis point out an interesting phenomenon: while it is true that human beings are jealous of each other's homes, careers, and money, they are never jealous of a bird's wings, a gazelle's speed or a cat's nine lives. Why are we jealous of people but not animals? Why don't we see more pet owners in rivalry with their parakeets, who can fly around the house while we can only watch in wonder? The explanation is that people are only jealous of those things which are in the realm of possibility. If we cannot make a claim to something in our mind, we do not make a claim to it with our hearts or hands either.

The same is true of how to purge jealousy from our being. Since jealousy entails desiring what we think belongs to us, accept in your mind that you have your own corner in the world. In the same way that you would not want anyone to mess with your corner, you cannot mess with anyone else's. Learn to accept the fact that what belongs to your fellow is his, *not yours in potential.*

In other words, jealousy is combated through respecting borders. You have your own destiny to fulfil, your own dreams to live. Stop living someone else's destiny. It usually takes only a moment of honest reflection to realize the invaluable blessings that God has bestowed upon each and every one of us, and to reclaim our lives as our own.

19

Ambition

THE MOST PAINFUL EMOTION

*But what will not ambition and revenge descend
to? Who aspires, must down as low as high he
soared.*

John Milton, *Paradise Lost*

*The higher the ape climbs the more he shows his
rump.*

French proverb

I once recommended a very bright student for a top position
at a bank. The man hiring was a friend, and I wanted to help
him recruit the best possible candidate. To my surprise, my
friend turned him down after the interview. When I asked
why, he responded that his bank was known above all else
as a people's bank and they were proud of the team spirit
that existed among their employees. 'There's no way this
guy is going to work with anyone else', he told me. 'He's
good, but he's too hungry. So I must sacrifice talent in order
to get principles.' My friend was obviously of the mind set
that ambition and principles could not coexist within the
same person.

In Britain, this distrustful attitude is common. Ambition
is treated here like a four-letter word. As a prime example,
when Tony Blair ran for Prime Minister as the second
youngest candidate in Britain's history, the press repeatedly
referred to him as 'ambitious', as if it were some kind of
incurable disease that he had acquired.

In general, we associate ambition with ruthlessness and

greed. Take talented investment bankers, for example. Because they are constantly approached by other banks, even their own managers do not trust their loyalty or integrity. The only way to guarantee that these highly ambitious young people remain with the company is by withholding their money until the end of the calendar year, paying them in bonuses rather than salaries, a practice known in the corporate world as 'golden handcuffs'. Savvy computer programmers are well known for accumulating stock in one company only to switch to a new start-up company once they have exercised their options.

Ambition propels us forward

These examples describe some of the negative aspects of ambition, but let us consider the positive ones too. First and foremost, ambition is, like jealousy, a powerful engine capable of propelling mankind forward. Without it we have laziness and mediocrity. If a doctor has no ambition, the sick will never be cured. If a researcher does not aspire to win the Nobel Prize, chances are we will not find a cure for AIDS.

Ambition is what produces excellence, and we have yet to discover a more reliable human engine that produces such lofty results. Would you hire a lawyer with no ambition to succeed? No, you want someone representing you who wants the victory for himself as much as for you. The bottom line is that ambition is necessary and good because it leads to self-awareness and improvement.

Incidentally, religion may have become so irrelevant in the modern age because people cannot stomach ambitious clerics. Religion, which was once the most compelling force in the Western world, has today become a joke, assumed to be practised only by those who need a crutch to make it through life. Indeed, ever since Marx, religion has been dismissed as an opiate, the respectable man's Prozac.

In the modern world, business has become the new religion, attracting the best minds and exciting the highest passions. Wall Street has become the new Wailing Wall, the stock exchange the new cathedral. I am firmly convinced that one of the reasons business has overtaken religion is that ambition is expected in business while in religion it is stifled.

Ambition grants us no rest

Still, it would appear that ambition is far more *de*structive than *con*structive. Like all true emotions, it is an inner compulsion that requires external release. When we feel ambitious, we feel restless to change something in our lives and to gain the recognition we feel we deserve. Indeed, ambition and satisfaction are inversely proportional, so that the more ambitious we feel, the less satisfied we are, and vice versa.

Ambition is, from this point of view, the most painful of the emotions as it invariably leads to insatiability and frustration. The old saying goes that there is no rest for the wicked; the truth, however, is that there is no rest for the ambitious. Those who are really ambitious are condemned to a life of endless running. Because they can never satisfy their hunger, they produce results but rarely know any happiness. They cannot take satisfaction for any achievement because they are already working on the next goal.

The paradox of ambition is as follows: If I want to get ahead then I'm not happy where I am, but if I'm happy where I am, I have no ambition to achieve more. So can we be happy and ambitious at the same time? Moreover, doesn't ambition directly contradict the Talmud's fundamental teaching: 'Who is rich? He who rejoices in his portion?' Aren't we meant to be content?

The answer depends on how we define ambition. If we see ambition as an appraisal of our God-given talents, our lives have the potential to be filled with happiness when we maximize those talents. When we waste that potential, on the other hand, our lives generally are filled with misery and discontent.

As Rabbi in Oxford, I noticed something interesting about the most accomplished students. The truly bright ones who perform exceptionally well in exams are also the most masochistic. I was once playing squash with Joseph, a Marshall scholar. Joseph was in the process of having his PhD dissertation – a thesis on international law – published by one of America's leading houses. But on the squash court, every time he lost an easy point he would quietly berate himself, 'Come on, Joseph.' When he lost a difficult point, he would scream, 'Joseph, you can do better than that.' Students like Joseph cannot give themselves a break. They constantly struggle to rescue themselves from the abyss of nothingness they feel inside.

I know this type of person well because it is me. This is why I have always admired those who rise above this trap, people who find an intrinsic sense of self-worth that transcends their professional accomplishments. My favourite country in all Europe is Italy, where people seem to take it easier and still achieve a great deal. The reason is simple: it is the home of 'Mediterranean man', defined as the man or woman who is prepared to forgive themselves for being human.

When insecurity fuels ambition

So which is it, then? Is ambition a beneficial or a destructive emotion? Does it afford us glory when we achieve it, or pain and frustration as we inevitably fall short? The answer is that there are two kinds of ambition, which we will call Ambition A and Ambition B. Ambition A is based on the idea that the individual is unworthy and must therefore seek achievement in order to distinguish himself. Ambition B, in contrast, is based on the idea that every human being is born special, with a precious gift to contribute to the world that only they can offer. They therefore have an obligation – to themselves, to society and to God – to contribute it.

The difference between the two is like the difference between Napoleon and Einstein. Born to a noble family that lost its wealth, Napoleon was riddled with lifelong insecurities. He became a conqueror not because he believed himself to be superior to others but because he felt himself to be less worthy. Like many, he spent his life trying to prove a point. Einstein, on the other hand, was born feeling endowed with great gifts. He knew that he was born special and that special people have an obligation to make an outstanding contribution to the world.

Ambition A is the most common form of ambition. Born of a profound feeling of unworthiness, it is predicated on the idea that doing and owning will compensate for being; that knowing famous people will compensate for our sense of anonymity and nothingness; that having control over others will compensate for lacking control over ourselves. In sum, it is fuelled by our insecurities.

Insecurity, however, cannot be so easily dismissed as it is responsible for not only the bad things we do, but the good as well. As I mentioned before, it is the scientist with low self-esteem who strives to win the Nobel Prize by finding a cure for cancer. Insecurity is also what leads us into loving relationships with other human beings, since we do not feel adequate alone, so crave the affection of others.

Ambition A

Consider the following metaphor to illustrate Ambition A. An individual life is like a number line, each one containing a different value. When we are born, we begin at the very beginning of the number line, a big zero. Because we have zero value, it is only natural that we want to transform ourselves from a nothing into a something. Indeed, we feel that we have something to prove to all of those who doubted our abilities: the teacher who expelled us, the parent who said we would never amount to anything. How do we become a one instead of a zero? With acquisitions. We acquire money, high-flying jobs, lovers, any trophy that will lend significance to our existence.

Nevertheless, beneath all these status symbols lies a bottomless pit that can never be sated. Underneath all the possessions is an emperor with no clothes. Because while ours is the world's most ambitious generation ever, it is also the most insecure. And although we try to fill the void with love, relationships and wealth, we consistently fail in this endeavour. An inner feeling of security and achievement is hardly ever attained.

When we substantiate our identity with external markers, no inner transformation takes place. Instead of gaining a sense of pride in the centre of an ever-expanding circle of possessions or awards, this centre remains a big, insecure zero. That's why Ambition A is insatiable. We'll work ourselves to the bone and probably die working before we ever achieve any real satisfaction. One would think that the more our insecurities fuel accomplishments, the more our self-esteem would grow, but precisely the opposite is true.

Take the rich and famous as an example. Nearly all the world's great screen actresses had turbulent childhoods. Greta Garbo grew up in terrible poverty in Stockholm. Madonna lost her mother as a child. One would expect that once these women had made it to the top they would have been satisfied. But insecurity follows on the heels of their success at every turn. Garbo became a legendary recluse. Bette Davis published an autobiography entitled *The Lonely Life*.

The survival of the fittest

Ambition A is in part the result of living in a market economy where proving oneself to the world is a constant battle and each possession a small victory. In such a predatory environment where only the fittest survive – there is a reason we call it the rat race – colleagues become competitors, allies antagonists. In this world, a person is ambitious because he feels threatened by those whose achievements seem greater than his own. Thus, weakness and insecurity, rather than strength, push him up the ladder of success.

He typically climbs that ladder alone, looking down on those he had to step on in order to reach his height. Like Melville's Ahab, the person motivated by Ambition A is often self-obsessed and tyrannical, unable to form meaningful relationships because he views others only as a means to his own end. Indeed, he drives away those who are closest to him because his insatiability strips the sensitivity from his spirit. Although he may lead the crew to new heights in search of the great whale, he will also sink the ship rather than admit defeat, so great is his ambition.

Ultimately, however, instead of earning the respect of his peers, he elicits enmity and jealousy. Others secretly pray for his failure. And because his insularity breeds suspicion rather than admiration, he condemns himself to a life of loneliness, imprisoned within the shell of his ego.

Take Kaiser Wilhelm II, the Emperor of Germany at the turn of the twentieth century. The grandson of two great dynastic rulers – Kaiser Wilhelm I and Queen Victoria – young Wilhelm was born with a withered left arm that affected his balance. To suffer from a glaring physical handicap and be unable to ride a horse was certainly not easy to swallow for a boy destined to rule a stern and disciplined nation. Wilhelm's character never recovered from the colossal insecurity that this engendered. Consequently, he exhibited the most unhealthy competitive streak throughout his lifetime.

As a boy, his competitiveness manifested itself on the playing field, as a man, on the battlefield. Because he felt intimidated by the British Empire, he engaged in a meaningless arms race with it, building huge battleships that Germany scarcely needed. As most historians point out, it was his relentless attempt to equal the strength of the British navy that eventually led to the outbreak of the First World War.

Ambition B

In contrast, Ambition B is predicated on the idea that all humans are born with infinite value. The rationale is that I am created in the image of God so I am *intrinsically* and *infinitely* unique and special, as is every other human being on this earth. Thus, while I am never more important than anyone else, neither am I any less worthy. I have no need to prove myself because I am born valuable. My colleagues' achievements never infringe upon my own because the world is large enough to contain *all* our ambitions.

Whereas with Ambition A the scenario is win/lose, with Ambition B it is win/win. I look upon my fellow human beings as comrades not competitors. Moreover, because there is an integral plan for creation and I am central to it, *as we all are,* God endowed me with a special gift to give to the world that only I can contribute. I do not have to estab-lish or earn my place in society by doing because *my essence is in my being* and not my *doing.* And although I know that without me the rest of creation is flawed, I consider myself not superior to others but an interdependent component of the universe.

Consider how the different types of ambition play out in our role as parents. Western parents have extremely high ambitions for their children, and it is all too common to compare our children with others. In addition, we typically classify development as achievement, believing that there is some merit in how fast a child walks, talks, or potty trains, when all of the above will occur naturally even if totally ignored. After all, these are characteristics of a biped: unless there is some physiological problem, all children eventually walk, talk, eat and sleep through the night without nappies, no matter how gifted they are, no matter how ambitious their parents.

Indeed, we incorrectly assume that there is some correla-tion between how early a child walks and how fast he will run. Nevertheless, you hear a proud mother describe how her daughter was walking at nine months and you wonder why your son is 'lagging' at thirteen. Or you hear a proud father tell you how little Bennett knows all of the alphabet while your little Betty shows no interest in letters at all.

All of these feelings and actions derive from Ambition A. We want our kids – even as infants – to get ahead in a highly competitive world. One mother even told me that she had to buy a computer for her four-year-old daughter out of fear that she would not have a competitive edge in kindergarten!

The parent motivated by Ambition B also wants her child to succeed but measures success in a different way. She does not want to pick the fruit before it is ripe; she is willing to wait as long as it takes for it to fall naturally. She knows that her son is a something, that he has his own special God-given talents that will manifest by themselves if given the proper environment and encouragement. She does not treat him like a block of marble to chisel away at. Therefore, she will not force little David into taking piano lessons in order to satisfy her own ambitions for him of playing in recitals and winning awards. Instead, she will encourage him to develop the interests he seems to gravitate towards on his own. She will be far less interested in the grades her son receives than in the substance of what he has learned. Finally, she will be far more impressed by how he develops his own potential than how he compares with others in the marketplace that is called a school.

In sum, whereas Ambition A derives from a desire to prove oneself in a competitive arena, Ambition B is born of one's obligation to maximize one's potential, whatever that may be. And whereas the goal of Ambition A is to overcome *nothingness*, the goal of Ambition B is to overcome *selfishness*. Finally, whereas Ambition A drives us to crave the recognition of our peers, Ambition B drives us to crave the recognition of our Creator who has endowed us with these very precious gifts that He wants us to share with humanity.

Not knowing your name

Many Jewish legends tell of 'the wise men of Chelm', a city filled with fools who thought they were clever. Mendel was one of these very wise men. One day, he went to the communal bath house. As he was about to enter the bath, it suddenly occurred to him that the moment he took off his clothes, he would cease to exist. Observing all the other naked men in the bath who looked just like him, he felt certain that he would forget who he was.

To prevent this, he decided to tie a red string around his toe. While soaping himself, however, the string fell off and slipped on to the toe of another man. When Mendel came out of the bath, he was distraught. Because there was no string on his toe, he had forgotten his identity. He scanned the room and soon found the red string on the foot of another bather. Mendel walked over to him and said, 'I know who you are. You're Mendel the water carrier. But tell me, who am I?'

When our identity is dependent on some external marker for validation, there is no guarantee that we will keep our bearings. Chances are in fact that we will drift far from our intended path. That's why Ambition A leads to permanent insecurity and over-achievement. We are always standing atop the precipice trying to keep ourselves from falling into the abyss of anonymity. Achievement and a sense of security are never internalized because everything on the inside is made of quicksand. Ahab's marker was Moby Dick; without the great whale, his life had no purpose.

Similarly, when someone becomes wealthy thinking that money will validate their existence, they live in permanent paranoia. They are convinced that all who befriend them do so only for their money, because deep down they feel that without their money they are worthless.

Paul started his own insurance company and sold his stake of the business thirty years later for what the newspapers reported to be over two hundred million dollars. His only son, Mark, was dating Wendy, a nice enough woman, yet Paul never showed her any warmth. When Mark asked him why, he replied, 'She is only interested in you for your inheritance.'

Although Mark and Wendy eventually broke up, Paul ended up treating all of Mark's subsequent girlfriends in the same way. When I met Paul, I told him that his money had become a curse. 'You worked so hard to give your family a better life. But here you are destroying the lives of those you love most because money is the only thing on your mind.

Because you're so obsessed with money, you believe that everyone else is just as obsessed.'

Blind ambition

Based on the above, we can identify three kinds of ambition: the bad, the neutral and the good. Let us begin with the bad: blind ambition. As the name implies, blind ambition occurs when you charge ahead with no identifiable destination simply to get noticed. You run not towards any particular goal but away from something, particularly the inner fear that you are worthless.

Look how many people in America today are prepared to go on national television and be utterly humiliated just in order to get their fifteen minutes of fame. Celebrity at any price has become the motto for a generation prepared to acquire recognition even at the expense of their own dignity. This is running towards existence rather than towards any vision or dream. You simply want to be, but you are too blind to see that real being is an internal affair and can never be achieved externally.

Neutral ambition

The second kind of ambition is neutral. While I can be ambitious for something totally self-centred, I can also at least try to achieve success in the name of something higher than myself while also placing myself in the limelight. The Pope, for example, can rebuild the Catholic Church and teach its members spirituality at the same time as going down in history as the most accomplished Pope of the millennium.

Neutral ambition can be compared to a plough on the back of an ox. I am a bold and ambitious ox: I want to be something; I want to be remembered. I could go into a china shop and destroy the china, but instead I put a plough on my back and trudge ahead, and in the course of my coming first, the whole field has been ploughed.

The problem with neutral ambition is that it is not really neutral at all. Take Bill Clinton. Here is a man who always wanted to be president, and succeeded. While on the one hand he is accused of self-indulgence and opportunism, on the other he has done an incredible amount of good for his country. Indeed, the American economy is stronger than ever and the country is at peace. Nevertheless, many people think that his ambition has degraded a great office because it is about him not the country. Although this kind of ambition is not inherently destructive, neither does it necessarily inspire others to advance a noble cause. Those who possess neutral ambition end up being remembered in their lifetime but quickly forgotten thereafter.

Good ambition

Finally, there is good ambition. This is when you realize you are special, you become ambitious for a cause and you subordinate yourself to that cause. Any action you undertake is for the sole purpose of promoting your goodly cause. Mother Teresa, for example, achieved worldwide fame and recognition, but for the purpose of enlisting the world community to relieve human suffering. In good ambition, the cause and the individual who works to advance that cause are one and the same. The believer and his beliefs become inseparable.

Unlike other religions, Judaism does not subscribe to suffocating ambition. In contrast to Christianity, which preaches that 'it is harder for a rich man to reach the Kingdom of God than it is for a camel to pass through the eye of a needle', Judaism teaches that we are born to distinguish ourselves. However, although Judaism encourages ambition, it views wealth and fame not as ends in and of themselves but as means to the end of promoting eternal values.

When Jacob flees the wrath of his brother Esau, he offers a prayer to God, 'If God will be with me and protect me along the path upon which I now embark and give me bread to eat and water to drink, then I will make the Lord *my*

God.' Sounds like a horse-trade, doesn't it? And what if God didn't give Jacob these things? Would he start worshipping idols? The real meaning behind this verse, as Maimonides explains it, is: 'If you give me the essential materials of life, O God, then I can get on with the job of worshipping you. But if I am starving for bread and have nothing to eat myself, how will I be able to give alms to the poor and raise children?' Jacob was in fact asking God to give him the tools to advance his belief system and spread the knowledge of God to the far corners of the earth. His prayer for wealth was to facilitate his divine mission and not as an end in itself.

A modern case of such commitment is Jody Williams, who won the Nobel Prize for Peace in 1997 for her contribution to the landmine campaign. On the day she won, she criticized every world leader who did not sign the petition banning landmines. Had she not condemned them for failing to take the threat of landmines seriously, she would have been treated like royalty. However, she sacrificed this personal honour in order to further her cause.

Passing the torch

Few people are as selfless as Ms Williams. Indeed, most people start out believing in a cause but end up believing in themselves. How do we know if we are ambitious for ourselves or for a larger cause? The answer lies in our ability to let go. If we find it easy to pass the mantle to someone more capable than ourselves to take the cause forward, the cause takes precedence. If, on the other hand, we cannot let go of the reins but insist on retaining control, the cause was only the means to promote our own personal ambition.

A case in point was Moses. Although he led the Jews through the desert for thirty years, when it came time to pass the torch to Joshua, he did not hesitate. Righteous prophet that he was, he quietly retreated from the stage of leadership without fanfare. There were no guards of honour, no twenty-one gun salutes. He was buried alone with only

God in attendance. Indeed, part of Moses' greatness lay in knowing that the needs and unique mission of the Jewish people superseded his own.

A more contemporary example is Nelson Mandela. Although at eighty years old he easily could have run again for re-election as President of South Africa, and won, he stepped down in favour of a younger leadership that would better serve the purposes of his country and his cause.

In contrast, I offer the example of Margaret Thatcher. A truly great leader in her time, she possessed the courage and assertiveness to save Britain from a continuing downward economic spiral. However, when her sell-by date came, she would not stand down gracefully so she was forced out. Although she was much admired while in office, history will forever debate whether or not she was good for Britain. Indeed, there is a general feeling that while she started out serving the interests of her country, she ended up placing her own first. It started with Britannia and ended with Thatcherism. She held on just a little bit too long.

In parenting, the same dilemma exists. Do we have children because we subordinate our existence to that of something we love, or is it because of our insecurities and need to feel love? Do we have children in order to give or to take? The only way of knowing for sure is when it comes time to let go and allow them to be people in their own right. Those parents who can never let go view their children's freedom as their own loss. Because of their insecurities, they treat their children like possessions. But those who are prepared to allow their children the freedom to develop their own personalities can, on the other hand, be assured that it was always the child who was paramount.

Subordinating ourselves to God's will

Judaism teaches that while we must all believe in ourselves, we must doubt ourselves at the same time. Indeed, the Talmud makes contradictory statements about ambition and self-appraisal. It says that a person should carry two statements in her pockets. In the right pocket, it should say, 'The world was created for my benefit', in the left, 'I am nothing but dust and ashes.' Balance is achieved only by the eternal tension of these two postures, the belief that we are everything, yet nothing. Therefore, while we want to be ambitious, we must never get carried away with ourselves. While we should always yearn for distinction, we must do so in subordination to a higher cause, the highest cause of all being God.

This explains the great paradox of Moses, who is described on the one hand as the greatest of all the prophets, but on the other as 'the most humble man who walked the earth'. Most people become arrogant when they reach for greatness, but Moses was different. The more he achieved, the more humble he became. His achievement pulled him closer and closer to God. As he was absorbed into the great infinite presence, he lost more and more of himself until his identity was no more.

Hence, even when Moses spoke the amazing words in Deuteronomy (11:13–15) promising that *he* would reward the Jews for their faithful service, this was not seen as heresy:

> *If you will only heed his every commandment that I am commanding you today – loving the Lord your God, and serving him with all your heart and with all your soul then I will give the rain for your land in its season, the early rain and the later rain, and you will gather in your grain, your wine, and your oil; and I will give grass in your fields for your livestock, and you will eat your fill.*

Aren't these words odd? Moses is speaking as though it were in his power to reward and punish. The Talmud explains that the Divine voice spoke through Moses, such was the degree of his subordination to the Divine will.

What few people understand is that a belief in God is a

statement of true humility because one realizes that no matter how far one climbs in life, the best one will ever be is number two. Without a God to whom we subordinate our ego, all of us would want to become God. Look at how many people throughout history have declared that they were gods, kings, fascist dictators – even distinguished religious leaders such as Thomas Becket, Archbishop of Canterbury. They began promoting a cause but ended up promoting themselves.

Unrestrained belief in the self is *at best* arrogance and at worst dangerous psychosis. Any man or woman whose ambition is unchecked by a force from above has been cut loose from all restraining forces of morality and is not to be trusted. Therefore, in order to tame ambition and ensure that goodness will prevail, it is necessary also to have subservience to God. Accepting that we are God's creatures born to execute *His* will ensures that we never become lost in our own fantasies of divinity.

Cultivating the art of gratitude

Putting limits on the ego while retaining our ambition and upward mobility is a prerequisite to a successful and satisfying life. One of the ways in which to achieve this careful balance is to ascribe our achievements not only to our own efforts, but to the gifts with which God has endowed us and the support of all those who have nurtured us. The arrogant man is always an ingrate. He is not only full of himself, but also shows no appreciation to all those who have facilitated his success. Cultivating the art of gratitude is the most useful means by which to guarantee that our ambition will always be a blessing to us, as we shall explore in the next chapter.

20

Gratitude

OVERCOMING THE IMPULSE TO SELFISHNESS

Ingratitude is treason to mankind.

James Thomson

Gratitude is not only the greatest of virtues, but the parent of all others.

Cicero

Gratitude is one of those emotions that begins strongly but then slowly weakens. When someone does us a favour, we initially feel immensely grateful. It would make sense that if they do the favour once and we feel grateful, if they did it fifteen times, we would be fifteen times more grateful. But the truth is that the more times someone does the same favour for us, the more we come to expect it.

When my wife gave birth to our first child, I was so grateful for the blessing she had brought into our life that I went out and bought a huge, expensive bouquet of flowers. I spent all my time in the hospital with her, and when she came home, I did the vast majority of housework. The same was basically true for our second daughter. But by the time our third was born, I was much busier with work, so I went to the hospital only in the mornings and the evenings. In addition, when my wife came home, I was not as helpful as before, so I hired a nanny to fill in for my absence. It was only when my mother came to see her new granddaughter that she told me how warped my thinking was. 'If you showed appreciation for Debbie when she had one child, do you realize how much more appreciation you have to show when you have three? It's simple mathematics, Shmuley.'

I thought to myself, 'That's easy for you to say, Mom, because you don't have to change the nappies, forgetting for a moment that she had changed mine.' But her point was well taken.

Gratitude as thanks

There are three levels of gratitude: thanks, trust and truth. The first level is simply to offer thanks to someone who has shown us kindness. If we are indebted to someone, we must have the courtesy to both acknowledge and show it. The emphasis is on the *recipient* of the favour to do the right thing. Remarkably, the Bible even teaches that this applies to thanks owed to animals and inanimate objects that help us in some way.

For example, because the River Nile saved him from slaughter when he was a baby, no less a personality than Moses was forbidden to transform the river into blood. Therefore God visited the first of the ten plagues upon the Egyptians through his brother Aaron instead. Similarly, because Moses was indebted to the dust of Egypt for saving his life when he buried the Egyptian taskmaster who beat the Hebrew slave, Moses was forbidden in the third plague to strike the dust and change it into lice. God again enlisted Aaron in his stead.

I have my own experience of gratitude for an inanimate object. Because my parents quarrelled much when I was a child, I would in my morning prayers ask God to help them get along better. One time, my father called home in the late afternoon to tell my mother that the old jalopy of a delivery truck he drove had broken down. He needed my mother to go to where he was and have her car push his truck back home. My parents certainly could not afford the expense of a tow-truck, and I was afraid that if my mother's car could not do the job, my parents would have another argument. I prayed to God that her car, half the size of my father's truck, would be strong enough for the task. We all went with my mother. Little by little, her small car pushed the big truck all the way home. My parents had averted an argument, and I was ecstatic.

I remember going to her car after everyone had gone inside and thanking it from the bottom of my heart. I even kissed its forward chrome bumper. Of course, you can dismiss this action as the naïve behaviour of a six-year-old. Or you can view it as the innocent gesture of someone uncorrupted by cynicism who was simply offering thanks for services rendered.

Gratitude as trust

The second level of gratitude is where the emphasis is not on the recipient but on the *provider* of the favour. We all have a moral obligation to ensure that a benefactor does not become cynical by feeling taken advantage of. If we expose ourselves to someone else to give them love, but they rip out our heart, we feel abused and will not be as trusting or giving the next time around.

Women who have been in abusive relationships find it very difficult to trust men again. Whereas they were once soft, these women become hard after their terrible experiences, warriors who protect themselves from all men. The net result is that they cannot conduct a successful relationship. Instead, they learn to do something highly unnatural: they reconcile themselves to living on their own. It is not that they enjoy loneliness, but they think the pain of loneliness not as bad as the pain of betrayal.

Showing gratitude upholds trust in human relationships and society at large. Remember the movie *The First Wives' Club*? We all identify with the scorn of a woman who has been abandoned by a husband who can show no gratitude. The saying goes, 'He owed his success to his first wife, and his second wife to his success.' How many men make it to the top only to trade in the wife who stood by them when they had little money or prestige? This, in turn, leads otherwise benevolent women to be less giving in relationships. If we want someone to trust us, we must show them that we do not take them for granted.

Gratitude as truth

The highest level of gratitude involves giving credit where credit is due. It is about establishing the truth. Until now, we have painted gratitude as a moral imperative to show thanks and an ethical responsibility to foster trust. However, gratitude is more than this: it is truth itself.

Dimitri was a medical student who came to Oxford from the USA with his wife Esther, a lawyer. While Dimitri was doing advanced research on mad cow disease, he was entirely supported by Esther. Every morning, she would take the 6 a.m. bus to London in order to arrive at her law firm by 8. After a full day of tedious law work, she would take the bus back and get home by 10 p.m. Esther undertook this onerous task with glee because she loved her husband and knew that, given enough years of research, he would become an outstanding doctor.

Esther's long absences led Dimitri to become close with Penelope, a young doctor at the hospital. Their relationship started with innocent lunches but quickly escalated into a full-blown affair. It didn't take Esther long to find out. Devastated by her husband's infidelity, she promptly flew back to her parents in the USA.

I told Dimitri that he had to get on the first plane and try to win his wife back. 'You owe her everything,' I told him, 'and this is a pretty pathetic way of showing your gratitude.' But Dimitri just didn't get it. 'It's not just I who owe her. She also owes me. There was plenty that I did for her too.'

Here Dimitri showed his shallow understanding of gratitude. In his mind, gratitude meant showing thanks. His wife did things for him, and he did things for her. He showed his thanks, and now that she was angry at him, he could turn his back on her and just move on. The truth was, however, that Dimitri was nothing without his wife. His success was her success. He owed her everything. By paying homage to his wife and showing her love and fidelity, he was not just showing his thanks but establishing the truth.

Human beings love to be original and hate having to borrow ideas from somebody else. We delight in the ingenuity of our success and love it when we can take sole credit for some great achievement. Showing gratitude is therefore as unnatural as being monogamous. In both instances, we are robbed of novelty. The imperative to show gratitude is, therefore, one that compels us to always tell the truth, despite the consequences for our originality.

Many Oxford students come from wealthy and accomplished families. This naturally gives them a head start on the other students, but they hate it when people point it out. If they get into Oxford, it's on their own merit. If they get a great job, their father had nothing to do with it. Because we all want to be our own person, we are prepared to compromise truth in the name of originality.

It is for this reason that the Talmud teaches that we must publicly attribute a source when quoting someone else's material not only in a speech or essay but even in everyday conversation: 'He who learns from his fellow man even one chapter, one rule, one verse, one expression or even one single letter, must pay him honor' (*The Ethics of the Fathers*). The ancient Rabbis further said that 'All who quote the name of the person whose material they are using bring salvation to the world.'

Anyone who is a public speaker will know the terrible temptation not to attribute sources of jokes, quotes and their best lines. However, by withholding that information you are guilty not only of not showing gratitude, but of lying. Thus, the ultimate reason to show gratitude is the preservation of truth.

Gratitude for our existence

If we are obligated to attribute the source of our information, we must certainly attribute the source of our very existence. Indeed, the Bible's grave insistence on honouring our parents at all times is ultimately predicated on the idea of gratitude. Because our parents have endowed us with the ultimate blessing of life, our existence must always stand humbled by that gift.

Unfortunately, however, children today will catalogue a thousand and one ways in which their parents have short-changed them. These childish complaints overlook the simple fact that without their parents, there would be no 'them' to hurt. In incorporating the commandment to honour one's parents, the Bible is thereby establishing the fact that one of the ten most important rules of holy living is always to show gratitude.

The Rabbis teach that our feelings of gratitude to our parents are the means by which we come to experience similar feelings, at an even greater level of intensity, towards God, our ultimate parent. The first words a Jew is supposed to utter upon awakening, for example, are of gratitude: 'I gratefully thank You, O living and eternal King, for You have returned my soul within me with compassion.' Even upon hearing bad news, we praise God for being the true judge of the world.

The holiest day of the Jewish calendar is Yom Kippur, the Day of Atonement. On this very serious day, all material pleasure is prohibited: food, drink, sex – you name it. It is a day on which man emulates an angelic existence by refraining from all sorts of material dependency. So what do Jews do over this twenty-four hour period? We go to the synagogue and pray. And why? To teach us an important lesson. Throughout the course of the year, we can easily be led to believe that what sustains us in life is the physical: food, money, possessions. Yom Kippur, however, serves as the supreme reminder that we are ultimately dependent on God alone, and therefore have an obligation to show gratitude.

Similarly, Maimonides argued that the rationale behind the commandment to pray was for man always to acknowledge his dependency on God, even for his most basic daily requirements. As the Bible teaches us:

He humbled you by letting you hunger, then by feeding you with manna, with which neither you nor your ancestors were acquainted, in order to make you understand that one does not live by bread alone but by every word that comes from the mouth of the Lord. (Deuteronomy 8:3 NRSV)

Ingratitude is self-worship

We may thus understand how one of the greatest insults possible in the Jewish religion is to refer to someone as a *kafuy tov*, an ingrate. Judaism spurns the ungrateful person who refuses to acknowledge that he is the beneficiary of someone else's love and kindness. There is, in fact, a direct correlation between ingratitude and idolatry.

Judaism's principal goal from its inception has been to uproot idolatry and instill the knowledge of God deep in the human heart and in the four corners of the earth. Of course, rare is the person who worships idols in the way their pagan ancestors did, prostrate before lead or marble. Idolatry is, however, still alive and kicking in the great secular religion of the ego, where worshipping idols has been replaced with worshipping the self. Few people today feel the need to give thanks to God. Instead, they pat themselves on the back and say, 'My power and the might of my own hand have gotten me this wealth' (Deuteronomy 8:17).

The essence of gratitude, however, is to establish the truth by acknowledging that our success is the result not of our own effort but of the collaboration of many others, beginning with the Almighty Himself and continuing with those in our lives who have showered us with the love and confidence to go forward. Gratitude constitutes our ability to be touched by someone else and thereby build a relationship. It is when we understand that whatever gifts we have in life are really loans, which we repay by giving thanks, by establishing trust. Every person wants to be recognized. And when they do something good, they have a right to derive pleasure from it and feel good about it. To rob someone of the satisfaction of goodness is a great crime.

Just think about all that our parents do for us. Until I became a parent myself, I had no idea what a Herculean feat it was to support a family. We take a lot of garbage from a boss just to earn a pay cheque. After a hard day's work, we come home with no energy left and sit down to do homework with one kid after another. All that a parent wants in return is for the child to love him, respect him and never judge him. He does not want rent or a promissary note for a percentage of the child's later income. He just wants to be assured that he will be always accorded a portion in his child's life.

When friends fall out

What destroys gratitude? When after someone does us a million favours, showing endless encouragement, they do one thing wrong and we forget all the rest. I see this all the time. It's called 'falling out'.

Justin and Webb were best friends who started a restaurant together. They had a big fight over the issue of live entertainment and would not speak to each other first for months and then years. When some of their friends tried to reconcile them, each pointed out the animosity that had been generated over this last incident. 'But don't you think that one incident pales in comparison to all the good things your friend did for you?' No way. That argument did not work because whether or not we are obligated to show gratitude is in our minds entirely dependent on our last interaction with someone. We rarely look at a relationship in its entirety.

This is why so many people show little gratitude to their

parents. Instead of focusing on twenty-five years of nurturing, they focus only on the big fight they had with their parents over money or the guy or girl they were dating. As soon as that happens, their entire memory is wiped blank. Of course, they hurt only themselves. The person who is not prepared to acknowledge the goodness that others perform on their behalf is condemned to loneliness.

Arrogance: the opposite of gratitude

If gratitude means that we recognize the role another plays in our success, its opposite is arrogance. Arrogance is when we think that we alone are responsible for the success we enjoy. As such, it is the most egocentric of all the emotions. It is also one of the most unhealthy, leading directly to mental illness and possibly mental breakdown as the mind begins to crumble under the weight of its own sense of self-importance.

Arrogant people always think of themselves in a detached way as if they were objective bystanders peering down at themselves. They always wonder what it is like for other people to meet them. I remember how this happened to me when I first published *Kosher Sex*. Never having assumed the book would enjoy the popularity it did, I was unprepared for the crowds that came to see me whenever I lectured on it. I gave one lecture in London where they expected about fifty people and nearly seven hundred came. I still remember walking down the street thinking a most unhealthy thought: 'There goes this noted author. He's walking down the street.' It was like I was two different people: the normal, humble me that had existed before and this new arrogant me that the old me was watching. It felt awkward; it felt shameful; and I knew it had to stop.

Many celebrities think of themselves in this highly self-conscious way. If they do not get the right table at the restaurant, they tell the *maître d'*, 'Do you know who I am?' They have an internal and an external self: the part of them which is natural and the part of them which is this star. But the fact that someone can actually think of themselves as a detached person shows a corrosion in the integration of mind and body.

Arrogance ultimately signifies the denial of God. Indeed, the opposite of theism is not atheism but arrogance. The more someone bloats himself up, the more he denies God. He becomes his own maker and his own authority. He feels beholden to none but himself.

The ripple effect of ingratitude

Ingratitude is problematic not only because it isolates and wrongfully inflates the ego of the ingrate, but especially because it leads to diminished acts of kindness. After all, most people's natural reaction to dealing with an ingrate is to swear that they will never practise another act of kindness. Indeed, nothing undoes our desire to help people more than when we feel taken advantage of and unappreciated. Thus, one person's ingratitude is a dangerous event that pours over onto the entire community since it lessens our natural desire to assist a fellow man.

Charlie and Helen were a middle-aged couple who owned a house in Oxford. After their kids moved out, they rented out several rooms to lodgers, one of whom was a young widower named Helmut, whose wife had been killed in a rock-climbing accident. Helmut had a young daughter, Julia, but at first he moved in without her because Charlie and Helen would not allow children. Later, however, when Helmut asked if he could bring Julia to stay with him, Charlie and Helen did not have the heart to say no. Everyone warned them that the landlord–tenant law strongly favoured a father with kids and that they were putting themselves at a significant disadvantage. Still, they thought this was the right thing and agreed to the family being reunited under their roof.

The father and daughter lived in the house comfortably for two years. But when Charlie and Helen informed Helmut that they were selling their house in order to move closer to their recently married daughter, Helmut refused to move

221

out. They gave him three months' notice, but he went to the local housing council and complained that he and his daughter had no place to live. The council sided with him, and Helmut remained there for months on end. Because of Helmut's intransigence, Charlie and Helen were unable to sell their home. After they lost three prospective buyers, the price of their house plummeted. It took them two more years to get Helmut to move out. Exhausted with their ordeal, Charlie and Helen swore they would never help another person again.

Taking advantage of our parents

In the Bible, there is a curious commandment whereby long life is promised for the simple act of sending away a mother bird who is sitting atop her young in her nest. One is allowed to take the eggs, but only after the mother bird has been sent away. Why so great a reward for so seemingly inconsequential an act? The explanation is that every mother possesses a motherly instinct, and in order to protect her young she renders herself vulnerable. Capturing her while she sits on her chicks is relatively easy because she will not abandon them even at the expense of her own capture or destruction. God tells us that we cannot capture her while she is caring for her young because we cannot take advantage of her devotion to her eggs.

It is like the difference between the following two robberies. A man walks down a dark alley and gets mugged. He is very upset, but at worst the consequence is that he will never walk down a dark alley again. The second man walks down a dark alley and sees an old man in front of him keel over with a heart attack. He rushes to his aid and tries to give him mouth-to-mouth resuscitation. Just as he does so, the old man puts a knife to his rescuer's throat and demands that he hand over his money – the rescuer swears never to help another person again.

Nietzsche objected to goodness because it makes us soft and vulnerable. Love makes us put down our defences. And when we get hurt specifically through loving, we swear to ourselves, 'I will never let my guard down again.' Slowly but surely, we harden our hearts into stone in order to protect ourselves.

As one of five children raised by a single mother who worked two jobs to support us, I know precisely what the Bible means. Children raised in single-parent homes often exploit the vulnerability of their parents. And my mother was so starved for the love of her children, whose custody she fought so hard to procure, that we knew we could take advantage of her softness. We could extort from her the exorbitant allowance that our friends received, even though she did not have the money to give it. We ignored her protestations to do our homework, knowing that she would never follow through on her threats to punish us. And we left her alone on Saturday nights while we went out with our friends, knowing full well that no matter how much selfishness we exhibited, she would always remain selfless.

I write these lines with profound pain in my heart knowing that at that time I hurt the woman who showed me infinite devotion. Sure, I was only a kid, but I still did not reciprocate her immense devotion and can only try to make amends now. (And I try to do that, by bringing her grandchildren to see her as much as possible since you can enjoy grandchildren without having to assume the responsibility or the work.)

Many of us are, lamentably, guilty of the same thing. Indeed, while we would not dare scream at our friends for fear of abandonment, we are prepared to yell at our parents because we know they would never forsake us. I remember, when studying to be a Rabbi, discovering the teaching that said the way we treat our parents is the manner in which our own children will treat us. 'Whooaaa . . .,' I thought, 'I'm in big trouble.' I was terrified because I knew that, as a son, I had taken advantage of a supremely good and vulnerable woman who would do anything to advance my welfare.

What a little thank you can do

If ingratitude leads to diminished kindness in the world, the converse is fortunately also true: hearing or reading the words 'thank you' encourages us to continue performing acts of kindness. The opposite of a *kafuy tov* is a *makir tov*, a grateful person. A *makir tov* shows gratitude for the good efforts that have been made on her behalf. As a result, she increases acts of goodness because, when people see how much their sacrifice is appreciated, they desire to do even more.

I often agree to trudge out to some city at the end of the earth to give a lecture. The invitation will come to speak to four old men and a goat in Armpit, Nowheresville. I'll agree to go because I think to myself, 'Stop being arrogant and only going for the prestigious venues.' Then as the day approaches, I regret my decision and think of a million ways to cancel: 'I can call them and tell them I died. No, I had better get my secretary to tell them that.' Or, 'I'll tell them the real me was abducted by aliens and if they want the real me to speak, they'll have to pay the round-trip airfare from Alpha Centauri.'

But then, unable to come up with a believable excuse, I drag my tired bones all the way to Armpit. Sure enough, the only people who have turned up are four guys and a goat, but I am not dissuaded. I will make no compromises in my delivery. I speak for forty minutes as if I were speaking to a crowd of at least ten. At the end, they offer me heartfelt thanks, and that really does make it all worthwhile. It's incredible, and it happens every time.

Gratitude is, therefore, the necessary pause that must come in between acts of goodness in order to further our desire to continue such acts. In the same way that being taken advantage of makes us hard, being shown gratitude makes us soft. A little gratitude can transform a heart of stone to a heart of flesh. It can literally turn an enemy into a friend overnight.

Gratitude in our relationships

This is the single greatest lesson of relationships. When God gives Adam Eve as a partner, the Bible describes her as *kenegdo*, a 'partner against him'. However, 'partner' seems to be undermined by 'against him'. What is the difference between a wife who serves as a partner and one who serves 'against' her husband? The difference is discerned only in how much gratitude is shown.

I have watched many couples fall in love and marry. At first all goes well, but when the pressures of everyday living begin to encroach, they forget to take the time to show each other appreciation. The result is two people who live together but who begin to resent each other. Soon, they are at each other's throats instead of in each other's arms.

Katie and Peter had been married for two years and had a baby girl. One night, we were all guests at a dinner party hosted by a mutual friend, Janine. Throughout the dinner, we watched in amazement as Katie unrelentingly disparaged Peter. She was so verbally abusive that it soured the entire meal for the rest of us.

After dinner, a despondent Peter came over to me and said, 'Look, the truth is we didn't just come for dinner. Janine told us that you counsel couples and I thought you might be able to help us. You can probably see from Katie's invective what the problem is.' In Peter's mind, their troubles were entirely caused by Katie's mean-spiritedness. He gave absolutely no thought, however, to what could have so turned his wife against him. I offered to speak to Katie the following afternoon.

Katie immediately admitted her mouth was out of control. 'I know I'm wrong for my behaviour. But doesn't Peter understand that this is all a cry to get his attention? When we dated I used to love him so much. He was the most caring guy in the whole world. But after we married, I gave up my career to look after Suzanne, and since then he has become the biggest ingrate in the world. He comes home and the TV goes straight on. I also need someone to talk to. I'm going crazy at home listening to *Sesame Street*.' 'Does he ever thank you for all the sacrifices you've made?', I asked. 'Thank me?' she responded incredulously. 'Why, he barely knows I'm alive.'

While her hurt feelings did not justify Katie's behaviour, it was Peter who was responsible for turning a loving partner against him. The old saying 'Hell hath no fury like a woman scorned' should be amended to 'Even hell is a pleasant place compared to a woman ignored.'

I told Peter, 'The situation is easily salvageable. You have to show your wife extravagant love over the next few months. Go to the opposite extreme. Give her too much attention. Make her the centre of your world, and you'll win her back. And it won't be hard to do. Call her up during the day and thank her for being such a great wife and mother. Bring her flowers at night. Three times a year, go away for the weekend and leave the baby with your parents. Above all else, show gratitude for everything she does for you and take nothing for granted.'

At first Peter listened to my advice, and for a few months the relationship improved. But then he reverted to his old ways and decided to remarry the television. His wife, fed up with this silicon mistress, fell in love with the car mechanic, ran off and lived happily ever after. Peter, of course, did not, but he still has his remote.

21

Compassion

WHAT MAKES US BOTH DIVINE AND HUMAN

No deep and strong feeling, such as we may come across here, is unmixed with compassion. The more we love, the more the object of our love seems to be a victim.

Boris Pasternak

We hand folks over to God's mercy, and show none ourselves.

George Eliot

Men and women today judge their success in terms of material prosperity rather than the quality of their relationships. Indeed, a man who is the chairman of a major multinational corporation is considered a success even if he is on his third marriage and his children from marriages one and two refuse to speak to him. No one seems to consider that you are hardly a success when the people who mean the most to you think the least of you.

So many of the young women at Oxford complain to me that men are no longer romantic. They long for the gentle guys who know how to treat a woman kindly. Yet, whenever I find just this kind of guy for them, one who has a job working as a part-time nightwatchman, they show absolutely no interest. 'What happened to the guy you were going to introduce me to who works at Goldman Sachs?', they ask. 'Oh,' I respond, 'you mean the one who works twenty-hour days and travels six months of the year?' It seems hypocritical for them to complain that no guy believes in love, when all they are interested in are the big earners.

This cultural conditioning begins in childhood. After all, how much more energy is concentrated on what our children will do professionally than on how they will turn out emotionally? How many parents say that they do not care whether little Joey becomes a street sweeper so long as he is a kind and compassionate person? Indeed, in today's dog-eat-dog world, compassion is often seen as a sign of weakness.

Contrary to today's Wall Street norms, Judaism teaches us to measure our assets not by the quantity in our bank account but by the quality of our relationships with our fellow man and with God. When appraising our success, we should look not at what we own but at the number of close friends we have and the contribution we make to the lives of others. Isn't that what will be mentioned in our eulogy? The ancient Rabbis taught: 'Anyone with whom his fellow men are pleased, God is pleased with him; but anyone with whom his fellow men are not pleased, God is not pleased with him' (*Ethics of our Fathers* 3:10). From this point of view, compassion is far from weakness. Indeed, it is one of our most humanizing attributes because it draws us outside the shell of our individual egos and connects us with humanity.

Abraham, paragon of compassion

The first Jew was Abraham, but Noah would initially appear to be a more probable candidate for the job. After all, in addition to the fact that Noah preceded Abraham, he was also the only one chosen to be saved while the entire human race perished. Indeed, the Bible attests to the fact that Noah was redeemed because he was a *tzadik*, a righteous man. The Rabbis of the Talmud, however, were very critical of Noah, and their negative view seems to be corroborated by the simple fact that the world had to wait another ten generations for Abraham to be found worthy enough to sire a nation that would be given the divine mission of disseminating ethical monotheism. So why is Noah the father of humanity but not of the Jewish nation?

Both men are faced in their lifetime with the prospect of wide-scale destruction, but their reactions differ radically. When the Almighty informs Noah of His intention to destroy the earth's inhabitants because they have 'corrupted their ways on the earth', Noah makes no objection. He bows his head, resigned to the fact that earth's inhabitants are doomed to drown.

Can you believe this? Imagine if it were you. God comes to you and says, 'I'm going to nuke the world. Everyone will be toast. But don't worry because I'm going to place you and your family in a nuclear bunker where you will be safe.' What would you say? Thanks for saving my skin while incinerating six billion other people? Yet this is Noah's reaction. He feels fortunate and begins to construct his ark as commanded. Upon disembarking from the ark, Noah's first action is to a plant a vineyard from which he later becomes intoxicated. Like modern man, Noah's very first impulse after survival is the pursuit of personal gratification.

Abraham, in stark contrast, never places his personal pleasure above the plight of others. When God reveals His plan to destroy nearby Sodom and Gomorrah with a terrifying display of fire and brimstone, Abraham does not resign himself to their suffering and head on to greener pastures. Although he knows that the inhabitants of both cities are deserving of their fate, and they have a pernicious influence on the rest of society, Abraham nevertheless objects. He lifts his fists to the heavens and exclaims, 'Will not the Judge of the entire earth also practise justice?'

As the world's first defence attorney, Abraham defends even those who seem indefensible. He begins by negotiating with the Almighty to cut a deal: 'Perhaps there are fifty ... forty ... thirty ... twenty ... ten righteous men in the city', by whose merit the rest can be saved. So now it seems obvious why Abraham is the first Jew: he has *chutzpah*! First he dictates to the Judge of the entire earth how to administer justice and then he tries to bargain with Him. What nerve! He places the welfare of others before his own.

But *chutzpah* is not the reason why Abraham fathered the Jewish nation. Rather, he had compassion. While Noah was concerned only with his own welfare, Abraham was concerned with that of the entire world, trying to recruit others to the calling of goodness. Indeed, Abraham was chosen as the first Jew because he understood the principal calling of the Jewish people: to serve as a light unto the nations and teach the world about God, morality and loving kindness

Compassion liberates us from selfishness

Compassion is perhaps the most pivotal of all Jewish values, and Abraham distinguished himself primarily by his compassion for all living things. Indeed, even while in terrible pain from his circumcision, he demonstrated unparalleled hospitality: 'And Abraham lifted his eyes and saw three strangers. He ran to meet them . . . and pressed them to enter his tent. "Let a little water, I pray you, be fetched, and wash your feet, and rest yourselves under a tree. And I will fetch a morsel of bread and comfort your hearts." ' Abraham could have had his servants go in his stead but he wanted to perform the kindness himself. His compassion was so great that it sprung him out of his own shoes and into those of his guests.

Abraham's example of hospitality was so venerable that it is to this day commemorated at every Jewish wedding. When a couple marry, they stand under a canopy, a *chupah*, which consists of a roof with no walls. This teaches us that, like their patriarch Abraham, the couple should strive to build a home without boundaries, a home that is open to guests and strangers alike. So often a couple's love becomes exclusive rather than inclusive, and through their love for each other, they learn to shut the world out. At the Jewish wedding ceremony, we aim to counter that inclination. Moreover, because the attribute of compassion is considered to be a genetic inheritance to all Jews from

Abraham, Maimonides, in an extraordinary legal ruling, wrote that the lineage of any person who claims to be Jewish and yet demonstrates mean-spiritedness should be checked.

We again find this compassionate reaction in one of Abraham's most illustrious descendants, the prophet Moses. When informed by the Almighty of His intent to devour the Jewish nation for their sin of the golden calf, Moshe lays his life on the line in one of the most dramatic showdowns of the Bible: 'If you do not forgive their sin . . . blot me out, I pray you, from the Torah which you have written' (Ibid 32:32). Where else in the history of apocalyptic literature does a person have the gall to admonish the Author of the universe and demand that his name be removed from his divine work rather than be associated with failing the victim?

Religious man is sensitized to the bonds that unite humanity

Like Abraham, *homo religiosus* – religious man – is someone whose entire life is dedicated towards acts of kindness. Having experienced the pervasive influence of the sublime in all matters, religious man is sensitized to the spark of God that lurks within created matter, especially human beings. As such, he feels a kinship with all of creation, demonstrating compassion also for plant and animal life.

The Czech writer Milan Kundera said that our civilization will ultimately be judged by how we treat our animals because they are defenceless. However, the Bible preceded Kundera by a few thousand years when it comes to protecting animal rights. Indeed, it instructs us to show the same solicitude for animals that we show our human brethren, the mandate for which is summarized in the Talmudic phrase, '[relieving] the suffering of an animal is a biblical law'. We are thus, for example, commanded to raise up an animal that is prostrate under its load. The intricate laws of kosher and animal slaughter were also designed to prevent the animal suffering what is otherwise a very painful death.

231

Indeed, a Jew is not permitted to hunt for sport because we are allowed neither to destroy animal life indiscriminately nor to inflict pain callously.

It is interesting to note that, according to Midrashic literature, both Moses and David were chosen to lead Israel because of their kindness to animals. So many mistakenly believe that the first trait of leadership is courage or fearlessness. What we see here is that the real hallmark of leadership is compassion.

By the same token, the Bible is filled with verses imploring man to show compassion to the earth. Not only are we forbidden to cut down trees unnecessarily, but we are actually commanded to celebrate the New Year for the Trees, the festival *Tu Bishvat*. Indeed, perhaps the greatest statement of the Torah demonstrating humankind's kinship with nature is the verse in Deuteronomy (20:19): 'For the tree of the field is man's life'. Just as we must never take a human life for granted, so too must we appreciate nature for the bounty it gives us.

Finally, one of the gravest prohibitions in the code of Jewish law is *baal tashchis* – to waste or destroy anything useful for human consumption or utility. I remember how strongly my father would admonish us whenever we threw out good bread. Compassion towards the earth means that we are all environmentalists because we care about what happens in the world and act upon that sentiment.

Judgementalism: the enemy of compassion

Although compassion is one characteristic of the faithful, so all too often is its opposite, judgementalism. This occurs because people wrongly assume it is their role to arbitrate over the less meritorious. But if religion should humble us, why are there so many judges and juries in the camps of the believers? Why is there malice rather than mercy, cruelty instead of compassion?

Judgementalism is the very antithesis of the religious experience. At its essence, it is closely related to religious extremism and, like its often violent cousin, is disturbingly on the rise. It seems ironic that one of the first steps of many Jews who return to their roots is feeling threatened by what they see as the licentiousness of secular culture, to judge the values of those who are less observant. Instead of going out to the world with their positive message from a position of strength and confidence, they prefer to retreat to an insular world buttressed by fear of the outside.

Similarly, in the USA, the Christian Right spends much of its time condemning the loose mores of the population in general and Hollywood in particular. Now, it is not that I agree with the negative influence that film and television have on our lives today, but I do not think that judgementalism is the way to combat it.

I have always hated judgementalism, believing it to be one of the ugliest of all human character traits. The judgemental person, with little humanity, does not seek to share with their fellow man but to condemn him. Few things are as off-putting as people who show scant regard for the average person's daily struggles and rush to dismiss them with impunity.

The purpose of religion is from a Jewish perspective not to condemn the world as it is but to offer a positive yet realistic vision of the way the world ought to be. Rather than judging people unfavourably, religion should show them a glorious vision of what they can become. Moreover, religion must inspire people to realize that vision or at the very least take a few small steps in the right direction.

Most importantly, religion should provide a means by which the individual can draw closer to God. And it would seem logical to assume that the closer one draws to God, the more awed one becomes with God's perfection and the more humble one becomes. Indeed, the truly spiritual person finds it difficult to dismiss any person or thing because she perceives God to be wherever her eyes roam.

Changing the world one kind act at a time

People who are judgemental clearly have not learned the lesson of Abraham because what is most evident from studying Abraham's life is his refusal to judge others. Indeed, Abraham sees himself as a defence attorney not a prosecutor. Judaism firmly asserts that there is only one Judge, the Almighty Himself. Therefore, our task is to serve not as judges but as agents of understanding and clemency.

The Talmud states that when God created the world, He initially decided that justice would be the operative attribute within His creation. However, because He foresaw that the world could not endure on justice alone, He mixed with it the attribute of mercy. Thus, in the spirit of *imitatio dei* we must always seek to promote loving kindness.

How do we achieve this positive yet realistic balance? By having compassion on others, never by judging them – although by all means, judge their actions. Do not merely condemn the wrong way, but in kindness show your fellow man the right way: we all know that positive reinforcement is far more successful and life-affirming than its negative counterpart. So don't accuse people of violating the Sabbath; like Abraham, invite them into your home to share the Sabbath with you. Don't blame Hollywood for teaching children violence; be an involved parent not just in your own family but in your community as well, modelling goodness and holiness in word and deed for all.

Remember, because God is compassionate and we are all created in His image, compassion is one of the emotions that makes us most human and most Godly at the same time. Therefore, compassion, sharing and love should be the guiding principles of our lives, and through this we will become a blessing to our immediate circle of influence and all humanity.

22

Happiness

THE MOST ELUSIVE EMOTION

Happiness is a perfume you cannot pour on others without getting a few drops on yourself.
Ralph Waldo Emerson

There is no duty we so much underrate as the duty of being happy.
Robert Louis Stevenson

———————————

For many years, I believed that happiness was a foreign god and an unworthy goal. I thought that happiness meant inner contentment, and that inner contentment was nothing more than a recipe for ordinariness and mediocrity. Why should we try to be happy if it would make us lose our hunger for greatness? I also used to think that because the pursuit of noble goals in life often entails pain and sacrifice, what right do we have to be happy? Happiness in my opinion was weak, the very opposite of lofty ambition and aspiration.

Since then, however, I have radically shifted my views. I now understand what true happiness is and how it is part and parcel of achieving noble goals. I was mistaken in believing that happiness had no redeeming qualities. And I was gravely mistaken when I thought that happiness was about selfishness. The truth is that only the selfless can achieve happiness. Let me explain.

The elusive nature of happiness

Although the American Constitution tells us that its pursuit is our inalienable right, no goal is more difficult to achieve than happiness. The disparity between how strongly we wish to be happy and how seldom we achieve this is truly astonishing. Consider one of the greatest paradoxes of our generation: although we are materially far better off than our ancestors, few if any would say that we are happier. Indeed, many people today would agree with the words of the prophet Jeremiah in the Book of Lamentations (3:17): 'My soul is bereft of peace; I have forgotten what happiness is.'

Unlike children, adults seem to need a reason to be happy. In a recent poll, published in the *International Herald Tribune*, 67 per cent of all Americans admitted that they were 'unhappy' much of the time, some 30 per cent admitting being 'significantly unhappy' more than half the time. These figures alone are staggering, but add to them the statistics on depression, and we have an epidemic of discontent.

One reason for happiness eluding us is that we tend to make its existence contingent upon future success. Students often tell me they will be happy if only they pass their exams, or if they get engaged to the wonderful person they are dating. For a while this anticipatory happiness works, but as soon as their expectations are fulfilled, they need to find other reasons to be happy. In many ways our generation is addicted to happiness like a junkie is to a drug, experiencing a series of brief highs and lows and always waiting for the next fix.

A second reason is that we all too often make happiness contingent upon material pleasure and acquisition. Happiness becomes something outside ourselves and we empower external devices to confer internal happiness upon us. Indeed, an even more astonishing finding of the *International Herald Tribune* poll is that consumerism is the number one way in which people rid themselves of depression: 53 per cent of respondents said that when they were unhappy or depressed they bought themselves something. Your boyfriend broke up with you? Buy a new dress, it will make you feel better. Your boss promoted your secretary instead of you? Go out and buy a new stereo. The logic here is that an object can somehow compensate for hurt feelings.

However, the nature of all this is such that the moment a physical possession has been attained, it immediately beckons us onto other things. Since the satisfaction evaporates so quickly, the curse is one of insatiable desire. Hence, the Rabbis of the Talmud said that a person dies with less than half of their desires fulfilled. What they meant is that our desire persuades us that we will only be happy by doubling our original desire. Indeed, modern man has become a glutton for endless material acquisition and sensual pleasure, as if he were always trying to fill the bottomless pit of his empty existence.

Yet we all know that material possessions are ephemeral and quickly become boring. None of us would ever trade our children for all the money in the world: if we lost all of our possessions we would still recover from financial ruin, but if we lost our children, our lives would be devastated forever. We could still smile somewhere down the road, but never with the same intensity.

Although we need money to support ourselves, it can never bring us any lasting satisfaction because its pleasure is fleeting. Consider the story of Randolph Hearst, the subject of Orson Welles' epic film *Citizen Kane*. Hearst achieved wealth beyond compare from his journalistic enterprise. The hundred odd rooms of the Hearst Castle are to this day filled with the priceless treasures he acquired from his travels around the world. But with all of his money, Hearst could not buy happiness and love. Indeed, all the material pleasures of the world could not fill the void inside him, which was larger than the castle he built.

I once counselled a couple who were fighting largely because of their financial difficulties. In short, the husband spent way too much money. The previous week, he had told his wife that he just *had* to have the Lamborghini sports car his friend was selling. He honestly told her that he would die without it. Of course, just weeks after he had spent a large portion of their savings on this must-have item, he became completely bored and ended up selling it for half the purchase price. As all physical pleasure, even its memory, can only be experienced for a few moments or a few days, it always leaves us vacant, yearning for more.

Compare for a moment physical pleasure with a spiritual pleasure, like a true friendship or enjoying your family. Even after a relative has died, we experience immense joy just thinking about the good times we spent together. Similarly, a rewarding book borrowed from the library will provide deeper and longer-lasting pleasure than any day out shopping.

Perhaps the greatest example of all is sex. Without love, without a soul, sex is instantly forgettable. In many instances, it will even generate pain and disillusionment, embarrassment and regret. But uniting the physical and spiritual aspects of sex brings deep enjoyment and lasting fulfilment. Thus, in terms of depth and longevity, spiritual pleasures are superior to their physical equivalents.

Living in accordance with our inner will

Judaism says that true happiness can come only with complete contentment. Indeed, the very experience of happiness is one of deep and pervasive fulfilment and satisfaction. What brings contentment in life? The end of all internal tension. Man often feels he is a hybrid creature, pulled between heaven and earth. The secret to happiness is a *total integration of self*, all of our contradictory forces – body and soul, mind and heart, emotions and intellect, selfishness and altruism – being brought into harmony. Happiness is where our ambitions and our values meet, where our outermost actions match our innermost convictions, leading to a life of productivity and pride.

The antithesis of happiness – inner tension – is when our

inner and outer selves are at odds with each other. Thus, the less tortured we are on the inside, the more happy we are on the outside. So in order to be happy, we must appease our conscience, which represents our innermost desire to be decent human beings. Thus, people who are wicked may know power and prosperity but they will never know happiness because their actions are at odds with their inner Godly nature.

Imagine a businessman who works day and night to succeed. He commutes three hours a day in order to maintain his palace in the suburbs. Because he often works at night, there are some days that he does not even see his children. On Sundays, he is so tired that he sleeps half the day or he goes to play golf. Consequently, as the kids grow up, his relationship with them is distant. As they become teenagers, this begins to bother him. After all, what is the point of having a beautiful home if the family is never together to enjoy it? What is the point of the luxurious car if everyone heads their own way all the time? Pangs of conscience tear him apart and he regrets that he did not spend more time with them.

How should he make amends? Although one can never make up for wasted time, he should immediately attempt to repair his relationship with his children in any way possible. This would bring harmony to his simultaneous desires to prosper materially and be close to his children. After all, without a family to benefit from his exertions, of what use is his sacrifice? Therefore, his relationship with his children serves as both the engine of his success and the key to nurturing his soul. By pursuing this noble goal, he synchronizes his inner and outer desires.

Unfortunately, instead of recognizing that what our children need is more of our time, most parents try to compensate for their absence with more toys or more money. We try to replace ourselves with objects and hope this will suffice. Amazingly, we do this even with the smallest of infants. Ninety per cent of the gadgets for sale in a baby store are mechanical stand-ins for parents: the mechanical

swing, the infant carrier, the bouncy chair, all are replace-
ments for human arms. And sadly, we continue to raise our
children by keeping ourselves at arm's length. Instead of
addressing the deeper needs of our relationship with them,
we all too often place superficial salves on internal wounds
and later wonder why our relationships have broken down.

Happiness is a balancing act

I do not believe that people who lived in monasteries knew
happiness. They might have felt inspired by their religious
devotions, and might have achieved a certain inner peace.
However, because they denied their physical needs, I maintain they could not have been happy. The ascetic chooses
to live a life of principles but, in doing so, robs himself of
any possibility of inner and outer integration. Rather than
bringing all of himself under a canopy of harmony, he
decides instead to kill part of himself off.

At the other end of the spectrum, our generation finds
happiness elusive because, as the first great secular age, we
are obsessed with our bodies and virtually ignore the needs
of our souls. Again, an unhealthy imbalance is created. Gyms
today show a better attendance than churches and synagogues. Similarly, we spend infinitely more time choosing
our clothing than pondering our values or in meditation or
prayer. Of this kind of happiness, King Solomon wrote in
the Book of Ecclesiastes (2:2), 'What use is it?' And we might
add, 'How long does it last?'

I once appeared on a television show to debate commitment-free relationships. The question posed was whether
women could enjoy commitment-free sex as freely and
easily as men. A divorced mother of three children called
up and said that she was having casual sex with two men.
She didn't love them, and they didn't love her. She was
happy with the situation because it did not interfere with
raising her children.

My response to her was that every person has a body and
a soul. The body craves sex and the soul human intimacy.

While the sex she was having might bring sensual pleasure, it would never bring her true happiness since it did not fuse together her body and soul. 'Tell me,' I asked her, 'would you not be much happier if you had one decent man who offered himself to you as a faithful husband and made you feel like the most desirable woman in the world?'

We often forget that there are levels of happiness. What this woman was experiencing was the very lowest level, consisting of ephemeral distractions that allowed her to forget her pain, like going to a movie. But happiness pursued in the form of physical pleasures virtually excludes the needs of the soul. And this is not real happiness.

Uniting the body and soul

Happiness means leading a life of balance in which each of our needs is satisfied without overwhelming one or starving another. In the same way that man cannot be happy while suffering extreme heat or cold, he cannot be happy indulging in spiritual or physical extremes. However, the most assured road to happiness comes not from addressing the needs of the body and then the needs of the soul in a distinct and compartmentalized way, but by catering to both simultaneously. How do we do this? By undertaking activities that bring about internal and external harmony as part of the same effort.

Going to the gym and exercising the body may, for example, make us feel better about ourselves. Leaving the gym and going straight to church or synagogue may satisfy the needs of our soul. But one of the problems with this approach is that it makes us into yo-yos, bouncing from extreme to extreme. Leading a compartmentalized life will not produce lasting happiness. But, unfortunately, this is the way most people spend their lives.

There is a way in which we can nurture both body and soul simultaneously. I call it the integrated path. For example, bike-riding hundreds of miles for the benefit of starving children will bring tremendous satisfaction to body and soul at the same time. Jogging in the fresh air with one's son instead of on an inanimate treadmill in the gym brings far deeper fulfilment. We are not just looking to pump up our bodies; we want to pump up our relationships. Reading a great work of literature and then going to pray will cater first to the mind's need for mental stimulation and then to the soul's need to commune with God, but reading the inspiring stories of the Bible achieves both at the same time. Cordoning off ten per cent of our earnings for the benefit of a deserving charity allows us to satisfy the material needs of ambition while simultaneously ensuring that others profit from our exertions.

Judaism makes every attempt to both recognize and unite the cares of the body and soul. Before we eat a piece of bread, for example, we wash our hands and make a blessing to acknowledge God's provision for us. Thus, in one act we satisfy two hungers. Of this kind of happiness, the deep contentment born of nurturing the body and soul, Solomon said:

> *So I commend happiness, for there is nothing better for people under the sun than to eat, and drink, and enjoy themselves, for this will go with them in their toil through the days of life that God gives them under the sun.* (Ecclesiastes 8:15 NRSV)

Here the ancient Rabbis explain that Solomon was referring to the kind of physical pleasure that involves a spiritual celebration, like the wedding or birth of a child.

Judaism's prime example of an activity that unites the care of body and soul is perhaps observing the Sabbath. Unlike the rest of the week, on the Sabbath we do not wolf down packaged pizza from the microwave on our way to evening meetings and activities. Instead, we prepare special meals consisting of several courses for dinner on Friday night and lunch on Saturday. Even though the meals are delicious, we do not eat like hedonists in pursuit of gourmet pleasure. Instead, we sit like royalty at a beautifully set table surrounded by our family and friends, saying blessings, singing songs and speaking words of Torah. In this way, we elevate the body's need for food by joining it with the soul's need to be with our loved ones and God.

Meaning is essential to happiness

Misery results from a feeling of meaninglessness. There are few things that can snuff out happiness like the feeling that our lives are arbitrary and inconsequential. Even a manual labourer who works in the boiling hot sun fixing roads can achieve a high degree of satisfaction and happiness from his job and his life. If, however, he were to discover that nobody was ever going to drive on that road, if he would be unfulfilled. It is primarily purpose that brings pleasure.

We can only surmount pain positively if we understand its purpose. No mother in the excruciating throes of labour, for example, thinks to herself, 'All this pain, and it's for nothing.' On the contrary, the pain can be managed only because it gives rise to life. But when we endure pain for no purpose, we are easily defeated because there is nothing to support us.

Without believing that all our actions are directed to some higher purpose, it is impossible to be happy. Consider Simon Wiesenthal. Even at ninety years of age, he would never consider retiring from his holy work of bringing Nazi murderers to justice. I visited him several times in Vienna. You walk in and see this man who is nearing a century yet he goes into the office every day and seeks out monsters who have been in hiding for over fifty years. Wiesenthal would have been miserable had he not devoted himself to tracking down Nazis. He turned his pain into something life-affirming and purposeful: the affirmation and preservation of justice. He once told me he does this because otherwise he would not have a satisfying answer to the question, 'Why did I remain alive when so many who were better than me perished?'

That higher purpose we must find in life in order to

achieve happiness can be our children, our devotion to a worthy cause, our friendships or the acquisition of knowledge. But there is one thing it cannot be: ourselves. We will never be happy if we live only for numero uno. The goal is too constraining, the cause too limiting. Even we will soon get sick of taking ourselves too seriously. Every human being lives with an innate desire to lose themselves in a lofty and noble pursuit.

The role of Divine Providence

A critical factor in achieving happiness is believing in Divine Providence. Providence dictates that God runs the world, and everything happens for a beneficial purpose as part of His Divine plan. So when something bad happens, we must always try to find the greater purpose.

Among the ancient Rabbis of the Talmud, there was a very special man named Nachum Ish Gamzu, distinguished by his belief that *gam zu letovah* – everything that transpired was for the best. Whatever happened to him – good or bad – he always believed was for a higher purpose. Even when he was being tortured by the Romans, he possessed enormous faith that his suffering was in God's plan.

The person of faith feels her existence to be pervaded by awe-inspiring meaning at every moment so she is cushioned from despair because she knows she was born to achieve feats of glory. The very first four verses of Psalms (NRSV) declare:

> *Happy are those who do not follow the advice of the wicked, or take the path that sinners tread, or sit in the seat of scoffers; but their delight is in the law of the Lord, and on his law they meditate day and night. They are like trees planted by streams of water, which yield their fruit in its season, and their leaves do not wither. In all that they do, they prosper. The wicked are not so, but are like chaff that the wind drives away.*

Those who are happy have a deep inner contentment, born of an attachment to something higher. Their 'leaves do not wither', they never burn out, because their happiness springs from the deepest part of them.

In contrast, those who seek happiness purely through their own selfish desires become like chaff in the wind. They quickly burn out. Sad to say, this is what I witness with so many young people today. Because they lack a sense of balance and have not plugged into something lasting and meaningful, they quickly run out of energy and hope for the future. One of their goals becomes retiring by the age of fifty because life is a race from which they will ultimately drop out. Wall Street has a very high burn-out rate; charity work does not.

A matter of perspective

Running a charity means constantly facing financial difficulties. Unlike a traditional business, our charity the L'Chaim Society has no regular source of income. We have no endowment, and every penny has to be raised from sponsors. And because we provide constant activities for the students, we incur large expenses. Like so many of us, I used to think that I would be happy if only the money problems would disappear.

Summers are particularly difficult because, when people travel, it is hard to raise funds. One summer in particular, our cash reserves were so low that I worried how we would meet our payroll, so much so that I could not sleep. Then, after returning from a trip abroad, I started seeing blurred. My first thought was that it was nothing, but when after a week the blur remained, I went to see the doctor.

He referred me to a top eye specialist and what she said scared the life out of me. She told me that I had contracted an unusual virus in my left eye that burns holes in the cornea. Because the situation was not healing but was leaving permanent scars, I stood to lose forty per cent visibility in that eye. Talk about depression. That night my wife and I went out for a prescheduled dinner with friends, but all I could do was sit like a zombie. Who cared about money problems now? My only concern was what would happen to my eye.

Miraculously, it completely healed, yet just two days later I was again worrying about our money troubles. As I was saying my morning prayers, I slowed down upon reading the prayer of thanks offered to God for being the One who 'opens the eyes of the blind'. This suddenly held new meaning and I thought, how can someone be unhappy as long as they can see? What could possibly get him down?

During another stressful period of financial hardship, Larry joined us for our Sabbath dinner. A successful investor in satellite communications, Larry once had it all. After making millions in his twenties and marrying in his early thirties, he had two beautiful children and three impressive homes. But, almost out of nowhere, things started to go awry. Larry developed a drug habit and took a mistress. Then, after squandering his money on capricious investments, he was ripped off by a few employees and was cuckolded by his wife.

'My, you sure look miserable', he said to me. 'What's wrong with you?' Forgetting that Larry was no stranger to misfortune, I started to tell him my woes. 'I just feel so forlorn. I've got nothing, no financial security, no guarantee that I can always provide for my family. What can I point to in my life and say is mine?' He looked confused and said sarcastically, 'Well, Shmuley, there is the small item of your wife and children.' 'Well, there is that, I suppose', I conceded humorously. Then, as if to bring me to my senses, he slapped me. It was well deserved. Because of my self-indulgent pity I had overlooked the most important blessings in my life.

Counting our blessings

Another point about happiness is that we must always keep in mind our deepest ideals through all life's vicissitudes. If a man loses a lot of money on the stock market, his natural reaction is to become immediately depressed, but when he remembers that he never stole or cheated, that his wife and children are healthy and safe, and that he is still in possession of all his powers, he will not become really unhappy. In fact, this minor setback may cause him to focus on his blessings. Thus, achieving happiness involves always seeing the whole picture all of the time.

There is a moving verse in Psalms that reads: 'From the constraints I called out to you, O God. And you answered me in the broad places.' Happiness is found in the wide spaces. Happiness means never allowing our vision to be so constrained that we see the dark forest and never the green trees. It is about never allowing ourselves to become so absorbed with our own concerns that we cannot shine our light on those who are currently in darkness.

The ancient Rabbis said that one of the keys to happiness is engaging in spiritual activities such as prayer. Why? Because prayer helps us put our lives into proper perspective. It empowers man to be thankful for the little things that so easily get taken for granted. Once man perceives how God accompanies him in every area of life, he no longer overlooks simple mercies like awakening with his hearing and eyesight intact. Whatever niggling problems afflict him through the day are easily put into perspective.

When we pray, we focus on the truly important things in our lives, none of which can be bought or sold in the market-place. We pray for life, health, wisdom, forgiveness, peace and the welfare of our loved ones. Unlike the material things we accumulate, these blessings do not weigh us down; because they make our burden lighter, we carry them with us wherever we go.

Most of us think that we would be happy if only we could win the lottery. But what we rarely consider is how we do win the lottery, and much more, each day. After all, if we had millions of dollars but could not walk or see, which would we want more? What we must understand is that happiness is not just a matter of perspective but actually a *conscious choice* that we make.

In the film *The Deep End of the Ocean* Treat Williams and Michelle Pfeiffer play a couple whose four-year-old son has been kidnapped. Nine years later the boy is found and returned to his parents, but his mother is not happy because of all the difficulties they face in trying to integrate a thirteen-year-old boy into a family of essential strangers.

At one point in the movie, the husband says, 'Beth, you have made a career out of being unhappy. I've decided that I have one shot in this life of being happy and I'm going to take advantage of it.' Most people overlook this point. They think that happiness is some incredible emotion that, like a wave covering a sandy beach, simply washes over and overtakes them. So many of us who really have the opportunity to choose happiness choose instead, by focusing on trivialities, to remain miserable, often without good cause.

Part of this choice of being happy is choosing to under-take activities that bring lasting happiness and satisfaction. We must choose to spend more time with our children and less time making money or building our careers. We must choose to spend more time volunteering for our community and less time playing cards with our friends. In short, we must choose those pursuits that bring lasting happiness rather than short-term distraction.

A recommendation to recapture happiness

Here is a recommendation for whoever thinks they have reason to be sad. List ten principal reasons for your unhappiness, and then sum up the courage to show this to one of your close friends. Few of us would be brave enough to reveal that list full of insignificant gripes and grievances. We would be ashamed of being exposed as shallow, immature and petty. Would we dare to show our list to a survivor of the Holocaust or someone else who has experienced tremendous tragedy in life?

This idea came to me when we had the great honour of hosting Elie Wiesel, the Nobel Peace Laureate, at Oxford, where he addressed over two thousand students. We flew him and his wife over from New York. Because of my enormous respect for him, I arranged everything first class: Concorde air fare, five-star hotels, the works. I felt that this was our obligation since he had waived his honorarium in his desire to address Oxford's students about the Holocaust.

Nevertheless, I was once again worried how we as a small student society would cover the expense. However, as I heard the eloquence of his speech and the haunting tales of both tragedy and hope, it suddenly struck me, would I have the courage to sit with him over a beer and complain about my petty financial woes?

Our life is a great journey. Sometimes the road is smooth; sometimes it is terribly bumpy. But we must always invite joy and enthusiasm to dictate our actions.

Inhibitors of happiness: jealousy, lust and glory

The ancient Rabbis said that there are three emotions that most interfere with happiness: jealousy, lust and the pursuit of glory. Each is an example of an insatiable desire. Jealousy causes us to want what we do not have, leaving us feeling permanently deprived. Lust and greed heighten our desire to acquire possessions and respect, in the end outstripping our ability to acquire them. Finally, the limitless search for glory deprives us of inner satisfaction since we are at the whim of others. There is no quicker road to unhappiness than to place our locus of happiness in someone else's control.

Having realistic expectations

Since happiness entails balance, we must learn to balance our expectations. Without strong expectations and dreams, we would never achieve anything in life, but with unrealistic expectations, we live with permanent disappointment. Realistic expectations mean never being too hard on ourselves and always looking for the bright side of life. Always finding the light at the end of the tunnel, without believing that it is an oncoming train. That's why I love visiting Italy. Italy has bred the unique strain of Mediterranean man, someone who is prepared to forgive himself for being human. People whose attitude is, 'I'm gonna try to get this thing done. But if it doesn't happen, nu? There will always be another opportunity. In the meantime, let's sit down and have a cappuccino.'

OK, so that's a bit simplistic, but you sometimes discover that the greatest things in life are actually the simplest. And happiness is a simple, yet elusive formula. Here are the ten basics you should set before your eyes. Do it literally, by pasting it on to your wall:

1. Determine your essential goals, values and ambitions
2. Live according to that plan
3. Forgive yourself when you mess up
4. Forgive others when they mess up
5. Spend as much time nurturing your soul as you do your body
6. Never lose sight of the 'little' things in life that bring much joy, especially time with family and friends. Play with your kids a lot
7. Work hard but play hard. Always give yourself *meaningful* recreation. Read enriching literature; listen to uplifting music
8. Don't compare yourself with others. Retire from the rat race while still endeavouring to be the best you can be
9. Give fifteen per cent of your time and money to

charitable and worthwhile causes
10. At least once a week, lift a glass of whisky – preferably a good single malt – and raise your glass and toast life – L'Chaim!

And if you ignore my simple ten-step plan for happiness and end up miserable, I reserve the right to say 'I told you so.'

23

Joy

THE MOST SPIRITUAL EMOTION

Serve God in joy.

Psalm 100

I sometimes wonder whether all pleasures are not substitutes for joy.

C. S. Lewis

Only a life lived for others is worth living.

Albert Einstein

The meaning of joy

If happiness means a pervasive inner contentment, joy is the unbridled and unfettered release of that contentment. The aim of religion is to help man transcend his natural human constraints and rise up towards God and out towards his fellow man; in other words, to close or at least narrow the quantum gap that separates heaven from earth. This task cannot be accomplished, however, when we remain weighed down by the gravity of our lives. In order to un-shackle ourselves from the mundane, we need joy. Indeed, there is no greater ingredient in the recipe for success than joy, because *joy is man at his most spiritual.*

Joy is when we anticipate the next hour, the next day, the next year, with optimism and enthusiasm. When we are truly joyous, we feel lively and energetic. When we feel that no goal is beyond our reach. Joy is about expansion and increase. Conversely, depression is about shrivelling into a little ball. When depressed, we find ourselves incapable of discharging even the simplest chore. Our horizons have contracted and our will is narrow.

The difference between a depressed man and a joyous one is like the difference between a cloudy day and a sunny one. I lived in Britain, where the days are almost always cloudy. In America, there are weekend forecasts; in Britain, we have millennia forecasts. They have accurately predicted that the weather over the next thousand years will be grey, cloudy and wet. The law in Britain is that if you see the sun you are immediately obligated to report it to the police!

Anyhow, the British countryside is one of the most beautiful places on earth. As Wordsworth attested, the rolling hills and the deep greens of nature evoke an image of paradise. The beauty is, however, rarely noticed because the clouds hover drearily over the landscape. No matter how beautiful the room, no matter how brilliant the tapestries, what good is it if you cannot see? Even if there is light but it is still cloudy, you can only see partially. When the clouds disappear and the sun comes out, however, everything sparkles.

Joy is the strongest weapon in the armoury of the religious man, a shield that renders man impregnable to the suffering of the world. Whereas mystics of other religions believe that meditation on man's worthlessness leads to piety, Jewish mystics have underscored that only in exultation does man tap into his infinite essence. While feelings of helplessness are one legitimate rung on the spiritual ladder, man's ultimate objective is to transcend those feelings and bask instead in the omnipresence of God. Only in joy can we do this, because only in joy do we find the strength to surmount all obstacles.

Joy means life

Having served at Oxford for eleven years, I think it is fair to say that an unusually large number of students here experience depression. They scamper in and out of my office, not really wanting to talk about why their lives are not as they want. They just seem to stare blankly out the window. Exam time, unsurprisingly, seems to be the height of the depression season.

Because Oxford respects academic performance above all else, the pressure to succeed is immense. Moreover, there is no shortage of talent among the student body, making the competition at times overwhelming. Students who were shining stars at their secondary schools or other universities suddenly become average; students who did not need to push themselves to excel back home must suddenly work extremely hard just to pass. Add to this the fact that seeking counselling is often seen as the step before failure, and you can see why depression is so prevalent.

It comes as no surprise then that I spend so much of my time encouraging the students – and myself – to be more joyous. Every Friday night, I devote at least one of my short speeches at the Sabbath table, accompanied by a L'Chaim – a toast 'to life' – to pointing out that Judaism is a celebration of life and calls for constant joy. In the daily liturgy, God commands us to serve him in joy and even obligates us to feel heightened joy at certain times of the year, such as on Simchat Torah, which translates as Joy in the Torah. Indeed, on this festival Jews are *required* to dance and sing.

The commandment to feel joy is so serious that God even threatens to withhold His blessing if we do not obey it properly. In the Book of Leviticus, He warns the Jewish people of the dire consequences of breaking His covenant. Amazingly, the ninety-nine harrowing curses end with the following words: '[All of this will befall you] because you did not serve the Lord Your God with joy and gladness of heart after all the good that He has shown you.' Rabbi Isaac Luria, foremost of the Jewish mystics, declared that even if the Jews keep the Covenant but do not do so in joy, the same curses will befall them. One cannot find redemption without joy. The meaning of this is quite literal. A life lived without joy is itself a curse. You will have money but without joy it will bring misery. You will have possessions but without joy they will be like tormentors. For joy is the ultimate blessing.

Can joy be summoned on command?

In the chapter on depression, I mentioned that Ronald Reagan had been due to open our new L'Chaim Society Jewish student centre. Just eleven days before his scheduled arrival and after six months of preparation, we were dancing at my house at Simchat Beis Hashoeiva, a pre-emptive celebration a few nights before Simchat Torah. We had a live band and large casks of apple cider. The evening was rocking.

When the presidential aide with whom I was liaising called from Los Angeles, I thought it was just to confirm some details, but instead it was to drop the bombshell that Reagan was cancelling his visit. Three days later, it was Simchat Torah. Having poured six months of my life into this project and drained so much of the organization's finances, I was not really in the mood to dance. To say that I was upset would be to employ classic British understatement. Nevertheless, Jewish law commanded me to be joyous on Simchat Torah, and I returned to the party to dance. Lucky we had all that apple cider.

Is God justified in demanding that we be joyous even if we have no good reason, particularly as we cannot predict the events preceding a day like Simchat Torah? It does seem a bit unfair. Emotional obligations are certainly more difficult to fulfil than those involving action. It is one thing to command people what to do, like give charity. You may be stingy but you give because you can still summon the willpower to pull it off. But to command someone how to feel is a different story. Indeed, although a boss can order an employee to work hard in the business, he cannot order him to enjoy the work. That would just not be reasonable or fair.

By the same token, imagine a traditional community where the custom is for the parents to choose their children's spouses (a custom, incidentally, that has *never* been practised in Judaism). The children are not consulted but instead bow to the authority and wisdom of their parents. Yet while a parent can direct their child to marry the person they have chosen because they have the interests of their offspring at heart, it would be unfair to tell them to love their betrothed. A young person cannot be expected to heed even the call of their parents where love is concerned because love cannot be manufactured, only freely given.

It is for this reason that commandment number five – 'Thou shalt honour thy father and mother' – says nothing about love. The Bible in its wisdom understands that because of the intensity of feeling that exists in families, a child may not feel love for his or her parents at all times. It is the nature of the human condition that the child often feels anger and frustration, perhaps even bitterness, towards his parents. And this is perhaps unavoidable in a relationship that is ultimately predicated on authority.

What the Torah teaches, however, is that although one may possess such feelings, one must nevertheless honour one's parents. Indeed, if we were commanded to love at all times, virtually all humanity would be faced with an unavoidable transgression. So why is it fair to command people to feel joy?

Joy is our natural state

This question works only if we presuppose that joy is not our natural state. However, the congenital human disposition from our earliest years is joy. Simple observation demonstrates that children are naturally joyous. Instead of requiring a reason to be cheerful, they need a reason *not* to be so. Deny them chocolate and they may cry, but otherwise they basically follow Newton's first law of motion, frolicking very happily until some greater force comes along and impedes them. And although a child has needs and can often act spoiled, he is naturally joyous and playful as long as his parents give him their time and love.

One of the reasons adults envy this state is because a healthy childhood is filled with memories of running amok, free from worry and responsibility. But as we grow older, the pressures of life gradually begin to erode that joy. For example, I remember as a kid how happy and free I felt as my last class ended on Friday. On Saturday and the first half of Sunday, I would play ball and go to the park. But as Sunday evening approached, the bliss began to fade. Gone was my freedom, and hovering above me were hours of tedious studying and homework.

If school can cause a child such agony, the greater pressures we face as adults can certainly lead to despair. We have to support families and face all the bills that flood in as if out of nowhere. Add to that office politics and worries over advancement. Then add concerns about our children and how best to raise them. The anxiety caused by such responsibility is indeed considerable, sometimes enough to drain the life out of even the most optimistic. Indeed, there is almost an inverse proportion between degree of responsibility and the amount of joy we experience in our lives.

Nevertheless, joy, like innocence, is our most natural state of being. The daily anxieties we experience are only veneers that overlay it. Like a curtain that blocks out the sun, these pressures can, when extreme, deaden our inner joy. Yet the joy still remains within us no matter how cloudy the surface becomes. This is why, in commanding His children to be joyous, God does not ask us to manufacture an artificial emotion: he merely asks us to *be ourselves*. In commanding us to be happy, God is telling us to stop taking our worries so seriously and focus instead on our blessings.

Leaving the mundane behind

Perhaps the greatest contribution the Jews have made to civilization is the gift of the Sabbath. Indeed, every seven days a Jew is commanded literally to take a rest from the pressures of the working week. The average American has, unfortunately, interpreted this day of rest as a day of shopping or watching football. But this is not what the Master of the Universe intended. In the words of Abraham Joshua Heschel, the Sabbath is a day to liberate ourselves from toil and 'especially care for the seed of eternity planted in the soul'.

It is not only transgressive to work on the Sabbath, but even inappropriate to talk about work. Instead, we are instructed to celebrate joyously with friends and family over festive, Sabbath meals. In celebrating this way, we are celebrating life, which is one of the reasons that Jews traditionally toast L'Chaim, 'to life', with wine and whisky. The purpose is not to induce an artificial state of joy through drink. Instead, by lowering our defences we seek to allow our true selves to shine through. The purpose of the drink is to weaken that curtain which obscures our joy.

So if our joy is like the sun pouring out of our heart, and our responsibilities are like an opaque curtain that blots out the light, we need to puncture holes in the curtain and let the light shine through. Even better, let's make the curtain translucent. After all, our worries are not going to disappear no matter how much joy we feel. But who says that we have to view them as worries? Why not see our responsibilities as God-given opportunities to maximize our inner potential?

How joy transforms the self

As I dreaded school, you probably wonder how I endured to become a Rabbi. You see, I only dreaded my school work until I was fourteen. Before that, I had to spend much time on subjects that did not in the least interest me. However, when I switched in order to learn in a *yeshiva* – a Jewish rabbinical seminary – I began to realize the glory of education. Indeed, I began really to thirst for knowledge. Instead of depressing me, my studies uplifted me. Weekends were a time not to escape from learning but to indulge in topics that interested me further.

I recall one time when all of the students had to evacuate

the building in our Yeshiva because of a fire alert. In my earlier years, the green light of freedom would have blinked in my mind on such an occasion. I once even set off ten stink bombs in the elevator of my junior high school to try to shut the school down for a few hours (I succeeded only in getting excluded for a few days). This time; however, I was totally upset that I had to miss class and waste time. A different perspective had clearly taken something depressing and made it joyous.

Hayley was studying accounting at an American university. She chose this subject primarily because there were other accountants in her family and it had been drummed into her head that accounting was a good way to earn a living. Although generally an excellent student in high school, Hayley's college performance was far from stellar. As hard as she tried to concentrate, she could not muster any enthusiasm for what was, in her opinion, a tedious subject. Although she would trudge off to the library determined to study, she usually fell asleep within the first hour.

Hayley had friends who studied far more interesting subjects, such as art and literature, but because she wanted to be able to earn a living when she graduated, she stuck to her business curriculum. She would listen with envy to how her friends spent their days with poets instead of debits and credits. It wasn't until she finally searched her soul that she decided to switch gears in her last year and study the subjects that she had always loved.

Without any previous course work in English literature, in two terms she enrolled in ten courses that would provide her with enough of a grounding to apply for graduate school in the field. As she expected, she simply fell in love with learning once it became interesting. When she went to the library now, there was no time to sleep; there was simply too much to learn. Her friends and family could not get over this; in experiencing her new *joie de vivre*, Hayley became a new woman.

The ancient Rabbis said that at the wedding feast of an only son, a father will dance even with his worst enemy. His joy allows him to surmount even the negative feelings that have cut him off from his human brethren. Joy liberates us from the confining cage of jealousy, bigotry and hatred. It is precisely because of its transformational character that joy is man at his most heavenly.

Joy knows no loneliness

Unfortunately, most people find joy too elusive. The far easier path is to submit to the laws of gravity and let the petty things pull us down. The primary reason we are burdened by our worries is because we feel that we experience them alone. Indeed, our problems make us feel isolated and abandoned. Thus, loneliness is a prime inhibitor to joy.

Jeffrey runs a pawn shop in New York City. One time, a man came in to sell some jewellery. Because he had certificates to prove that the pieces were bought from a legitimate wholesaler, Jeffrey felt certain they were not stolen and purchased all the merchandise. The following week, the FBI arrested him for buying stolen goods. A thoroughly honest man, Jeffrey was devastated. The FBI claimed that he should have recognized the documents as forgeries. As they led him away to jail, Jeffrey felt lower than ever before.

After he was released on bail, his father came to see him and told him not to worry, making light of the entire situation: 'Put a smile on your face, son, we're all behind you. Everything's going to be all right.' His father then hired New York's top criminal lawyer to defend him. 'By the time we're finished with them,' the lawyer told him, 'they'll be issuing you a public apology. Don't worry. I'm here for you and we're going to beat this. You're not going through this thing alone.' Jeffrey was instantly comforted.

So the first part of the solution is to surround yourself with loved ones. Just the presence of Jeffrey's father made all the difference in the world between hope and despair. The second part is to surround yourself with your Divine parent. If we feel the presence of God under every rock and behind every leaf, we can never feel alone or abandoned.

The spiritual soul is joyous precisely because he experiences the presence of God in all His ways and never feels forsaken. The man of joy is a man of vision because he sees that which others do not see. While others focus on what they lack, the man of joy focuses on his abundant blessings, on the hand of God.

Your joy is my joy

When I was sixteen, I was a rabbinical student in Jerusalem. One evening while I was walking home from school, I saw a large commotion surrounding a white Mercedes taxi. A pretty little girl who could not have been much older than eight had been hit by the car and lay unconscious in a pool of blood. Everyone was afraid to touch her because we all thought she was dead. I was devastated.

I looked up to the heavens and said in my heart, 'God, this is the holy city of Jerusalem. I was walking so merrily through the streets just a few moments ago. Why would you have given me such a terrible sight to behold? How could you have allowed this tragedy to happen?' I then offered a prayer: 'Lord, if you give this young girl life, I will dance and sing to you in the streets of Jerusalem.' I watched her, and a few moments later she suddenly moved her hand. Then, she moved her head and groaned.

It was the most joyous moment of my life. I felt that I had somehow had a hand in saving her life. I went bananas. I ran to the nearest alleyway and started to sing and dance in abandon. The neighbours opened their windows to see the spectacle – but they didn't call the police! So infectious was my joy that some even started to sing with me the words from Psalm 84: 'My heart and my flesh sing for joy to the living God.'

Because I had prayed in a totally disinterested manner for the welfare of a fellow human being whom I would never meet again, I had made her joy my joy, her welfare my welfare. I had never felt so liberated in all my life. Joy had set me free.

I have experienced similar feelings of elation when counselling couples. The greatest feeling is when I meet a couple intent on divorce and then, upon my intervention, they decide to give their marriage a second chance.

Lisa and Sheldon were just such a couple. The night before Lisa was scheduled to meet with her lawyer to initiate divorce proceedings, Sheldon invited me over to their home. I pleaded with them the entire night to give their marriage another chance. There were no major issues to divide them, save stubbornness and an unwillingness to compromise.

In the early hours of the morning, Lisa and Sheldon fell into each other's arms and apologized for their pigheaded-ness. It was 7 a.m. by the time I returned home. Without a wink of sleep, I was walking on air, more awake than I had ever been in my life. I felt that my being alive made a difference.

In both instances, I had tapped into the great joy that comes from selflessly caring for others. Unlike depression, which makes us close ourselves off from our fellows, joy opens an infinite reservoir of love that we seek to share with our fellow beings. Unlike the unhappy person, who is shackled by anxiety and enslaved by guilt, the joyous person is truly free because his spirit is released and allowed to roam at will. He is liberated from the rigid and narrow confines of self-centredness and experiences the exaltation of feeling one with the universe.

In order to make joy a part of our lives, we must liberate ourselves from our own selfish concerns by focusing on how to feel someone else's joy. If we sit around just waiting for good news for ourselves, chances are we will wait a very long time. But if we also await good news for someone else, we have a million more opportunities to experience bliss. Lord Byron said, 'All who would win joy, must share it; happiness was born a twin.' In short, it's a numbers game – the more joy we feel for others, the more we will receive in return.

24

Love

THE MOST HUMANIZING EMOTION

For one human being to love another; that is perhaps the most difficult of all our tasks, the ultimate, the last test and proof, the work for which all other work is but preparation.

Rainer Maria Rilke

Love is the only sane and satisfactory answer to the problem of human existence.

Erich Fromm

You can give without loving, but you cannot love without giving.

Amy Carmichael

Finally, we arrive at the last stop on our tour of the human emotions. So what is the connection between joy and love? There is a joy in selfless giving. And when we give of ourselves selflessly, we begin to know what it is to love.

What we talk about when we talk about love

The word 'love' may just be the most abused word in the English language. As often as we use it to describe our relations with people, we use it to describe our affection for objects. You hear a man say, 'I love my new car'. Kids tell you how they love chocolate ice-cream or the latest video game.

Commercial advertising perpetuates the abuse by correlating love with the commodities they want you to buy: 'I love what you do for me, Toyota.' Popular love songs often abuse their subject by failing to provide any substantive meaning to the term. Consequently, although the word is used much, it signifies little. After all, if we love every*thing*, we love nothing.

Moreover, how can the same word that describes my relationship with my dog be applied to that with my wife? And how can the same word that describes my relationship with my wife refer to my relationship with my mother or daughter? The Romance languages at least differentiate between the act of love and the receipt of pleasure. In Spanish, one uses the passive language *me gusta* – it pleases me – to describe liking something like chocolate or dancing. When speaking of loving a person, on the other hand, one uses the active verb *amor*, to love, suggesting an effort put forth. Nevertheless, the issue is far more than lexical. On a deeper level, the problem with the word 'love' suggests a confusion with loving as a much broader cultural phenomenon.

To borrow the title of the Raymond Carver short story, it seems imperative to know precisely 'what we talk about when we talk about love'. Even with self-help manuals, a veritable industry of their own these days, very few have attempted to tread these uncharted waters. If you search the shelves of your local bookstore, you will find virtually no titles dealing directly with the subject of love under the rubric of 'self-help'. You will find 'Six Hundred Steps To Achieve Personal Success' and '1001 Ways To Improve Self-Esteem'. You will be insulted to find out that everything you have learned since kindergarten has been a waste of time, but you will not find a valuable discussion on what love means.

This is because self-help is exactly what it declares itself to be. Even when describing how to be a better friend, it usually does so in the name of self-promotion. (Take, for example, the never-out-of-print-since-its-first-publication *How to Win Friends and Influence People*.) The premise of the self-help genre is how *I* can be better, not how I can extend beyond the boundaries of my own ego and unite with another, which is the essence of love.

Nor, surprisingly, will you find such a discussion on love in the section entitled 'Sex and intimacy'. Among the recently reprinted *Kama Sutra* and all its contemporary copycats, you will find countless ways to seduce and reproduce, but you will find little discussion of love, or even of intimacy for that matter. Even Masters and Johnson's encyclopaedic text *On Sex and Human Loving* devotes only one chapter in twenty to 'Loving and being loved'. In this, the authors actually confess that 'few sexologists (including ourselves) have addressed this subject in any detail. Nevertheless, we have all felt love in one way or another' (p. 213). The other nineteen chapters deal with types of sexuality, sexual behaviours and their dysfunctions, in other words with issues of the mind and the body but not of the heart.

Love is . . .

In a recent lecture, when I asked the audience to offer a synonym for love, the first response I received was 'compassion'. Compassion, an emotion that is truly necessary for humanity, is what we feel for someone else who is suffering. We learn this from the etymology of the word, which comes from the Latin *cum* which means 'with' and *patior*, which means 'to suffer'. An example of compassion is what most of us have felt for the recent plight of the Kosovar refugees. We have said to ourselves, 'How terrible, it shouldn't be this way; what can we do?' But these feelings, while noteworthy, are not love.

Love is when we feel the suffering of another as if it were our own. There is a wonderful story about one of the great Rabbis of the twentieth century who accompanied his wife to the doctor. When the doctor asked what was the matter, the Rabbi answered, 'Our leg hurts, and we won't be able to continue walking for much longer.' The doctor said, 'Now wait a second, whose leg is injured?', to which the Rabbi responded, 'Ours'. The Rabbi was literally in pain to see his wife in pain. The border between self and other had dissipated.

The essence of love is the expansion of the borders of the ego to embrace another. The Bible actually commands that 'you must love your fellow man *as yourself*'. The greatest and strongest love is self-love, and all love begins from this point. Love is not where you begin to find something compelling or exciting about the other party. That is attraction. Rather love is where the individual develops an elasticity and is able to expand his or her self to encompass the other individual as well. Stated in other words, love is where you begin to discover that the other person *is* yourself, that all human beings are children of the one God and comprised of the same cosmic stuff. Love is about discovering the affinity between yourself and the stranger, and when that happens there is an automatic expansion of the ego that embraces and encompasses the stranger that has now become your brother, so that you can love him as yourself. It follows that real love cannot be selective. Since love is about discovering the underlying unity that encircles all of humanity, it is impossible to love one of our human brothers and hate another.

The paradigm of this type of pure and selfless love is the parent's love for the child. When the parent sees her child in pain, the parent is in pain. The parent cannot distinguish between him and herself and the child. The parent's suffering is worse because the parent's love is deeper than the child's wound.

The Rubins had been friends of my family since my own childhood. When Gary was born, he was diagnosed with a very rare disease and was not expected to live past the age of ten. His childhood was spent not on the playground but in and out of hospital.

Gary's parents, whose previously normal lives were devastated by the constant care their son required, never even once considered placing Gary in a home. They lived their lives with Gary's pain and never gave up seeking out possible treatment. Although many parents would have been unable to persevere with such suffering, the Rubins demonstrated their undying love for their son every single day of his life. For twenty-five years, they felt his pain as if it were their own.

The same holds true for joy. When the parent sees the child experiencing joy, the parent feels overjoyed. Never does the loving parent feel envy or jealousy. In fact, the parent gladly spends endless hours tending to the needs of her baby – feeding in the middle of the night, countless nappy changes – and is ecstatic if she receives as much as a smile, contented if she receives nothing more than a sleepless night. While raising a child is one of life's greatest challenges, it is at the same time one of life's foremost pleasures because there is a joy in selfless giving. And when we give of ourselves selflessly, we begin to know what it is to love.

This should not be mistaken as love deriving from sacrifice. The pleasure here does not stem from a denial of the self. The Bible does not command us to abrogate and stifle the self in order to love the other. Rather the joy and the pleasure here derives from the *expansion* of the self, from becoming larger than our own life from gaining an elasticity of being.

So if I had love for the Kosovar refugees, I would not be able to watch the news on television and then return to my usual evening of dinner and helping the kids with their homework. Even if I were to take the time to write a letter to my congressman to intervene on behalf of the refugees, this would be a step in the right direction, worthy political action, but it would not be love.

If we loved the refugees, if we felt their pain *as if it were our own*, we would not remain spectators of their plight. Instead, we would translate that love into action and our every waking moment would be spent trying to help them, as if they were our own children. Thus, while compassion moves us to great heights of consciousness, love has the power to move us to Godliness.

The difference between lust and love

Another common misconception about love is that it is closely related to its horny cousin, lust, but these are not members of the same family, not even of the same tribe. Love is when we want to give to someone else. In other words, we gain by the giving. Lust, on the other hand, is when we desire to possess or 'use' someone else for our own gratification. So whereas love is the supreme expression of selflessness, lust is the supreme expression of selfishness.

Whereas love is the supreme acknowledgment of another's individuality, lust is its supreme denial. Whereas love is about recognizing the humanity of the one we love, lust is about turning them into an object. We could not care less about the pain or trauma of the object of our lust because lust makes us entirely self-focused.

When we love, we want to join with another and become one. The supreme act of love is the embrace. The act of hugging involves creating a circle with our arms; it speaks our desire to create space within our own lives for the person we love. We recognize that they are their own person and we symbolically tell our beloved that we are happy to love them on their terms. Because love acknowledges the depth and profundity of human feeling, those who love fall more and more in love with the object of their love as time progresses.

Lust is not an emotion because an emotion involves connecting with something outside ourselves. When we lust, we seek to appropriate the other into our own identity. In lust, we do not connect as much as control. Indeed, the supreme gesture of lust is not the hug but the grope. No circle is made when we grope another person. We do not give the other any space but instead insist that it is our way or no way.

The difference between lust and love is like the difference between the two kinds of sexual desire: hormonal and erotic. Lust, like hormonal desire, is all about releasing an inner need. A person engages in hormonal sex simply because of a hormonal build-up within the body that needs to be released. Hormonal sex usually ends up boring and uninspired because it engages only the outer, animalistic layers of being. It is all about what I call 'sexual ventilation'. Like lust, it pulls us into ourselves and renders sex a form of masturbation with another.

Love, on the other hand, is all about satiating an inner need. When we feel erotic desire, we want to make love because we find our lover irresistible. Indeed, we cherish and respect someone to such a degree that we wish to share our innermost self with them. Love, like all true emotions, draws us outside ourselves, teaching us that real fulfilment can only be achieved with a fellow human creature.

Indeed, erotic desire signifies the transcendent longing to become one flesh with the object of our desire. Never animalistic, the capacity to feel erotic desire is one of the characteristics that makes us fully human. Whereas an act of lust keeps our bodies, minds and hearts separate for an instantly forgettable experience, an act of love *integrates* our bodies with our minds and hearts and provides the most satisfying of sexual relations. That's why lust is general and love is specific. When we lust for sex, almost anyone can fill the need. When we love someone, only they can satisfy us.

Love is unity

It is told that a man once came to Hillel, the great Hebrew sage, and asked him to teach him the entire Torah while standing on one foot. Hillel's reply: 'That which you hate do not do unto your fellow man. This is the whole Torah; the rest is commentary.' All religions preach that you should love God, and love your fellow man as yourself. Goodness is the whole purpose of religion, and love is the supreme human emotion, but why? Why is love goodness?

On a physiological level, we could say that love feels pleasurable and heightens our sensations. Hatred, the opposite of love, makes us simmer. But recreational drugs also make us feel good, and for the sadist, cruelty feels good.

Just because something feels good, however, does not mean that it is good.

One reason why love is goodness is because love means being at one with humanity. This is what we mean by brotherly love or love for our fellow man. Not coincidentally, in the Hebrew language the words for 'love' (*ahava*) and 'one' (*echad*) contain the same numerical value, indicating that the terms share common value. And common value is indeed what love is all about. It is when we look at another person and see not difference but the essence that unites all human creatures.

Love gives us not only the wings to rise above artificial differences and achieve unity, but also vision. It affords us the power to see the all-encompassing unity that underlies creation. A parent loves their child because when they look at the child see not someone different from themselves but an extension of themselves.

Love is the belief that all humanity shares a single soul and that we all come from a single source. In the Kabbalah, the soul of *Adam Kadmon*, the first man, was a collective soul subdivided into minute components. Each human creature possesses a fragment of the soul while being at the same time part of the collective soul. Thus, as the paramount act of unity, love is the ultimate demonstration of the absolute unity of God.

Conversely, every act of hate is an act of alienation, of separation, of saying we are 'other'. The Talmud says, 'Someone who is arrogant and someone who shows hatred is an idolater.' This is because every person who hates denies the unity and wonders of God. Hate is when someone sets himself up as an independent entity outside God's community. Hate is when someone imprisons herself inside her ego and refuses to recognize her self in others and the other in her self. On the individual level, such emotional confinement leads to at best prejudice and at worst mental illness. On the collective level, it leads to genocide.

Understanding self-love

Finding that all-encompassing unity is not only critical to the social order and the macrocosm, but also essential to the inner world. Self-love is an often misunderstood concept. Most people think it means liking yourself. True self-love, however, is the ability to love and bring together all our inner disparate parts. It is about achieving symmetry between the mind and the emotions.

There are times in our lives when we feel chaos inside, that our minds are at odds with our hearts. When our intellect and our emotions conflict, we are in a state of disharmony, disjointedness, unhappiness. Conversely, people experience the opposite virtues of harmony, connectedness and happiness when they find inner peace between the two faculties.

How do we know that we can be in control of our lives and actually lead a fulfilling life? The answer is that, ultimately, we believe ourselves to be one organism; we do not separate our minds from our hearts. The same is true when it comes to our selves and others: we do not believe that Jews and Arabs, for example, are unrelated, separate entities. We believe that the world of man is all one. The same is true of our inner world: we believe that man is in harmony with nature, including his own human nature.

Uniqueness and unconditional love

Most people, asked whether they would prefer to be loved conditionally or unconditionally, would respond 'unconditionally'. But this simple response overlooks the virtues of conditional love. Let's contrast the two. Unconditional love means that I love you no matter what. Whatever vicissitudes arise in our relationship will have no bearing on what we feel for each other.

The paradigm for this kind of love is once again parental love. The mother loves her baby despite the fact that he entirely rearranges her life for many years. The child is loved purely for the virtue of kinship, not because he is particularly special or unique. Indeed, Mummy does not objectively love Johnny because he is good or kind or intelligent; she subjectively loves him because he is her son. This unconditional love is precisely what Johnny needs in order to grow up emotionally healthy and content, so it is a perfect match.

When the boy becomes a teenager, however, Mum's unconditional love becomes inadequate: he wants to be loved because he is special. He wants some girl who was previously a stranger to appreciate and admire him because he is handsome, kind or humorous. Created in the image of God, we all feel ourselves to be Godly in some way. Indeed, perhaps the greatest human desire is to be loved and appreciated for our special qualities. Love, from this point of view, validates our individuality. After all, who wants to be average? Since Johnny's parents cannot provide this kind of discriminating love, he seeks the love and approval of others: teachers, friends and especially girlfriends.

This conditional love corroborates his uniqueness and makes him feel worthy. When Johnny's father tells him he is a terrific ball player, it does not mean much to him. When the coach chooses him to be on the team, however, this carries weight. Similarly, when Louise chooses him among fifty other boys in the class to be her boyfriend, the love means something.

A critical point to be made here is, however, that even the parent's love is not entirely unconditional once the child becomes responsible for himself. If the child's behaviour is truly egregious, for example, the parent may feel hard put to generate love. Consider the case of the prodigal child. I know a family where the son has not taken his own children to meet his parents for ten years because of the hatred he harbours for them. The parents have firmly stated to me that they do not want to have anything to do with him because too much hurt has transpired. For some parents, the unconditional love of the childhood years can seemingly disappear.

If the parent's love is not entirely unconditional, certainly no other human relationship could be based on unconditional love. This is not as bad as it sounds, however. After all, if my wife had loved me unconditionally when we first met, I would not be at all flattered. If she could have chosen any other in my place, I am average and undistinguished. If all love were unconditional, we would mate indiscriminately like automatons or animals. Thus, we actually desire conditional love in order to differentiate ourselves from others.

The choice to give up choice

Here we return to an important point made in the loneliness chapter. What distinguishes us from others ultimately guarantees our isolation. We all want conditional love because we want to be unique. But uniqueness is a double-edged sword. On the one hand, it means that we are unlike any other person; on the other, it means that since we are unlike any other person, no one can truly understand us or fathom our pain. We will always be different from them.

The greatest form of loneliness in the world is feeling that you are not understood. The Torah teaches that God created love because He did not want man to be lonely. Loneliness is, however, not measured by the absence of company but is rather a feeling of ordinariness. After all, you can be married for twenty years and still be a stranger.

When Adam was created, he was surrounded by millions of animals, yet he was still lonely because they were different from him. He could understand them, he could eat with them, he could walk with them, but he could not love them because they were different beings. When we love someone we recognize that they are like us and that we are like them. Love saves us from loneliness because we then share an inner affinity.

It was only when God created Eve that Adam's loneliness was assuaged. She was a being like him. She was, however, at the same time profoundly different. She was a woman; he was a man. But they were of the same kind, so the loneliness could disappear, and each could also be enriched by the relationship.

So herein lies the paradox: we need conditional and unconditional love to coexist simultaneously. This contradiction is precisely what we pursue in marital love. When we first meet our spouse, we want their love to be conditional upon who we are. We start dating, and what causes us to gravitate towards each other is our date's unique gifts. We compare them with others we have dated before and indeed find that they are nicer, more attractive, more understanding. It is at that stage that we decide we want to marry them.

Once we are married, however, we desire our spouse's love to be unconditional, in spite of our peccadilloes. We want them to choose to give up choice. We don't want to be compared any longer. A wife needs to know that her marriage will survive an altercation with her husband. A man needs to feel assured that if he loses a lot of money, his wife will not run off with someone who is more successful.

Therefore, marriage involves *the choice* to render our spouse unconditional love. Implicit in the marital bond is the commitment never to evaluate our spouse against strangers. Thus, conditional love and an appreciation of the special gifts of our beloved lead us to make them a one-time offer of unconditional love. In other words, marriage is the educated choice to give up all other choice.

Falling in love with an equal who is an antagonist

So crucial is this paradoxical relationship between conditional and unconditional love that it warrants elaboration. In unconditional love the emphasis is not on the beloved, but on the one who harbours the love. The object is almost immaterial. What is significant is only the lover's capacity to love, a capacity which is infinite. Hence, when offered unconditional love one does not feel special or distinguished. A woman wants to hear a man say, 'I love you because you're beautiful', rather than, 'I love you because I have an infinite store of love within me. Although you're not distinguished or special in any way, I still love you endlessly.' People don't want love as a gift. They want to know they can earn it.

Conversely, the shortcoming inherent in conditional love is that its effects may not last. You may love someone because they are special, because they make you laugh, or because they are so bright. But this means that, first, your capacity to love them is limited to the cause – and after all, how funny can they be? – and second, your love may vanish with the cause. Your partner may experience tragedy, God forbid, and their humour will all but dry up.

So herein lies the paradox: we need both conditional and unconditional love to coexist simultaneously in a relationship in order to make it complete. Obviously, we all want to be loved unconditionally – to be adored by our partners regardless of how old and wrinkly we get, and independent of our financial and social circumstances. On the other hand, we also seek conditional love. Nobody wants another's affection simply because they have the capacity to do so, making the loved one replaceable and exchangeable.

And this is the key – and the beauty – inherent within the mystery of heterosexual relationships. For every heterosexual relationship comprises the same paradox. You are in love with someone who is your equal – they are human, like you – but who is also your *opposite*. The part of them that is similar to you represents conditional love. Because you are compatible and alike, you are able to comprehend and appreciate their beauty, their kindness and their humour. You are able to relate to them on the level of conditional love because you are both capable of assessing one another's virtues.

But then there is a part of the relationship that shall forever remain mysterious. You are a woman, he a man. You are diametrically opposed poles, who will forever represent an enigma and a riddle to one another. To love that part of your partner that you cannot fathom or appreciate requires unconditional love. You have to love them for what they are rather than for what they do for you. Indeed, parts of a woman's femininity will positively infuriate the man in her life, and vice versa. That's why there ae so many witticisms associated with gender difference, so many he said/she said films, so much fodder for Woody Allen and Nora Ephram alike! We make light of such gender differences, and yet as well we must honour them. For to dismiss the part of a woman which is inaccessible to a man is to reject the essential womanness in your wife, and will result in a flawed and crippled relationship.

And this is the mystery and profoundity of male/female love, a subject which endless poetry and prose have attempted to capture. But the puzzle is endless, wider than the furthest expanse of ocean, higher than the tallest peaks, deeper than a bottomless well. The great secret of a loving relationship is that it is all based on an abstruse contradiction. You love what you recognize in your partner. You have found someone with whom you can 'connect', who shares mutual tastes, who understands your fears, and who laughs at your jokes. When peering into the eyes of your significant other, you begin to see yourself. Your love is conditional upon these qualities that attract and engage you. It is why you loved them in the first place. And yet, there is always that little extra X or Y chromosome. Every man and woman will forever pose a conundrum to the other. Indeed, this is a great blessing of relationships since it guarantees novelty and freshness. Your partner can never be treated as a known quantity. You will forever remain curious and want to discover them further. The relationship, then, is an endless journey.

Thus, it becomes necessary to discover unconditional love. A man has to love the aspects of a woman that he does not understand. He must embrace that which he sees as unfamiliar, as convoluted, as irrational – even as agitating. No man has ever understood why women love to receive flowers. To a guy, they are a bad investment. One pays a lot for them and they die within a few days. And not only is the money lost, but the moment of affection withers as well. I have always told my wife – who insists on flowers for birthdays and anniversaries – that she cannot pull out of the closet any of the flowers I have bought in years past. And yet, all rationale aside, a woman loves to receive flowers. Hence it is for a man to accept, and embrace and let go of any attempts to understand. He must bask in the feminine radiance that attaches itself to things of natural beauty and colour. He cannot love *only* the aspects of a woman that he finds virtuous and that are apprehensible by a man; he must also love the mystery. And that is the essence of unconditional love: to give, even when your partner has not stimulated or elicited the love from you, but to give it rather as a free-flowing gift.

Why we need God's love

Looking at the problem as a whole, how can we reconcile this paradox of wanting to be unique yet without difference? The answer is that one leads to the other. When we have embraced someone unconditionally, we want them to develop conditional uniqueness. It is because we so love our children that we want them to develop their gifts and virtues.

By the same token, God offers mankind conditional and unconditional love simultaneously. He tells us that He is our Father and will love us no matter what. He grants us life and health whether or not we deserve it. But simultaneously, He tells us that we must obey His will and act virtuously.

Without God, there can be no true love because there will always be a degree of separation between two human beings. And while we can shower another with affection, we can never fully understand their pain. To love means to feel one's own being only through and in the being of another. To love God means to feel that one's own existence and activity are rendered possible and obtain value and significance through God and in God. Only God the Creator can reconcile the paradox of human uniqueness and the desire to be one, bridging collective and individual identities. Only God, the architect of our individuality, can understand that special part of us which no one else could ever understand.

This is why the quintessential act of love is prayer. Prayer is when we speak to the only Being who can fully understand us because He created us. In fact, prayer is referred to in the Bible as *ahavah*, which means love. If you do not pray regularly, you feel profoundly misunderstood. You feel lonely and unconnected. Far from merely being a religious rite, prayer is a psychological need. There is a requirement on the part of man to attach himself to his source and express himself to his Creator.

God is the ability to reconcile opposites, so what Adam and Eve really had was a triangular relationship. They loved each other through God, who was able to overcome their differences and create unity while at the same time not abrogate their vital individuality. That is why real love must possess a spiritual component. Love is the ability to reconcile opposites, to transform two people into one flesh, and to render them one without compromising their individually.

The Hebrew word for man is EESH and for woman EESHA. Each word is composed of three letters, two of which, the *aleph* and the *shin*, are common to both. The other two letters are the *yud* and the *heh*, which together compose God's name. Without these, we are left only with the *aleph* and the *shin*, which spell out the Hebrew word, *aish*, fire. This teaches us that when a man and a woman include God in their relationship they will have passion and communication, communion, holiness. If God is absent, however, all that remains is fire, opposition, irreconcilable differences. The love of a husband and wife is ultimately demonstrated in the child because there are three partners in the creation of a child. The parents together give the body, and God gives the soul.

The paradox of love: the coalescence of opposites

As parental love illustrates, one element of love involves the loss of self wherein one's own identity becomes submerged into someone else's – your joy is my joy, your pain is my pain. Love, from this point of view, is the act by which we transcend our ego and merge with another. On the other hand, paradoxically, love is also the act by which we affirm our ego.

Romantic love, for example, begins with a profound emphasis on self based on personal tastes. It is certainly not unconditional love. Our choice of friends is to some extent a reflection of ourselves. And the person whom we choose to marry will forever be the greatest personification of our most deeply held values, the affirmation of our ego. Indeed, the best way to know someone is to study who they married. As the relationship deepens, however, we want to give more and, consequently, lose more of ourselves. We begin to merge together.

Yet there still must be an act of differentiation between self and other. As Martin Buber said, the healthiest relationship is an I–Thou relationship. There has to be an 'I' who loves and a 'Thou' who receives and reciprocates my love. If one partner loses their identity to the other, they quickly tire of each other. Because they no longer have anything to give, they have nothing by which to enrich each other. Even in the parent–child relationship, if a parent sacrifices himself completely to the child, the parent becomes ineffective and the child spoilt.

The question to be asked, then, is how can love be an act of both affirmation and subjugation? The answer brings us to a deeper understanding of love. First, let us start with the premise that the only way to rise above a contradiction between two opposites is to find a third place where they harmonize. For example, when a man and a woman love each other, they have the potential to become one flesh and create a living being called a child. The child possesses attributes of each parent, making him the embodiment of

279

this coalescence of opposites. When the mother looks at her child, she sees herself, as does the father. They are both correct because the child is an extension of both parents, at the same time being his own unique, indivisible organism. Here we have the miraculous equation of $1 + 1 = 1$.

This is the case with love too: it exists as neither a promotion of self nor a denial of self but as a third, far more significant entity based on the coalescence of these two contradictory ideas. Love is the ability to have your own identity yet transcend it, to give love yet to feel someone else's love.

Moreover, it is only love that can achieve this coalescence of opposites because of its sublimity. The inverse of this statement is also true, that love is sublime precisely because it can unite opposites. Only love can achieve the union of male and female to create one flesh.

The paradox of God's being

The paradox of love mirrors the paradox of God's Being. On the one hand, God is infinite because He occupies the boundless expanse of space. On the other, God is present in the minute details of the universe, in the smallest creatures on this earth. So how is God's Being demonstrated? It is in His ability to be large and small simultaneously, in His ability to create a finite world yet remain infinite.

To illustrate the paradox of the finite and the infinite, there was in the Temple in Jerusalem a unique chamber called the Holy of Holies, which was twenty cubits square. Smack in the middle was the Ark, which was ten cubits in length. This means that when you measured from the end of the Ark to the wall on either side, you should have measured five cubits each side. Yet, if you did this, you got ten. In other words, the Ark was there, a measurable, physical entity, yet it occupied no space. There in the Holy of Holies, the holiest place in the world, God's greatest infinite power was demonstrated. The finite and the infinite merged and co-existed together as one.

Practically speaking: how can I feel love?

I have often been asked the question of whether one must have love in one's heart in order to love. The answer to this question is certainly yes. Whether that love is already present or must be planted and nurtured, however, is another question. It is my firm belief that even if love is not present in one's heart, one can teach oneself to love. Consider the physical heart: if you have an unhealthy heart, you have the best chances of improving your condition by eating heart-healthy foods and moderately exercising its muscle. The same is true of the metaphorical heart. Given the proper nutrition and exercise it, too, can be made into a healthy, loving heart.

If, for example, a person with an uncharitable heart sees a beggar on the street and thinks, 'I'm not going to give you any money; go get a job, you lazy parasite', the remedy is to give the beggar money, once, twice, a third time, even though this wrenches the person. Indeed, the Torah teaches that if you give charity, even if you do not feel the love that should accompany the act, the feeling will eventually come. In other words, action brings love. Maimonides employs this exact logic when discussing how to correct our character flaws in the Mishneh Torah. Basically, we must act with our hands in order to cultivate our hearts.

The converse is also true. Like the physically healthy heart, a naturally good and loving heart can deteriorate over time if not given the proper nutrition and exercise. Good deeds must be performed or else the heart begins to wither. Or it becomes so concealed that you can no longer feel it.

The river, the kettle and the bird

The Talmud says that he who dreams of a river, a kettle or a bird will find love. These are three metaphors for three kinds of relationship and three kinds of love.

A river relationship connotes a man and a woman, different and discrete like two separate towns, who are linked by the 'river' of marriage. This relationship may be functionally successful, producing children, a good household and shared values. In this kind of relationship, common interests keep them together. But deep divides still remain, causing loneliness and lack of fulfilment. These two distinct people experience no higher bonding.

A kettle relationship involves a closer collaboration of the clashing characteristics of man and woman. Men and women are opposites, like fire and water, which, through the medium of 'the relationship' (the 'kettle') become productive. The kettle helps them negate their differences and thereby achieve mutual goals. This is a higher level of unity because they are actually working together in harmony. Nevertheless, there remains a strong gap in intimacy since, in essence, she is fire and he is water. They have not overcome their gender differences but counteracted them, as in the Mars/Venus approach. Without the kettle, they would cancel each other out.

The bird metaphor describes the highest level of love, whereby man and woman retain independent identities while being orchestrated together as one whole. A bird has two wings. If both were on the same side, the bird could not fly. Similarly, male and female must retain their distinctive identities. There must be antithetical propulsion.

Nevertheless, this model indicates a mutual enrichment whereby gender differences are not merely overcome but transcended. The man and the woman have become one entity, the wings of a single bird working in tandem. Each retains their own identity while being joined together as a higher organism. The great sage Hillel neatly aphorized the paradox when he asked, 'If I am not for myself, then who will be for me? But if I am only for myself, then what am I?'

So many people talk of love but remain pathetically low on the ladder of love. We suffice ourselves with the river and kettle approach when we are capable of becoming the wings of a bird. We should soar and climb within the framework of love, rising high above the petty and superficial problems that separate us. And it is to this lofty ideal that we must always aspire. Only then will we experience the powerful words of Solomon mentioned in his great biblical song: 'Turbulent waters cannot quench love, neither can great floods extinguish it' (Song 8:7).

25

Love and fear

INCOMPATIBLE EMOTIONS

Crossing the finish line

All we do and say, all we feel and experience, all that makes us who we are, can be placed within these two headings: love and fear. For example, loneliness, which we have defined as the pain of no longer feeling needed, is an emotion inspired by fear. You may refrain from entering into a relationship because you think, 'What if one day my Tom no longer needs me? What if he replaces me with someone else?' Similarly, jealousy is an emotion caused by fear. It is the fear of my own inadequacies that makes me envious of others who outperform me. Likewise, that same fear of insignificance causes me to overcompensate when somebody wrongs me – how dare he hurt *me* – and lose my temper. And it is the fear of the stranger that causes me to hate him.

Conversely, compassion is an ability to feel love for someone who finds themselves in difficult times and dire straits. To feel compassion is to love the world and desire to make it a better place. To be happy is to love the world and to love life.

One of my key points from the beginning of the book is that there are positive and negative emotions. In sum, the positive emotions are those which draw us outside of ourselves, enabling us to create and sustain lasting relationships. The negative emotions are those which invert that process and pull us into ourselves, emotions like depression which make us indifferent to the world outside us.

Falling in love with love

Few cinematic events have evoked the 'wow' factor in me like the opening scene of *Saving Private Ryan*. I was mesmerized by Steven Spielberg's recreation of the Normandy invasion of June 1944. The rest of the film was equally spectacular and stunning in its achievement. I was sure that the movie was a shoo-in for the Best Film Oscar of 1999. It came, therefore, as a shock and a surprise when the prize was presented to *Shakespeare in Love*. To be sure, it was a humorous and romantic film abounding with beautiful Elizabethan dress and superb acting, and Judi Dench did a superb job as the grand old English Queen. But to rate it above an epic like *Saving Private Ryan*?

But it didn't take a fortnight for me to figure out why *Shakespeare in Love* stole the heart of the world. *We all love watching love*. Romantic love has become so absent from society that people are dying to witness even a faint flicker of it. And a movie that depicts it well will triumph over a war movie any day.

But what's stopping us from bringing that love into our own lives? To be sure, there are many reasons that romantic love has become a surreal fantasy that appears only in the movies. Among other things, sex without commitment, an insatiable appetite for 'the best' which makes us all feel unhappy with our partners, as well as a hyper human competitiveness which makes career so much more important than relationships, has driven love from our lives. But there is a stronger reason, more important than all the rest. Simply put, we have no love because we are all so afraid. And those who live in fear canot have love.

Crippled by fear, mired in cynicism

To be sure, every generation has been challenged by fear. In times gone by, there was the fear of disease, fear of constant war, fear of being exposed as a heretic and fear of early death. But our generation alone faces the mother of all fears, the biggie and the one that threatens to cripple us all: namely, the fear that life is meaningless. There is no plan and things ultimately just don't work. All around us it is chaos which prevails. With a 60 per cent divorce rate, we face evidence that love doesn't work, that one plus one doesn't equal two. With the deep generation gap that separates mothers and daughters, we begin to believe that all families are dysfunctional. We live in the constant fear that the Universe is fragmented to its very core and that no one can fix it. Sure, we can *escape* from the pain of arbitrariness and meaninglessness, and we do by drinking and pursuing other mind-numbing activities like watching endless television and movies. But we are all ultimately doomed to loneliness because the one thing that can save us from our desolation, love, has been proven to be a fake. Candace Bushnell even argued in her trend-setting bestseller *Sex in the City* that women today are becoming more attached to their children than their husbands because they believe in biological but not romantic love.

No wonder that we are so cynical in regards to relationships! The fact that we have lost a belief in the potency of love has left us bereft of its warm and soothing glow. We are left stranded in the cold, shivering in terror. Just look at how many fears affect modern male–female relationships: there is fear of commitment, fear of betrayal, fear of rejection, fear of not measuring up (literally), fear of being unfavourably compared to a rival, fear of marrying the wrong person, fear of marrying too soon, fear of marrying and then meeting someone better, fear of monogamy, fear of intimacy, fear of failure and the fear of getting fed up and bored early in the marriage.

Learning how to love again

So long as we continue to live in fear, we cannot love, for the two are utterly incompatible and represent antithetical emotions. For the opposite of love is not hate – it is fear.

The quintessential difference between love and fear is that

love is about amplification and expansiveness while fear is about contraction and shrinkage. Love makes us giants and fear makes us pygmies. The Bible commands 'Love your neighbour as *yourself*'. All love begins with self-love. Self-love is part of the human survival instinct. But once we love ourselves we are able to expand the borders of our own ego and bring others under the rubric of what we consider the self. For example, a mother loves her daughter. Ask her why, and she is puzzled by the question. 'There is no reason. It's just that she is *my* daughter.' Her daughter is her own flesh and blood. She *is* her mother, therefore the mother loves her child. When parents look upon their own child, they cannot distinguish between the self and the child. When we look at our child we have miraculously expanded. It is as if I don't end with *me* anymore. Whereas once upon a time I ended at the tip of my nose, now that I love this creature in front of me, I end where they end. They have become an extension of me. And if you hurt my child, it is not *as if* you are hurting me. You *are* hurting me, literally.

Love is the dissolution of borders and boundaries. An absence of love is about rigidity. I see a stranger and I do not love him because he is not me. I end here while he begins there. But love is where I remove the boundaries of the ego and I can now see myself in the stranger. I experience what we share in common and I am able to love him because he and I are the same.

Isn't this the essence of marriage? A man meets a woman. At first she is nothing more than a stranger to him. There is a firm line which separates them and they are both guarded at their initial encounters. But slowly, by sharing and communicating with her, he comes to know her, falls in love with her and marries her. Now he calls her 'his' wife. Whereas before he defined himself as ending at his extremities, now his wife has become his flesh. When he looks into her eyes he sees himself. He protects her the way he protects himself. He loves her as he loves himself because she *is* him. And likewise, he *is* her. This is the meaning of the Bible's pronouncement that he 'should cleave unto his wife and they shall become one flesh'.

Love is a feeling of expansiveness. When you are in love the whole world is bigger and brighter and filled with laughter. This is also why joy is the sister emotion of love. Wherever there is love there is joy and wherever there is joy there is love. Joy too is defined by expansiveness. Joy enlarges the heart and expands the ego. It bursts forth from within and causes us to dance. Notice that the posture of both love and joy is a natural extending of the extremities. When you are joyous you throw out your arms and dance. Your hands and your feet spread as wide as they can go. Your body swells and your lungs inflate as you sing and laugh. The same is true of love, which causes you to throw out your arms and offer a hug. And it's not just the body that expands with joy, it's the heart and the ego as well. The Talmud says that when a man dances at the wedding of his only son, he will dance even with his worst enemy. The previously constrained heart has now broadened and he welcomes his enemy as if he were an old friend.

Fear as a means to diminution

Fear is about a shrivelling of the body and a contraction of the ego, a narrowing, tightening and retrenchment of the self. The quintessential posture of fear is the 'fetal position' – the retraction of the extremities to protect the head and the torso. We physically become small. We cannot stomach the stranger. Rather than being a compatriot, each person approaches us as an enemy.

One could spend all day listing the fears harboured by men and women, which make it impossible for them to fall in love. But the greatest fear of all is the fear of being vulnerable, the fear that the moment we let down our shield someone whom we trust will strike. We cherish our supposed freedom and feel we must avoid dependency. After a while, we get encased in the shell of our own existence, afraid to expose our soft underbelly, and we settle into a surface existence of routine, isolation and artifice.

A woman sent an e-mail to my LoveProphet website, telling me something that I have since discovered is becoming increasingly common. 'I have been dating Brad for three months. We started having sex on the fourth date. I can't explain why this happens, but every time he tries to stimulate me to the point where I am about to lose control, I stop him. He finds this a real turn off.'

I wrote back to her telling her that her action is actually quite common. 'Who is Brad to you, anyway? A boyfriend? After how many other boyfriends? And what does boyfriend mean anyway? How serious is the commitment? How special is he to you that you should trust him to the point where you lose control? The reason you stop him is that you are afraid of lighting a fire that might burn the whole house down. Perhaps it will consume you. Or perhaps it will give Brad a control over you. You don't want him exercising that kind of dominion over you. So even when you make love, you insist on being in the driver's seat. You think to yourself, what if I fall in love faster or more intensely than him? What if he is not there to catch me when I fall? He is a boyfriend, and that allows him to end the relationship with the ease of a 25-cent phone call. Also, since you are not married, he is not *your* husband. That all-important act of possessiveness is not present. So you can't love him as deeply as if it were. And therefore you stop him. Because you are *afraid*.'

Fear and love: like mixing oil and water

It follows that those who live in fear cannot love. They are incapable of the necessary expansion that allows the ego to open out, so that it may bring another under its wing. Love is about throwing caution to the wind. It is about taking flight and being carefree. But fear is about being guarded, suspicious and easily offended. It is about weightiness and being unable to proceed. Those who live in fear are stuck in the mud. Hence, when singles ask me, 'Why can't I fall in love?', what they are really asking me is, 'Why can't I soar? Why have my wings been clipped?'

Samantha dated Sal for half a year. He ws utterly infatuated with her and asked her to marry him. Remarkably, although he was by far the nicest guy she had ever dated, she turned him down. Shocked and hurt, Sal ended the relationship. When I asked her why she had thrown away such a perfect relationship, Samantha told me, 'Nobody is that perfect. There had to be something wrong, some ugly side of his character. And I'd rather know about it before we marry than be stuck with a whole bunch of kids and only then discover that he has flaws that I might not be able to live with.' Pop.

And George doesn't even date anymore: 'I'm tired of women telling me that they just want to be friends.' When I gave him the number of a lovely girl named Erica who particularly valued 'the nice guy' stereotype, placing sincerity above charm and charisma, he refused to call her, despite my incessant prodding, because he feared rejection. 'My ego just can't handle another excuse about why she can't go out with me a second time.' Pop. Pop. Pop.

Fear is destroying our relationships.

Learning to be brave

Thus, I advise my single friends to actually verbalize the word 'courage' to themselves as they walk out the door for a date. Throughout the date, whenever they sense that unreasonable fears and anxieties are grabbing hold of them, they are to identify them as irrational and actively dismiss the thought. I give the same advice to men and women who find it difficult to say sorry after they have wronged someone. Afraid that their apology will be rejected, they find themselves too frightened to utter the vulnerable words. So I tell them, just before you say sorry, utter to yourself the words 'be brave'. And you know what, even if your apology is rejected, you'll survive. Because in addition to everything else, love also makes us strong.

Fears are apparitions and ghosts, and a life of anxiety is a life lived in the valley of death. We must choose to live in the land of the living. Turn away from the past, don't allow yourself to be spooked by ghosts. Look instead at the *real person* who wishes to share your life and offer you love.

I also advise those who seek my counsel to discuss their fears with a wise friend who can help them understand just how irrational their worries are. The best way to nip fear in the bud is to speak to someone who has endured something similar. Once you see that they have crossed over the Rubicon of fear and have lived to tell about it, you will see that fear is a shadow that quickly vanishes the moment it is exposed to the light of love.

There is no story of any great human achievement throughout history that did not first involve the overcoming of fear. And there is no story of loving and living happily ever after that did not involve the same.

www.loveprophet.com

Rabbi Shmuley is now available twenty-four hours a day, seven days a week on his web site at www.loveprophet.com. There you will find a one-of-a-kind matchmaking site, which includes not only listings of personal ads, but all the advice and guidance you need to follow through from a first date to a walk down the aisle. The site has an extensive database of questions and answers from readers and web browsers which serves as a treasure trove of relationship and life knowledge, always at your fingertips. You can also find an archive of Rabbi Shmuley's essays on topics ranging from finding a soul mate, discovering sensuality, raising a child, overcoming cynicism and gaining self-confidence to the social implications of various films.

In addition, you can find a schedule of Rabbi Shmuley's lectures and other public appearances, as well as the latest news on his current and upcoming books, tapes and other publications. Colourful, humorous and ever insightful, www.loveprophet.com is one of the web's most valuable properties.

www.matchnet.com

Rabbi Shmuley also serves as matchmaker-in-chief for Matchnet.com, one of the world's premier matchmaking sites. Follow the links to Rabbi Shmuley's bold venture into the dating world – www.americansingles.com, www.britishsingles.co.uk and www.jdate.com, a Jewish matchmaking site. Rabbi Shmuley has launched a number of exciting programs with Matchnet, so be sure to keep posted. You can reach Rabbi Shmuley by writing to him at shmuley@matchnet.com.

The Oxford L'Chaim Society

Rabbi Boteach is founder and dean of the L'Chaim Society, a high-profile education organization that hosts leading figures from around the world. Past guests have included Mikhail Gorbechev, Shimon Peres, Binyamin Nethanyahu, Jerry Springer, Yitzchak Shamir, Bob Hawke, Javier Perez de Cuellar, Elie Wiesel, Simon Wiesenthal, Boy George, Diego Maradona, Rabbi Harold Kushner and Professor Stephen Hawking. Rabbi Boteach founded the organization at Oxford University where he served as Rabbi for eleven years, becoming 'something of a legend' at the University. L'Chaim aims to spread understanding, love and tolerance, to strengthen marriages and relationships, and to create values-based leadership.

A frequent guest on television and radio, Rabbi Shmuley has appeared on all the major British, American, South African, Australian and Israeli television and radio shows and was the subject of an hour-long documentary in the BBC's prestigious *Everyman* series. In the United States he has appeared among others on *The Today Show*, *Good Morning America*, *The View*, *Politically Incorrect*, *Larry King Live* and the *Howard Stern Show*.

Some of the written publications that have profiled Rabbi Boteach include *Time* magazine, *Newsweek*, the *New York Times*, the *Washington Post*, the *L.A. Times*, the *Miami Herald*, the *New York Post* and the *New York Daily News*. Rabbi Boteach was also the subject of a New York magazine cover story in February 2000. An internationally acclaimed speaker, Rabbi Boteach won the highly prestigious Times Preacher of the Year Competition in London just days before the new millennium.

If you would like further information about Rabbi Shmuley Boteach and the L'Chaim Society you can write to: Oxford L'Chaim Society, 6 East 39th Street, 10th floor, New York, NY 10016, or at shmuley@matchnet.com.

Rabbi Boteach also publishes weekly essays on contemporary social relationship issues via the Internet. If you would like to subscribe and receive the essays, please email: shmuley@lchaim.org.